PEIRCE'S PRAGMATISM
The Design for Thinking

VIBS

Volume 107

Robert Ginsberg
Executive Editor

Associate Editors

A volume in
Studies in Pragmatism and Values
SPV
John R. Shook, Editor

PEIRCE'S PRAGMATISM

The Design for Thinking

Phyllis Chiasson

Amsterdam - Atlanta, GA 2001

The paper on which this book is printed meets the requirements of "ISO 9706:1994, Information and documentation - Paper for documents - Requirements for permanence".

ISBN: 90-420-1275-7
©Editions Rodopi B.V., Amsterdam - Atlanta, GA 2001
Printed in The Netherlands

For Dorothy (Dottie) Davis

CONTENTS 061102—5299D2

EDITORIAL FOREWORD

Pragmatism is fundamentally a theory of learning. Anyone investigating the mind's functions and the possibility of knowledge should concede, with pragmatism, that a theory of learning must be constructed first. But what is meant by "learning?" Too many philosophies would keep strictly separate the scientific methods of gaining new knowledge from the pedagogical methods of absorbing established facts. Against this artificial and harmful separation stands pragmatism's hypothesis that there is only one methodology of human learning. This methodology is complex, to be sure, having many skill levels, but there is a continuity between the lowest and highest levels. That continuity is provided by a basic pattern or form of intelligent inquiry.

The classical American pragmatists each explored the nature of intelligent inquiry in light of their own academic interests. William James was a pioneer of experimental psychology who investigated the widest variety of psychological phenomena. John Dewey was also a pioneer, in social psychology, and pursued philosophy's utility for a progressive democratic society. Charles Sanders Peirce (1839-1914) was a pioneer in logic, semiotics, and metaphysics, and formulated a highly original philosophy of natural science. While all three agreed that human intelligence is essentially about learning from experience, a basic tenet of empiricism, such an agreement alone could not have pulled them together into a distinct philosophical movement. However, they were further agreed that (1) while experience grounds knowledge, the mind transforms experience into objects of knowledge, (2) the transformation of experience aims at the relief of doubt and establishment of belief, which is a preparedness to act towards achieving a goal, (3) because the mind aims at practical belief, its transformation of experience is guided by experimental activity, and (4) the experimental process of creating sound beliefs can be logically evaluated according to its ability to guide us towards the reliable prediction and control of our environment.

Peirce's pragmatism developed a sophisticated logic of scientific inquiry. Because of the continuity between all levels of intelligent inquiry, this logic is highly relevant to learning at every level and thus could revolutionize educational philosophy. Peirce himself was interested in pedagogy and composed (but never published) basic logic texts that sketchily illustrate this continuity of learning. Phyllis Chiasson has undertaken the rarely accepted challenge of explaining in detail Peirce's great relevance to pedagogy. She has an exceptional educational background in secondary education. She also has vast practical experience translating her pedagogical expertise into theoretical models, which have been successfully applied in both business and educational settings. Her impressive qualifications and honors are ably enumerated in the "About the Author" page concluding this book. I will only add my opinion that few educators or philosophers possessing her high level of expertise could so proficiently teach us the lessons of Peirce's thought for the classroom.

As she recounts in the text, Chiasson discovered that many of the fundamental principles of learning, gleaned from decades of teaching and tested in consulting, can be found in Peirce. More significantly, this study of Peirce displays how the wider philosophical issues surrounding these principles can in turn illuminate remaining questions of educational theory. This reciprocal relationship between confirming practice in a philosopher's theory, and then testing that theory by trying to resolve further practical problems, exemplifies the pragmatic method and makes proper use of a pragmatist's work.

The pragmatic method is also exemplified in Chiasson's chosen mode of writing, the dialogue. While entertainingly engaging, her dialogue has the serious task of demonstrating learning methods while instructing the reader in Peirce's philosophy. Chiasson employs a full array of her considerable skills to safely escort both the philosophy novice and the education initiate safely through Peirce's terminology. However, this book will also impress and enlighten the Peirce specialist and the pedagogical theorist. By bridging together philosophy and pedagogy, Chiasson has performed a much-needed pragmatic service for which both fields shall be indebted.

John R. Shook
Editor, Studies in Pragmatism and Values Special Series

PREFACE

This book is an explanation, in dialogue format, of Charles Sanders Peirce's 1905 essay, "What Pragmatism Is." The entire text of the original Peirce essay, which first appeared in *The Monist*, has been reprinted in the appendix to this book with line numbers and a few silent punctuation changes. In addition, lines of the essay that are discussed within each chapter are noted on the first page of the chapter.

You may notice that the essay lines between 536 and 564 have not been explicated, nor have Peirce's notes or his postscript. I decided to ignore twenty lines concerning a logical distinction because they would require an extensive explanation of formal logic, yet would not contribute to my general purpose for writing this text. The information in Peirce's first two notes has been incorporated into the general explanation of terms without specific reference to them. His third note explains a distinction between the English and German concepts of the word "proposition." I have thoroughly addressed Peirce's meaning of proposition within the text but have not drawn a comparison to the German meaning of this term. Therefore, if you read German, you may want to refer to Peirce's third note concerning the difference between English and German meanings of the term "proposition." The postscript is of historical interest, since it reflects the frustration and isolation within which Peirce was forced to operate during the second half of his life. However, it is not part of the essay itself and does not add anything to his theory. For this reason, it too has been left out of the discussion.

As you read this text, you will encounter several references to the Relational Thinking Styles model, the Davis Non-verbal Assessment, and the Engaged Intelligence training program. These references are used to illustrate and clarify information in Peirce's essay. None of them has been explicated in a specific way within this text. More detailed information about each of these topics is available at the following web site: www.davisnelson.com

Port Townsend, Washington
1 January 2001

ACKNOWLEDGMENTS

This book probably owes its existence to the initial encouragement and ongoing support of Jayne Tristan. Without her insistence that what I had to say needed saying, I might have had neither the incentive to begin, nor the courage to continue this endeavor. Tristan also made herself available for my questions throughout the writing of this book and answered these queries with grace and precision. In addition, I thank H. G. Callaway for encouraging me to submit this manuscript for consideration by the Value Inquiry Book Series. His early support and his confidence in the philosophical sophistication underlying my often unsophisticated commentaries have been gratifying. John R. Shook (first as referee, and later, as editor for this book) has provided the best encouragement and support any author could desire. His enthusiasm and interest in this project have made my editing chores seem like a light burden. The continuing encouragement and editing skills of VIBS executive editor, Robert Ginsberg, have been valuable as well. I am grateful to Richard T. Hull, stylistics and format editor for VIBS, who answered my many questions with both patience and promptness. Joseph Ransdell provided editorial assistance with the early chapters of this book. He also patiently answered questions concerning Peircean terminology which arose during the earliest stages of my writing. Kelly Parker also provided prompt and helpful answers to my questions. I am also grateful to Jada Prane, whose thorough reading of the final manuscript resulted in many useful suggestions for clarifying difficult points.

My thanks to Adrianne Harun for her intelligent copyediting of this book; to Johanna Rienstra for her careful proof reading; and to Jane Wirth for her helpful suggestions following an early read-through of the original manuscript for this book.

Internet sources deserve special acknowledgement as well. As an unaffiliated researcher, it is likely that, without access to Internet discussion forums, I would have met neither the individuals mentioned above, nor any of the many other philosophers with whom I now exchange ideas. Most particularly, I thank all participants of Peirce-L (the C. S. Peirce discussion list) and Dewey-L (the John Dewey discussion list). These online discussion lists are moderated by Joseph Ransdell and Tom Burke, respectively.

Dorothy (Dottie) Davis, now retired, deserves a large share of credit for providing me with the underlying framework for the knowledge I have been able to acquire over the past twenty-five years. Her non-verbal model of Relational Thinking Styles comprises much of the basis from which I have come to understand Peirce's pragmatism. My association with Davis from 1976 until 1983 left me with basic information and methods for practical application of her ideas, as well as a solid foundation for the insights that I have since gained about Peirce's pragmatism. Janet DuBerry, my long-time friend and associate, is an important contributor to this work. She, too, has been involved with these ideas since the beginning. Now living in Madison, Wisconsin, she currently provides assessments and coder training in non-verbal thinking styles for the Davis-Nelson consulting firm and is a skilled trainer for the Engaged Intelligence program as well. Eldon McBride, another early supporter of Relational Thinking Styles, first encountered the non-verbal assessment in January 1980 while acting as a counselor and the director of a day-treatment program for troubled adolescents in Tucson. McBride, who assisted in the early field testing of the Davis Non-verbal Assessment, is now a high ranking personnel executive for a large aerospace company. He still maintains close contact with this work and uses these concepts for his day-to-day decision-making. Marlys Moeckly, now retired from the University of Arizona College of Nursing, devoted a full year of her time in the early 1980s, helping us to field test the Davis Non-verbal Assessment. Psychologist and vocational rehabilitation specialist, Steve Miller, also assisted in early field testing of the non-verbal assessment and, with Moeckly, helped to design the contextual analysis tool which we still use today. Also during the 1980's, philosopher and counselor, William (Bill) Collins, guided my early philosophical explorations and encouraged me to use dialogue and fables as a means for explaining my work.

My associate, Ruth Gordon recently moved to Port Townsend to enhance our collaborative work with Relational Thinking Styles. Almost daily, she reminds me of the importance of this information to children, adolescents, and for their parents and teachers as well. My thanks to Dr. and Mrs. James Clifton for allowing me to use their home-building experiences to illustrate an important concept in this book. I thank my daughter-in-law, Shannon Devlin Schwimmer, for allowing me to use her impressive baking skills to explain the concept of propositions.

My remarkable husband, Hal Leskinen, deserves as much credit as I do for the ongoing explication of the Relational Thinking Styles model and assessment tool. We have both been intensely engrossed in this work for many years and look forward to many more years of joint immersion in these ideas. Our children have also made significant contributions to this work: David Schwimmer, Amy Miley, Greg Leskinen, Tonya Watkins, and Andrea Schwimmer participated in many activities and experiments over the course of their childhood and adolescent years as we developed and tested materials.

PROLOGUE

"I hated that!" Hal said emphatically as we left the restaurant.

I nodded in firm agreement. We had planned to have dinner at the tiny Italian restaurant just around the corner from our home. However, just after a few moments of listening to the jazz musicians playing at the restaurant that night, we decided to cook at home and avoid having to listen to that particular vocalist during supper.

"I just don't like scat singing," I commented. We were walking past the few storefronts along the way to Aldrich's, our corner market.

"Scat singing?" Hal questioned. "Is that what it was?"

"Yes. They scooby-dooby-do the words up so much that I can hardly follow the music."

"That was Johnny Mercer," Hal offered.

"What was?"

"The song they were playing, 'Something's Gotta Give,'" he said. "Johnny Mercer wrote it."

The mention of Mercer's song brought to mind a subject I had been working on that afternoon.

"That song brings something to mind for me."

"Do you mean 'Something's Gotta Give'?"

"Yes. It reminds me of what I was working on today."

"What's that?"

"I was trying to find a simple way to explain what Charles Sanders Peirce means by the terms 'belief' and 'doubt'."

"Why would that song bring this to mind?"

"Because," I answered, "Peirce has a particular way of using these words. He says that 'all you have any dealings with are your doubts and beliefs, with the course of life that forces new beliefs upon you and gives you the power to doubt old beliefs.' In other words, everything we do involves our beliefs interacting with our life experiences. Whenever a belief and an experience do not match, 'Something's Gotta Give.' Today I was trying to come up with a simple means of explaining the way in which Peirce uses the words 'belief' and 'doubt.' I wanted to explain how the Relational Thinking Styles non-verbal model demonstrates different people's ways of believing and doubting as they interact with experience. This would help me to explain how Engaged Intelligence training improves reasoning abilities."

"I don't understand what you mean."

"That's probably because I have not figured out a way to explain what I mean. Mercer's song brought it to mind again. Do you see the connection?" I anticipated affirmative response. "'Something's Gotta Give'?"

"No," my husband said thoughtfully, "I do see the connection with Relational Thinking Styles, but I cannot say that I see any connection to Engaged Intelligence training."

By that point, we were at the checkout counter and required by unspoken local etiquette to visit with the local community. We bantered lightly with the stranger in line ahead of us, with the cashier, and with our neighbor in line just behind us, who had come in for garlic and wine. When we started back for home, I had forgotten what we had been discussing, but Hal had not. He is as interested in this work as I am, and we talk about it nearly incessantly. I usually do most of the talking when it comes to Peirce, though. Hal finds it impossible to understand Peirce's convoluted language and sentence structure.

As we were walking back home, Hal said, "Now, about the connection between 'Something's Gotta Give' and Engaged Intelligence training...."

"It's really more about belief and doubt," I interrupted.

"Belief and doubt?"

"Peirce's meanings of the words 'belief' and 'doubt,' which are not what you might think," I explained. "His meanings have to do with habits of mind versus uncertainty."

My voice trailed off here, as it always does when I try to paraphrase Peirce. Neither Peirce's written words, nor the concepts behind them, trip easily across the tongue. However, Peirce's concepts are important for all of us, especially in these times. Complaints about the failure of American schools to produce workers able to meet the demands of this information age are really complaints about the lack of an effective "design for thinking" to serve as the foundation of educational programs. Few people realize that Peirce's pragmatism underlies the logic of computer program design; even fewer realize that his is much more than a system of dry symbolic processes. Peirce's pragmatism is a rich and vibrant philosophy for which logic must be informed by both aesthetics and ethics if it is to produce right reasoning. I wanted to be able to talk with Hal about Peirce's concepts since, embedded within his theory, are keys to solving problems we are facing today. I envision Peirce's "design for thinking" as the keystone for building a world population of citizens able to reason rightly. I am most interested in the ways that Peirce's theory of pragmatism can be used to develop sound educational practices.

For me, this interest was born out of necessity in 1975, when, just before the school year began, I was abruptly switched from teaching ninth-grade English to teaching juniors and seniors. Upon arriving for teacher work-days in the fall, I discovered that all the books designated for use by juniors and seniors had already been reserved by other teachers. I would not be able to use a single class-set of anything until sometime in February. Until then, I would need something to do with five classes of more than thirty-five students each. The solution to my problem surfaced when I came across a stack of forty workbooks on a back shelf in the English department workroom. Not one of these books appeared to have ever been opened. The title of this set of workbooks was *Creative Analysis*, by Albert Upton and Richard Samson.

This workbook contained a series of graded exercises. Each section started simply, gradually leading to much more difficult levels. The text in the book was minimal, offering no rationale for the exercises. However, rationale was not an issue for me at that point. I was only using these books because they were available. I felt I had no choice but to continue, however intimidating the exercises might be. Never before had I encountered such rigorous intellectual stimulation. Working through the exercises provided an exciting roller coaster-like experience for the students and me. One moment we felt too dumb to continue; the next, smarter than we had ever been before.

Each morning I worked along with the first hour students as they completed the exercises for that day. During the rest of the day, I served as a resource while the other classes completed the same exercises. Sometimes it would be necessary to figure out something we had not understood during the first hour. Next day, first period received the benefit of our learning during the previous day. Then we started in on the next exercises.

By February, something remarkable had happened. All of us had become a whole lot smarter. Students who once thought they were much too dumb to attempt college started thinking about giving it a try. Without any specific writing training, writing skills started to improve dramatically. Without any specific literary analysis training, students could grasp the essence of a difficult poem or a piece of literature.

Amazing intellectual transformations took place in my classes during the 1975-1976 school year, but I had no way of explaining what had happened or why. It did not make sense in any linear way that these kinds of gains could have come from performing a series of workbook exercises. I had no one at my school to talk with about this. I persuaded my friend, Janet Duberry, who taught in a different school district, to begin using the *Creative Analysis* workbook with her classes. Since we were both raising children as well as teaching full-time, we had to limit our discussions to telephone conversations during our already crowded evenings. I had hoped to interest some of the other English teachers at my school so that we could exchange ideas and strategies during working hours. However, the few people in my department to whom I brought up these remarkable results dismissed them as impossible. "Besides," one English teacher sternly informed me, "that workbook is much too difficult for high school students. You should not be using it in the first place." I had amazing results on my hands, yet I could not convince my colleagues to even look at them.

Then, in the spring of that year, a group of teachers within the school came together to discuss what to do about a group of students who were falling through the cracks. The I.Q. scores of these students were too low for them to be considered learning disabled and too high to be considered educable mentally retarded. The school district offered no special services for them. About thirty teachers attended that meeting. One was Dorothy Davis, who taught dance in the physical education department. I knew that she had earned a doctoral degree a few years before, but had assumed that her degree was in an aspect of physical education. When I proposed to the group that we might want to teach thinking skills, the head of the special education department coldly stated that "no one can teach people how to think." Davis, however, reached across the man sitting between us to tap my hand and say, "I'd like to talk to you after this meeting."

The brief discussion we had after that meeting began the unfolding of Davis's remarkable theory of non-verbal reasoning habits. From the spring of 1976, until I left teaching in 1980, we met almost every morning before the school day and during summers as well. Over this time, we expanded and deepened her theoretical model so that I could develop materials for putting it into action. In the evenings, I would telephone Duberry and share with her what Davis and I had discussed that day. Over the course of several years, during our evening discussions, Duberry and I developed and tested practical applications of Davis's non-verbal theory. We also adapted *Creative Analysis* exercises so that we could use them with slower learners. We continued using the *Creative Analysis* workbook in our regular classes.

Two years after Davis and I had our first discussion, she devised an ingenious method for determining the reasoning habits of the students in my special classes. This method evolved into what is now the Davis Non-verbal Assessment. Because of this assessment, we have been able to test out many assumptions about learning styles and learning capabilities as well as make accurate predictions about how particular individuals will perform within certain contexts. The assessment has also provided me with a means for understanding Peirce's concept of abductive inference and John Dewey's concept of an empirically verifiable theory of valuation.

Davis, Duberry, and I recognized that *Creative Analysis* and the non-verbal theory were somehow related, but none of us could figure out the connection. *Creative Analysis* had been based upon *Design for Thinking*, a previous work of Albert Upton's. According to Upton, *Design for Thinking* was deeply indebted to *The Meaning of Meaning,* a much earlier text by Charles Ogden and Ivor Richards. We found no obvious similarities between Upton and any of the references Davis used to construct her thesis. We knew that a connection must exist, but what was it? Davis had built her model of non-verbal reasoning habits by using the theoretical model of her major professor. His model was a three-tiered cube-like structure, similar to the three tiers of content, context, and matrix in Upton's *Design for Thinking.*

The question of how these systems connected remained a mystery for several years. In early 1982, after a series of personal and medical setbacks, I abruptly became a single mother and the sole support of three children. We moved to the Seattle area in the fall of 1983, where I became a creative writer for a large corporation. My tenure there lasted an excruciatingly long eighteen months. In the winter of 1985, I met Hal Leskinen, a recent widower with two school-aged children. Though trained as a civil engineer, he had, several years before, become intrigued with Neuro-linguistic Programming™ (NLP). This is an interesting and uncannily effective psychotherapy system—which we later discovered originated from the same linguistic roots as Upton's *Design for Thinking*. In the spring of that same year, we formed a consulting agency, Davis-Nelson, using the Davis Non-verbal Assessment as our primary tool for management selection and training. By the summer of that year, we were a couple and, eventually, our business partnership extended into marriage. Davis-Nelson became increasingly busy over that first year—so busy that I felt we were in danger of neglecting our children. In February of 1986, we pulled out of the consulting business, except for a few customers, and began developing a computer analysis program that would enable me to teach others how to administer the Davis Non-verbal Assessment. We completed the final testing of this program in the fall of 1987. It has been in regular use since then.

Over those years of developing and testing the computer analysis program, we encountered many questions about the connection between our non-verbal assessment and an increasingly popular verbal one, the Myers-Briggs Type Indicator™ (MBTI). The MBTI is based upon the temperament typology of the psychologist, Carl G. Jung. I soon determined that the MBTI does not identify the same information as the Davis Non-verbal Assessment, which is not to say that information derived from the MBTI lacks significance. Anyone familiar with Jung's temperament theory is aware of its value as a psychological tool. In the course of my analysis of temperament, I became an expert in Jung's psychological types. This expertise resulted in the development of an online temperament assessment, the *Chiasson Temperament Indicator* (CTI). Midway into this study of Jung's temperaments, we encountered the Enneagram, an ancient and complex description of different motivational factors. We soon recognized that this system fills in the gaps that we felt were still left open after considering both temperament and non-verbal reasoning styles.

As we worked with these three systems, the connections among them became increasingly obvious to us. Enneagram information provides a category for the "whys" of what we do—the apparently innate core values that motivate us. Jung's typology provides a category for "what" we notice and prefer—the differing levels of emphasis (also apparently innate), that we place upon intuitive, sensory, affective, and logical modes of consciousness. Our preferred modes of consciousness allow in and filter out different aspects from the potential contents of an experience. Relational Thinking Styles (RTS) accounts for "how" we form and achieve purposes. In other words, RTS (non-verbal reasoning methods) accounts for the different ways in which we use the information that filters into consciousness (based on temperament) to form and accomplish our purposes (initially impelled by our core values).

However, none of this led me any closer to the connection between Davis's theory and Upton's *Design for Thinking*. Sometime during 1989, I tried to order a copy of *The Meaning of Meaning*, which Upton credited in his text. However, I was told that the book was out of print and that a new edition was due out later in the year. The bookstore promised to send a copy as soon as the new editions arrived. Meanwhile, I read all of the books that Davis cited in her dissertation. None had anything to do with Upton's three-tiered model. Only the model devised by her major professor shared that form. Someone suggested that I read *Wittgenstein's Vienna*, by the philosophers Alan Janik and Steven Toulmin. Indeed, Wittgenstein appeared to be asking the same questions that Davis's theory answered. However, after reading Wittgenstein's books, I saw that, though he was asking the same questions, he had not even attempted any answers. I was stuck. I had re-read several texts by John Dewey, and I had read Justus Buchler's *The Concept of Method* several times as well. I had also combed through Davis's references on aesthetics again. Still I could find no match between Davis and Upton.

Then, unexpectedly, my copy of the reissued edition of *The Meaning of Meaning* arrived. A cover blurb announced that this text included a new introduction by Umberto Eco. I had no idea that Umberto Eco was anything but a novelist—author of *The Name of the Rose* and *Foucault's Pendulum*. It turns out that Eco is also a highly regarded scholar in the field of semiotics, the study of signs and their meanings. I had never heard of the term "semiotic" before this, though the study of signs and their meanings is the foundation of Upton's *Design for Thinking*. I felt a palpable sense of amazement as I began to read Eco's introduction to *The Meaning of Meaning*:

> Perhaps the most conspicuous example of this pioneering imagination lies in the way in which Ogden and Richards address Peirce. Peirce was not only the greatest contemporary scholar of semiotics but was also...the greatest American philosopher of the turn of the century and beyond doubt one of the greatest thinkers of his time.[1]

I found a description of Peirce's theory of signs in appendix D, #6. This description corresponded to what Upton described in *Design for Thinking*. While lavishing much credit upon the work of Ogden and Richards, Upton had apparently failed to realize that his own work was based upon their interpretation of Peirce. Davis had not referenced Peirce in her thesis, either. Upon reading Eco's introduction and the description of Peirce's semiotic in the appendix, however, I became convinced that the connection between these two lay with Peirce. Hal and I promptly headed over to the University Bookstore to see if we could find anything written by him. The lady at the information desk said: "I'll have our Peirce specialist meet you in the philosophy section." (She pointedly corrected our pronunciation of his name, saying "purse" for Peirce.)

A Peirce specialist? The bookstore had a resident specialist in someone we had only just heard about that afternoon? What was going on?

Their specialist turned out to be a former philosophy student who had dropped out of college to give himself more time to study Peirce. He met us only seconds later, full of excited enthusiasm, and handed us several must-have anthologies, including one edited by Justus Buchler. I immediately recognized Buchler as the author of *The Concept of Method*. Though the connection between Davis's theory and Buchler's book is obvious, I had not seen Buchler's connection to *Design for Thinking*. Nor could I have known before this that Buchler's work had anything to do with Peirce. He referenced Peirce only once in *The Concept of Method*. As soon as I discovered that Buchler was a Peircean scholar, he became my Rosetta stone for connecting Davis's theory to Upton's text—and both of them to Peirce.

After the Peirce specialist piled us up with books, he said quite sternly that we must go immediately to the University's philosophy library and find a copy of *Peirce's Theory of Abduction* by K. T. Fann. "It is out of print," he said, "but you must get a copy. I am sure they will let you photocopy it."

We returned home that evening with our stack of Peirce anthologies and a photocopied manuscript of K.T. Fann's book. As I thumbed through Fann's text, I was amazed. Peirce's concept of *logica docens* matched up to what I had been teaching through *Creative Analysis*. I also suspected that, even though Peirce claimed instinctive reasoning habits (*logica utens*) could not properly be called reasoning, these would probably match up to Davis's non-verbal reasoning methods. Since I knew from years of using the Davis Non-verbal Assessment that these non-verbal methods can be demonstrated, altered, and enhanced, I realized that he might be mistaken in dismissing all of *logica utens* as not subject to self-control. I suspected that he might have been thinking of *logica utens* as a particular sort of habit, the one which we usually call "direct" and which is also known by the term "linear."

Next, I dug into the anthologies. The first essay that I read was an early one, "The Fixation of Belief." His four methods of fixing belief generally corresponded to the methods in Davis's theory. How could this be so? Nowhere had she referenced this man. Then I read "Logic as Semiotic: The Theory of Signs." Though the terminology was different, the concepts were familiar to me from *Design for Thinking*. Next, I read "What Pragmatism Is." This essay had an obvious connection to both Upton's and Davis's work. Finally, because of its intriguing title, I read "A Neglected Argument for the Reality of God." This last essay stunned me. The process Peirce describes there as "musing" is identical to the non-verbal process which Davis's model refers to as "multi-relational reasoning." I also recognized that this essay as a whole described the deliberate and complex process which Davis's model usually refers to as "meta-relational," and sometimes as "retroductive reasoning." The latter is a term that Peirce also used, with a slight difference in meaning.

I called Davis the next day to ask if she had ever heard of Charles Sanders Peirce. She recalled that one of his essays, "How to Make Our Ideas Clear," had been required reading for a course in graduate school. However, it was so difficult to read that she had given up on it.

I embarked upon an extended Peirce mission at that point. I bought more anthologies. I read Peirce's essays repeatedly. I drew comparisons from his work to what I knew about *Creative Analysis* and Davis's non-verbal theory. Between 1989 and 1998, I read, raised children, and wrote—without access to anyone else working on these ideas. In retrospect, I suspect that this isolation was good for me, forcing me to think things through on my own. Other than the authors I mentioned before, I avoided secondary sources and stuck to reading what Peirce himself had written. Though I do not pretend to grasp his mathematics or many of his technical terms, I still find Peirce's own writings much easier to understand than that of most of his interpreters. Davis now agrees that her model must have been built upon Peirce's theory. We have determined that her major professor's purportedly original model was little more than a graphical representation of Peirce's triadic theory of right reasoning. Just as Upton's *Design for Thinking* is a method for teaching Peirce's *logica docens,* Davis's non-verbal model is an expression of Peirce's *logica utens.*

Once I understood the connections among the works of Peirce, Davis, and Upton, I was able to put together the pieces of what we had been doing all those years. The Engaged Intelligence training program, which Janet DuBerry and I built out of our work with those three sources, teaches the verbal and the process skills for mastering Peirce's requirements for a formally trained method of right reasoning (*logica docens*). The Relational Thinking Styles model of non-verbal reasoning habits, developed by Dorothy Davis, describes the patterns of untrained reasoning habits that we all use in our day-to-day lives (*logica utens*). The Davis Non-verbal Assessment is a diagnostic tool which identifies the specific reasoning pattern that an individual habitually uses for making day-to-day decisions.

This brings us back to what I was trying to explain to Hal that evening during our walk to and from the market. Hal thinks that Peirce is as difficult to follow as Shakespeare is. Because of this, I have never been able to bring him to an understanding of how Davis's non-verbal model and the Engaged Intelligence training program connect to Peirce's pragmatism.

These days we have plenty of time to discuss such matters. Our children are all grown; the youngest is twenty-six. We are grandparents. It took me twenty-five years to be able to explain how and why, back in 1975, my students and I started becoming smarter from using Upton's system. At the end of my explorations, I find myself arriving back where I started and, as T. S. Eliot might have said, knowing this place for the first time. I am glad to be here. Now I can explain not only what I know, but also where it comes from and how I came to know it.

Later that same evening, Hal and I agreed to spend an hour or so together each morning until we could work out a way for me to explain one of Peirce's essays to him by translating it into everyday language. What follows is an account of our morning discussions, which ranged over a course of five weeks. May you find them as entertaining as we did.

One
SETTING THE STAGE

"Is this the name of the essay?" Hal asked as I typed out the title of Peirce's essay, "What Pragmatism Is."

"Yes, Peirce published 'What Pragmatism Is' in 1905. Since he died in 1914, this essay expresses a mature culmination of his philosophy. It is based on his sixty-odd years of intensive philosophical development."

"Maybe you should mention what you mean by the word 'pragmatism,'" Hal suggested. "People might be confused before you even start."

"But this essay is about what pragmatism means."

"I know, but I bet that most people think of the word 'pragmatic' as just doing something practical or expedient."

"Then maybe I should start off by saying what pragmatism is not."

"How come?"

"Because, as you suggested, some people react automatically when they come across this word. You are correct in saying that the word 'pragmatic' has more than one meaning, at least in common usage it does. Everyone probably has a personal sense of what the words 'pragmatic' and 'pragmatism' mean."

"Go for it, then!" he said encouragingly.

"Pragmatism does not mean a philosophy that is practical in the everyday sense of the word, nor does it mean utilitarian. Nor does pragmatism mean expedient as some people would have it mean. And pragmatism absolutely does not mean that you should head out full steam ahead, regardless of whatever ethical principles you have to violate in the process. It also does not mean dull, nor technical, nor lacking in beauty or goodness."

"That is a lot for it not to mean."

"I have more," I said. "Some people think the philosophy of pragmatism teaches moral relativism."

"What is moral relativism?"

"Moral relativism stands for the mental perspective from which right and wrong anchors to whatever is most appealing, popular, or expedient."

"That sounds like modern American society," he commented ruefully.

"I am afraid it does," I sadly agreed. "But, even though I consider moral relativism bad news, its opposite is at least as bad."

"What is its opposite?"

"Dogmatic fundamentalism. People using this perspective make doctrines into sledge hammers for pounding in authoritarian moral pronouncements. These pronouncements are usually based on a literal interpretation of some doctrine. Sometimes, though, the doctrines are just made up out of thin air, such as from someone's dream or a hallucinatory vision. Such arbitrary interpretations invariably disregard reason, compassion, and mitigating circumstances."

"I know what you mean. People even kill one another over these kinds of beliefs. Are you trying to say, then, that Peirce's pragmatism is neither too loose nor too rigid when it comes to morality?"

"In a sense," I said, then deciding against trying to explain Peirce's meaning of the term "ethics" at this early stage of our discussion, I continued. "At the same time, however, pragmatism is much more rigorous than either of those extremes that I just mentioned. Peirce's version of pragmatism holds that all choices in conduct, including scientific choices, should be guided by the most admirable aesthetic impulses and the highest ethical principles."

"What did Peirce mean by aesthetic impulses?"

"That is a topic that I do not want to go into right now."

He shrugged amiably. "Then, what about ethical principles?"

"Do unto others as you would have them do unto you, and do this from the perspective of unconditional love."

"That sure sounds familiar."

"That it does. However, I doubt that anyone always operates from the highest set of ethical principles. Peirce believed that we should always aim our behavior in that direction, though. The more you behave ethically, according to Peirce, the more it becomes a habit to do so. Ultimately you will have formed your character to habitually make ethical choices."

"Like being a bottisattva."

"Or a saint. That is why moral relativism does not fit in with Peirce's pragmatism one bit! Ethics is central to Peirce's theory of right reasoning. Only people who do not understand pragmatism will attach the moral relativism label onto real pragmatic thought."

At that point, I figured I had said enough of what pragmatism is not.

"Perhaps we should begin now with our discussion of Peirce's essay."

Hal nodded in agreement.

"Peirce starts out here by drawing a distinction between the mental perspective of people who are experimentalists and...."

"Experimentalists?"

"People who figure things out by means of experimenting, by testing ideas out in the laboratory or the real world to see if they work."

"Oh," Hal said as if startled by the obviousness of my response. "I see that. Now, who is Peirce drawing the distinction between?"

"He draws the distinction between the mental perspective of the experimentalists and the mental perspective of others."

"Others?"

"Others," I repeated. "Peirce is discussing pragmatism here in terms of being a scientific method, so he is referring to other sorts of educated people, or intellectuals. He is referring to those who get all of their learning out of books instead of testing ideas out in the real world."

"They must have had ivory towers in those days too."

"Probably even more than they do in our times. In Peirce's day, being educated, especially at the college level, was an elitist indulgence. Average people could not go to college. Many were never even able to attend high school. In the nineteenth century, an educated person was nearly always a man. He was someone who had learned facts and details about the ideas of long-dead people. No one expected him to do much with this information, except, perhaps, teach it to others just as it had been taught to him. The whole idea of experimenting was *déclassé* in those days."

"Hmmm."

"It still is in many educated circles."

"Such as?"

"Just think about the state of education in schools and colleges, even today. Other than for science education, teachers seem to have little understanding of the skills that students need for asking good questions and for figuring things out. I doubt if most educators even realize that students need to be able to do this. An experimentalist knows how to figure things out, regardless of whether the subject matter is science, literature, art, or auto mechanics. Few educators know how to help students develop the reasoning skills of an experimentalist. The essay we are discussing describes the process for reasoning like a good experimentalist. The methods for reasoning in this way apply to all thinking and to all subject matter, not only to reasoning in math and science. Those two just happen to have been Peirce's favorite areas."

"Maybe the problem is that teachers and professors do not know how to think this way themselves. You and I know teachers who completely lack intellectual curiosity. We also know more than a few professors out there who love to debate topics like 'how many angels can dance on the head of a pin'."

"We sure do." I knew exactly who he meant. "This society probably has the same proportion of experimentalists to educated people who are not experimentalists as there were in Peirce's time. Other than for the sciences, we do not expect scholars or educators to be experimentalists. We even reward students for not being experimentalists, for sticking closely to what their teachers and professors tell them to think and do. Those students are the ones who usually receive the highest grades."

"That is a good point. I had not thought of it that way before."

"Even curious and insightful educators may not realize that reasoning skills require mastery of a set of core basics, just like reading, writing, and math. As you know, I was completely unaware of these processes before circumstances forced an awareness of them on me. No one would expect a child to be able to read or write without knowing the alphabet. Even the most dedicated educators may not know what the core basics of reasoning entail, or even that such basics exist. We cannot expect people to fully engage in the learning process if they do not even know that these core basics exist."

"You are probably right about that."

"Now back to experimentalists versus others," I said, bringing us to the topic at hand. "Peirce has some strong attitudes about those others. He claims that, 'if those others just checked out an experimentalist's mind, they would discover that his disposition is to think of everything just as it is thought of in the laboratory, that is as a question of experimentation'."

"That sounds like a direct quote."

"It is a direct quote, but only partially. Peirce had a habit of putting everything he had to say on a subject into one sentence. What was not in that quote is Peirce's contention that those others are 'mostly unqualified to even check out the disposition of the experimentalist'."

"Because they do not know what to look for?"

"Probably. Peirce qualifies his general contention about experimentalists by saying that even an experimentalist would probably not be objective enough to be experimental in cases where his mind is trammeled. That is Peirce's word," I interjected, then continued, "...'in cases where his mind is trammeled by emotions or by his upbringing'."

"'Trammeled,'" Hal repeated. "That is an interesting word."

"A trammel is an impediment to free action. If your mind is trammeled, it means that you have a mental impediment to free action because of emotions or your upbringing. Maybe we should use the children's jargon and say 'whacked out'."

Hal laughed. "That is a much more descriptive term!"

"I think so too. Peirce is saying that even someone naturally disposed toward experimentalism will not be an experimentalist when he is emotionally whacked out, or when his upbringing gets in the way."

"Upbringing?"

"Suppose this experimentalist type of person is good at figuring out what chemicals do and why. Say, too, he has been raised since childhood as a fundamentalist Christian who is not supposed to believe in evolution. This person might be a terrific experimentalist when it comes to chemistry, but incompetent if he has to deal with hypotheses that disagree with the beliefs he holds against evolution."

"I see how that could happen."

"Peirce then qualifies his pro-experimentalist claims even more:"

Of course, no living man possesses in their fullness all the attributes characteristic of his type: it is not the typical doctor whom you will see every day driven in buggy or coupe, nor is it the typical pedagogue that will be met with in the first schoolroom you enter.

"What does 'pedagogue' mean?"

"It means teacher. When Peirce refers to the 'typical pedagogue,' he means the 'typical teacher'."

"Oh, I see."

I continued. "Then Peirce says that, 'when you have found, or ideally constructed on the basis of observation, the typical experimentalist'...."

Hal interrupted. "What does 'ideally constructed' mean?"

"He means that you have formed a set of descriptors that would apply to someone who is the most ideal of the typical experimentalists."

"Oh, that makes sense."

"Notice he says 'ideally constructed upon the basis of observation'."

"But that would just mean that you are not supposed to make up the descriptors out of thin air."

"Yes. An experimentalist of Peirce's sort would always form his categories and conclusions empirically, that is, on observations of real cases. An experimentalist would not rely upon untested assumptions."

"That makes sense. Where were we when I interrupted you?"

"Let me see," I said, scrolling up the page. "We are here. 'When you have found, or ideally constructed on the basis of observation the typical experimentalist....'"

"Then what?"

"Then you can observe him, Peirce says, and 'notice that, no matter what assertion you make to him, he will not take it as absolute truth'."

"Meaning?"

"Meaning that 'the typical experimentalist will take your assertion to mean that if a given prescription for an experiment ever can be and ever is carried out in act, an experience of a given description will result'."

"I know that must be a direct quote from Peirce because I cannot make any sense out of it."

I sighed heavily. "I guess you need a translation, then."

"Good idea."

"Peirce's 'typical experimentalist' will take your assertion as something that will end up asserting what you say it does, if that assertion is capable of being tested, that is. If something cannot be put to a test, then the typical experimentalist would see no sense at all in what you say."

"This sounds just like Bertrand Russell's philosophy, which you hate. I find it hard to imagine you siding with Russell."

"Peirce's pragmatism is not at all like Russell!" I responded hotly. "Just wait until we move a little further on. I know it might sound like Russell to you now. Trust me, this is different."

Hal grinned at my outburst. "I will trust you just for now."

I have nothing personal against Bertrand Russell, a twentieth-century British philosopher. However, Hal knows I have strong feelings against Russell's faulty interpretation of good scientific method. But I digress.

"Next in this essay," I said by way of continuing, "Peirce gives the example of a Mr. Balfour who spoke before the British Association."

"Who is this Mr. Balfour?"

"Arthur J. Balfour was a British philosopher who later became Prime Minister. Who he is does not matter all that much, though. Peirce is trying to make a point here based on what Balfour said."

"And what did he say?"

"Peirce writes that Balfour said that 'the physicist...seeks for something deeper than the laws connecting possible objects of experience.' Then Peirce describes Balfour as saying that this physicist's 'real object is physical reality unrevealed in experiments' and that 'the existence of such non-experiential reality is the basic, unalterable faith of science'."

"Non-experiential reality," Hal repeated. "What would that look like?"

"It would not look like anything, or sound like anything, or feel like anything, or...."

"Or taste, or smell like anything?"

"You are right! This was the big problem with the state of philosophy in those days."

"What was the problem?"

"Most philosophers back then believed that a reality existed that was incapable of being experienced and, therefore, incapable of being tested. If you attempted to construct a philosophy of science from that framework you would, like Mr. Balfour, have to defend a set of truths that you could never know and must take on faith."

"Some things you just have to take on faith," Hal argued, "like God, or re-incarnation, if you are Buddhist."

"That is one way of viewing things."

"And what about miracles? What about the double-blind studies that indicate prayer speeds up the healing process?"

"Peirce would probably have suggested that there may be something else at work there. He would have said that science needs to take a look at these phenomena using his methods. If these findings are accurate, then there may be some underlying principle that we have not discovered yet. People used to believe that basic chemical reactions were magical before the principles of chemistry were widely understood. However, even if we prove that prayer heals and even if we discover a principle that allows this to happen, science still would not be proving or disproving the existence of God."

"Why not?"

"Because scientifically proving that prayer heals would be like proving that exercise builds muscles. Science would be proving a basic law or principle that can be deliberately used by people to produce predictable results. Science could not conclude that God causes this to happen, which does not mean that God does not exist. It only means that, in the case of science, you cannot use God as an explanation for why some phenomenon does or does not occur. We will cover why this is so later on in the essay."

"That is fine with me," he agreed. "I will drop it for now."

"The world view back in Peirce's day was such that most philosophers, and even some people who called themselves scientists, operated from the assumption that a non-experiential reality existed. Certain truths about reality were not open to scientific inquiry. You just had to take them on faith. This belief affected the way people pursued scientific inquiry. Science is like everything else. The answers you get depend upon how you frame the questions. How you frame a question usually depends upon what you already know and already believe to be true or false."

"Like Mr. Balfour?"

"Yes. Balfour was describing a philosophy that would have been familiar to most educated people in the nineteenth century. Even for educated people in those days, beliefs came fully formed and based upon unquestioned absolutes. These absolutes were pre-existing truths not open to question or examination."

I could not resist getting a stab in at Russell at this point.

"Russell had a problem with framing questions, too," I added. "Like Peirce, he wanted to move away from absolutism as a basis for doing science. However, he went too far in the other direction. His version of scientific method held that, if you do not know how to count it, measure it, understand it, state it, or prove it with existing tools, then it must not be real. Therefore it does not matter and should not be funded."

"Then, did Russell close off science from the other end?"

"The other end?"

"Yes, the other end." I could see that Hal was struggling for words to explain what he meant, gesturing with his hands to indicate a scales or a seesaw. "Oh, you must know what I mean," he said finally.

"Are you trying to say that the Mr. Balfour types closed off science by saying, 'you cannot look into these matters because they are unknowable and cannot ever be proven'? And the Russell types closed off science by saying, 'if we do not yet know how to prove it, we should not look into it, because it is not a valid scientific question'?"

"Exactly!" Hal said gratefully. "Are we still on the topic?"

"I think so." I scrolled back up the page to where we had left off. "Let me see. We were talking about Balfour and his faith-based philosophy. Peirce says that this typical experimentalist would be color-blind to all such ontological meaning...."

"Whoa!" Hal said, before I could finish my sentence. "What does 'ontological' mean?"

"'Ontological' means proclaiming the existence of something just by thinking it up, independent of any experience of it."

"Then, does ontological mean something is not true?"

"Not necessarily. 'Ontologically-derived' means that something is supposed to be taken as true whether or not it can be proved. For example, most people would agree that numbers are not just 'made up.' Numbers are considered to have ontological existence, meaning that they are to be taken as true, whether or not you can prove that they exist. The branch of philosophy known as ontology is the study of the essence of things. For many philosophers, ontological truths reside in pre-existing essences, regardless of whether the matter is even capable of being proven."

"That sounds like religion." Hal believes in God, so I know he was not being disparaging when he said this.

"Religious beliefs are ontological. Faith is accepting fundamental premises as givens and choosing to believe in something that cannot be proven one way or the other. As I said, ontology is the study of the essence of things. Some call ontology the science of fundamental principles. Peirce even has ontological categories in his theory. He dismisses ontologically-based 'meaning,' but he does not dismiss the existence of ontological essences."

"Then, did Peirce believe in God?"

"I am sure that he did. In another of his essays, Peirce concluded that any sane person would work from the hypothesis that there is a God. However, Peirce was opposed to allowing religions and religious beliefs to dictate what can and cannot be examined or discovered. This has nothing to do with believing in God or not. Peirce's main contention was that a point exists at the beginning of the discovery process in which the exploration of any idea must be allowed full reign. If you start out with an idea that cannot be explored because it has already been set in stone, then you limit your ability to discover new ideas."

Hal appeared satisfied with my brief explanation so I left it at this. I did not want to bring in another essay here to explain Peirce's complex spiritual philosophy, nor did I want to try to explain abduction this early in the game.

"If meaning has been 'ontologically derived,' that means its meaning has been taken directly, without testing, from some irreducible, primary source. Such meaning need not be proved or disproved because it just is."

"And Peirce does not believe this?"

"No, he did not. Peirce says that an experimentalist would be 'color-blind' to any assertion that is supposed to be taken on faith."

"Why do you think he says color-blind and not just blind?"

I had not thought of that before. It was an unusual term to use.

"Maybe he uses 'color-blind' because an experimentalist would not be entirely blind to an assertion just because it had been 'ontologically derived'."

Hal squinted at me questioningly, so I added by way of clarification, "I mean, an experimentalist would not be entirely blind to an assertion just because it had been made up or taken on faith. The making-it-up part is not the big problem for Peirce's experimentalist. Peirce even has a theory about how an experimentalist would go about doing that. The having-to-take-it-on-faith part is what an experimentalist cannot abide."

I could see that this concept was not too hard for Hal, a perpetual experimentalist, to grasp.

"In the rest of this paragraph, Peirce sets himself up as an authority about the experimentalist mind. He writes that he had 'inhabited a laboratory from age six to well past maturity.' He had also spent most of his life associating with experimentalists. He says he has 'a confident sense that he understood them and that they understood him'."

"Is he establishing his credentials for us?"

"Maybe not for us, but he is placing himself firmly within the experimentalist category. The next paragraph in this essay is one long sentence," I said, while counting the lines. "It is nine lines long, to be exact."

"Nine lines long! How could anyone write that way?"

"Peirce did and that is why we are having this discussion. No one has ever claimed Peirce was a good writer, only that he was a precise and deliberate writer. He also has terrific ideas."

"And what is in this next one-sentence paragraph?"

"Peirce says that his life in the laboratory does not prevent him from becoming interested in methods of thinking. He also says that he, personally, exemplifies the experimentalist type, both in what he is saying now and what he will be writing later on in this essay."

"Is that it?" Hal asked hopefully, when I paused.

"No. Peirce also writes that when he first read metaphysics, it...."

"A definition of 'metaphysics' please," Hal said, interrupting me.

"Joe Ransdell, who runs the online Peirce discussion group, once told me that a librarian in ancient times arbitrarily assigned the title, *Metaphysics*, to an untitled work by Aristotle. The librarian gave the text this title because it was the next book on the shelf after the one called *Physics*. The word comes from the combination of two Greek words. 'Meta' means beyond or after, and 'physika' means of the physical or concrete in nature. The term 'metaphysics' covers a broad category and is used a number of different ways in philosophy. Peirce described metaphysics as the branch of philosophy in charge of 'giving an account of the universe of mind and matter'."

"I thought metaphysics has to do with religion."

"Religion is one way of 'giving an account of the universe of mind and matter.' However, it is not the only way. Metaphysics can have to do with God or any other underlying principles of the natural order of things. Metaphysics also covers things that cannot be experienced, yet can be proven to exist by reason alone."

"Then metaphysics must be ontological," Hal said, appearing pleased that he had found a situation for applying his newly acquired terminology.

"It depends upon whose metaphysics you are talking about. Ontology covers things that can be proven to exist by reason alone but cannot be experienced. But 'ontologically derived meaning,' as Peirce is using it, refers to taking meaning on an *a priori* basis, which means without testing or investigation. Peirce is opposed to 'ontologically derived meaning,' not ontology."

"I see the distinction now."

"Good. To continue, then," I said, bringing us back on course, "Peirce says that when he came to read metaphysics, 'much of it appeared to be loosely reasoned and determined by accidental prepossessions'."

"What are 'accidental prepossessions'?"

"Good question. Most philosophers use the word 'accident' to mean that something is unpredictable. The word 'prepossession' means a bias or a prejudice. The phrase 'accidental prepossessions' probably means a random reappearance of an already existing set of beliefs."

"That sounds like a plausible meaning."

"Peirce then says that, although most of the metaphysical work that he read appeared to be loosely reasoned, he did come across a few people who seemed to be thinking like experimentalists."

"Meaning?"

"Meaning that their writings made him think of the kind of reasoning that he used in the laboratory. Because of this, he felt he could trust them, as he trusted other laboratory men."

"Who were these people?"

"Kant, Berkeley, and Spinoza are the three he mentions here."

"Do I need to know about these people to understand this essay?"

"No."

"Thank goodness!"

"Our hour is up. Have you had enough for today?"

"Is this a good place to stop?"

"I think so. Tomorrow we will be discussing the reason Peirce chose the term 'pragmatism' as the name for his theory."

"Great!"

Two
THE NAME GAME

Essay lines 49-85

"Today is the name game!," Hal announced enthusiastically as we sat down to begin our next morning's work.

"Name game?" I wondered.

"This the day we find out why Peirce called his philosophy 'pragmatism'," he reasoned. "That means we are going play Peirce's name game today!"

"I would not call it play," I said glumly. This day's effort would include a paragraph that was twenty-four lines long and had only four sentences. The first sentence was nine lines long, same as yesterday's paragraph, only much more difficult to explain. Here we had barely started, and I was already beginning to think I had bitten off more than I could chew. I started out that morning's dialogue by referring back to what we had discussed the day before.

"Peirce describes his experimentalist versus other types of intellectual people to show why he names his theory pragmatism. He needs to draw a distinction between the ways in which these two sorts of educated people go about figuring things out. You need to understand this difference in order to understand why he needed to select a particular name for his philosophical theory."

"And what is that difference?"

"The difference is that experimentalists care about outcomes. They base their conclusions on results. The others do not. Peirce wants to differentiate between himself and those other kinds of intellects who do not need proof. The others believed in an unchanging, fundamental 'isness' which needs no proving, which cannot not be proved. This 'isness' supposedly transcended mundane things such as physical reality."

"And would this be an ontological 'isness'?"

"Yes. This is a good place to use that word."

"Are you saying then, that Peirce's basis for the difference between these two is that experimentalists rely on outcomes and the others do not?"

"Yes, and this basis is reflected by the way in which an experimentalist does science, as contrasted with just applying pre-conceived beliefs."

As I said this, I remembered a perfect example of the "experimentalists versus others" dichotomy.

"By the way," I added, as I began searching among my favorite quotes, "a classic example of the non-experimental approach to science comes from a seventeenth-century astronomer. Back when Galileo was trying to convince people to look through his telescope and see for themselves that four moons orbited Jupiter, he received a bizarre argument from the Florentine astronomer,

Francesco Sizzi. This argument was typical for the times, which makes it even more of a curiosity. Sizzi's wrote this as logical explanation of why he would not even look through Galileo's telescope. Here is what Sizzi wrote:"

> There are seven windows in the head, two nostrils, two ears, two eyes, and a mouth; so in the heavens there are two favorable stars, two unpropitious, two luminaries, and Mercury alone undecided and indifferent. From which and many other similar phenomena of nature such as the seven metals, *et cetera*, which it was tedious to enumerate, we gather that the number of planets is necessarily seven.... Besides, the Jews and other ancient nations, as well as modern Europeans, have adopted the division of the week into seven days, and have named them from the seven planets: now if we increase the number of planets, this whole system falls to the ground.... Moreover, the satellites are invisible to the naked eye and therefore can have no influence on the earth and therefore would be useless and therefore do not exist.[2]

Hal was laughing out loud by the time I finished reading this.

"This is an extreme example, but it does point out the type of conclusions a non-experimentalist might end up with."

"That is a memorable piece of reasoning," he commented, still chuckling. "I understand the difference now between experimentalists and others."

"The next thing Peirce says is that his theory holds that a conception...."

"A conception?"

"By 'conception' Peirce means the point or meaning of an idea," I said, then continued. "A conception, which is the meaning of an idea, 'lies exclusively in its conceivable bearing on the conduct of life'."

"Is that another direct quote?"

Since Hal was still having trouble with Peirce's phrasing, I struggled to find another way to say this.

"What Peirce means is that meaning resides in consequences which affect the conduct of life."

"That does not make any more sense to me than the other way did."

"I extracted that definition of Peirce's theory from one of his famous nine-line sentences," I admitted. "Shall I try again?"

Hal nodded.

"Do you understand what he is trying to get across by saying that the meaning of something resides in its consequences?"

"Not in the least."

I sighed at this and started over again.

"Back when Peirce was developing his theory, even educated people believed that things meant whatever they meant in-and-of-themselves. The goal of science, philosophy, or whatever, was to figure out what that pre-existing meaning was."

"I will bet that most people still believe that."

"Probably, but that is not the point here."

"What is the point?"

"The point is the mistaken belief that meaning is inherent in a thing or a word. Peirce cannot abide the idea of pre-existing meanings separate from effects. He contends that you cannot possibly know what something means unless you know its effects."

"And how would you determine that? You would have to wait until something was over to figure out its effects."

"Determine what?"

"Its effects," said Hal, ever the engineer. "Would that be like making blueprints and plans for a building?" he offered, then he looked confused. "But with meaning? With ideas? How are you going to know in advance what the effects of ideas would be?"

"Everything that someone does on purpose is the result of an idea."

"Everything?"

"Yes, everything. You cannot do anything on purpose without first having an idea. The meaning of what you do, which is always based on an idea, comes from its effects on human conduct. Some ideas are more concrete than others, which makes them easier to demonstrate in advance of acting on them. Blueprints are a way of expressing ideas so that you can deliberately change your conduct in advance of doing something. You can work out what you are going to do on a set of blueprints before digging a foundation and pouring the concrete. The meaning of your blueprints resides in how they affect what you do when you use them. If you have a set of blueprints, but ignore them and, instead, dig a free-form foundation, then those blueprints are not affecting your conduct. They are essentially meaningless."

"I see that."

"So, your question should not be, 'how are we going to know in advance what the effects of ideas will be?' We have many ways of expressing the probable effects of ideas in the physical world, like blueprints, scale models, and drawings. Your question should be, 'how can we know in advance what will be the effects of concepts, such as values, purposes, methods, and abstract ideas, that do not lend themselves to physical demonstrations?' No one had tackled that question before Peirce with any great success. His theory did for language and meaning what blueprints do for engineering."

"Which is?"

"We will deal with that later," I assured him. "Right now we want to find out why Peirce calls his theory 'pragmatism.' As I said before, in Peirce's time, people believed that meaning was intrinsic. They believed that things and words meant what they were supposed to mean independent of how they were used. Peirce is proposing a radical idea by contending that the meaning of a concept is determined by it effects upon the conduct of human behavior."

"Then would you say that he has a blueprint approach to life?"

"Yes, but probably not in the way you are thinking. Pragmatism is much more than simple and obvious practicality. It applies to all types of behaviors, including mental ones that are entirely invisible."

Hal seemed to be following, so I continued.

"Peirce said that if you can accurately define all of the conceivable consequences of doing or not doing something, then you will have the complete meaning of the concept. This means that, once you can accurately define all of an idea's possible consequences, you have the entire meaning of that idea."

"That is quite a mouthful."

"True. But Peirce said if you do that, then there is nothing more to the meaning of that idea. Once you have identified all of the conceivable consequences of an idea, the concept in question is complete. You have all you need for knowing what that idea means."

"All?" Hal asked skeptically. "That would be an enormous undertaking. Besides, once you did this, you would take away the interesting parts of life. You would take away all of the mysteries, which are fun to think about."

"Good science is an enormous undertaking. That is the whole point. It is so enormous, that it is much easier to throw up our hands and say that it cannot be done. Most people would not bother in the first place."

"Would they just take things on faith?"

"Yes. Taking something on faith, without examining the assumptions behind it or the consequences from acting on it, is much easier than inquiring into a topic the way Peirce would have us do it. Peirce proposes that everything that matters to the conduct of life should be open to inquiry, even things that everyone already takes for granted as being beyond inquiry."

"What about things that do not matter?" Hal asked flippantly.

"If something does not matter one way or the other, it is irrelevant. Irrelevancies have no place in Peirce's pragmatism. This is what he means when he says that the meaning of something resides in those consequences coming from it which affect the conduct of life."

"If it's not broke, don't fix it?"

"Not unless it would matter if you did. Maybe it would matter to fix something that is not broken in order to teach someone how to fix it, in case it ever did break," I explained. "However, you are wrong in thinking that Peirce's pragmatic theory would take the mystery out of life."

"How so?"

"Peirce's theory provides access to tools for exploring and examining the mysteries of life. We can use his theory to examine meaning in language and cultures, to present ideas logically, to explore things and ideas in greater depth.

Peirce's pragmatism is as useful for creating artistic masterpieces as it is for discovering scientific principles."

"But we digress?" Hal suggested.

"You are right," I agreed and returned to the text. "Peirce says that some of his friends wanted him to call his theory 'practicism' or 'practicalism,' but he chose the word 'pragmatism' for his own reasons."

"What were his reasons?"

"He says they had mostly to do with having learned philosophy by studying the German philosopher, Kant. Peirce writes that, in the German language, the meaning of the word for practical 'praktisch' and the word for pragmatic 'pragmatisch' are completely different. No self-respecting experimentalist, claims Peirce, would ever want to be associated with the word 'praktisch.' That is why he picked the term 'pragmatism'."

"Trying to impress the Germans, huh?" Hal said wryly.

"Probably not so much to impress as to get in step with them. Many of the great ideas of the modern age of Western thought originated in Germany. Peirce was especially fond of Immanuel Kant, though he disagreed with him on major issues."

"Was Kant a contemporary of Peirce?"

"Heavens no! Kant was born about a hundred years before Peirce."

"Why was Peirce thinking about using words like 'practical' and 'pragmatic' in the first place? He could have just picked a name he liked."

"Peirce wants people to know that his is a theory of reasoning based upon both reality and usefulness. Some say that you can categorize different kinds of philosophy into two sorts, realism and idealism."

"And Peirce's was realism?"

"Peirce's was grounded in realism, but he identified himself as an idealist. I see his philosophy as a bridge between the two, a combination of both."

"How so?"

"Proponents of pure realism say that you look at what you can prove and say this is what is true and this is all there is. Pure idealists claim that what you can prove is only part of the picture. Idealists hold that an ideal state of perfection exists to which you can aspire, but which you can never know."

"And pragmatists?"

"Peirce's sort of pragmatist says that you take what is and use it to inquire into what might be true."

"I guess that makes me a pragmatist."

"There never was a question in my mind about that."

Since we were still close to the beginning of the essay, I was going to leave the explanation at that. Then I thought better of it. I decided that I might create confusion later if I failed to set things straight here.

"As I said, Peirce considered himself an idealist as well as a pragmatist. I suppose you could say he was a 'realistic idealist.' He was not the type of idealist who failed to inquire into ideals or to test them against practical reality. For Peirce, the goal of inquiry is to uncover the 'ultimate ideal reality.' At the end of inquiry, which you can never be sure you have reached, you will have uncovered a truth that is waiting for you to find it. Not all pragmatists believe that an ideal reality exists, though. Some think that you make it up as you go. However, all pragmatists agree that inquiry should never end. We are human beings and, therefore, fallible. We cannot ever know for sure that we have reached an absolute truth."

I realized that Hal did not have enough information yet to disagree, or even ask questions. I decided it was still too early in our discussion to explain these positions any further, so I continued.

"Next, Peirce explains why he called his theory 'pragmatism'."

"And why did he?"

"Peirce says that the most striking feature of his new theory is its 'recognition of an inseparable connection between rational cognition and rational purpose.' This connection is the final factor that causes him to prefer the name 'pragmatism'."

"An 'inseparable connection'?"

"Like all pragmatists, Peirce holds that a thought and the purpose for thinking it are inseparably connected. Naturally, he means only rational thoughts and rational purposes, not such things as hallucinations or dreams, because these are irrational. They are not subject to deliberate self-control."

"I still fail to see any obvious connection between that statement and the reason Peirce names his theory pragmatism."

"Peirce means that no idea can exist in a vacuum. A rational idea is always connected to its purpose. It has a practical use-factor. What something means depends upon how it is used and to what end."

"Hmm," Hal was thoughtful at this. "Then pragmatism not only means that the meaning of something is in its effects?"

"Yes, it does only mean that. But the way we determine the effects of something is by looking through the lens of purpose."

"In other words, we have to know what we are after in order to know if we have gotten it?"

"Yes."

I had to make a judgment call at this point. Should I bring up the realist-nominalist dichotomy here? Or should I let it go until we begin talking about the Scholastics? I opted to let it go. I decided that such a discussion would take us off track if I tried to deal with those two perspectives now. I avoided the issue entirely by focusing upon the social and intellectual events that contributed to Peirce's context.

"You should probably be aware that Peirce lived in an era of crisis that would ultimately threaten both scientific and religious absolutes. The essay we are discussing was published in 1905. To put that into perspective, it might help to know that Darwin's *The Origin of Species* was first published in 1859, just two years before the outbreak of the American Civil War, which lasted until 1865. Peirce began writing about his ideas in 1867 when he was twenty-eight years old. The United States had been turned upside down both philosophically and politically by the time Peirce began developing his philosophy. Darwin's theory of evolution was far too revolutionary and too new for science to have fully accommodated its implications."

"Is that like the effects of quantum mechanics on the twentieth century?"

"Yes, it is much like that. Most scientists who sided with Darwin in those days ended up operating from the opposite end of the same pole as the religionists. The science end held absolutely that there could be no God. The religionists held to the opposite end of the stick, contending that there absolutely must be a God, one of a particular kind and denomination. Both sides pounded on each other with different ends of the same stick, absolutism."

"They are still pounding each other with that same stick. At least it seems like that to me."

"I agree. For Peirce, unquestioned absolutism is the problem, regardless of the end of the stick from which it originates. Now, this next sentence is going to be a difficult one. It is seventeen lines long."

"One sentence that is seventeen lines long! No wonder I cannot understand him!"

"Shall we give it a try?"

"Sure, why not?"

The next sentence was formidable. I was not sure I was up to the task.

"This sentence is about philosophical nomenclature."

"And what is that about?"

"Naming things and qualities that have to do with philosophical matters."

"It would have been nice if he had just said that."

"But then he would not have been Peirce, would he? Peirce says that, for years, he has wanted to say a few things on this matter of philosophical nomenclature. In particular, he has wanted to 'submit a few plain considerations' about this matter to the few philosophers out there who are not happy about the current state of affairs."

"What state of affairs?"

"The state of affairs concerning naming things and qualities having to do with philosophical matters."

"And this is something that matters?" Hal asked in a tone of incredulity.

"It matters a great deal! How can you possibly know what people mean if you do not know what their words mean?"

"Oh, good point."

"Peirce is assuming the existence of other philosophers, besides himself, who want to rescue the study of philosophy from its airy-fairy status. He is appealing to those who want to put philosophy on an equal footing with the useful studies of the natural sciences."

"Airy-fairy," Hal repeated, wincing. "That does not sound like Peirce."

"Not exactly," I admitted. "Peirce did use Shakespeare's term 'airy nothings' in another essay to describe these sorts of thoughts. Anyway, airy-fairy is what he is implying when he says that meaning should not be 'ontologically derived.' Peirce believes that philosophers should use the same methods as scientists for inquiring into matters."

"In that case, I will accept 'airy-fairy.' Go on."

"Peirce says that, instead of using up all their time scorning each other's work, philosophical investigators should cooperate and stand upon one another's shoulders. Investigators in the natural sciences do this. If philosophers did the same, they could build upon each other's findings the way scientists do and 'multiply incontestable results'."

He made a face at this. "'Multiply incontestable results'?"

"Peirce means that they could produce more and better philosophical understandings. Philosophy could then operate the same way science does, by using one person's discoveries as a tool for discovering other things and by replicating each other's experiments to validate findings. Then philosophers, like scientists, could build upon valid ideas, not gibberish."

"I find it difficult to think of philosophy as something that produces results. I have always thought of philosophy as made up of different people's opinions about things, not as something connected to any results."

"You are not alone," I assured him. "Peirce was different from most philosophers. He believed that philosophers should hold themselves to the same standards as scientists. Scientists must be able to repeat every observation. If philosophers were to operate as scientists, then one observation, like a flash of insight, a personal experience, or an isolated event, could not be used as the basis for constructing a general rule or principle. The observation would have to hold up to scrutiny. It would have to be repeatedly tested by others first and verified against experience."

"So, no more *Books of Revelation*?"

"St. John the Divine would probably have had a few problems meeting Peirce's requirements. Peirce also has something to say here about forming hypotheses, too."

"What do you mean by 'hypotheses'?"

"Peirce uses 'hypothesis,' 'proposal,' and 'proposition' interchangeably throughout this essay. You can also think of the word 'goal' in this same sense as well."

"I will keep that in mind."

"For Peirce, a hypothesis is a provisional explanation for something. What he means by this is that you can only know if a provisional explanation is correct if it works. You know it works 'if it has been remarkably borne out by experience.' The experience that Peirce refers to here is one in which the hypothesis correctly predicts what it is supposed to predict. However, even then, even if a hypothesis has been tested out in experience and has correctly predicted what it is supposed to predict, Peirce says that a hypothesis should only be trusted provisionally."

"Why only provisionally? Is it impossible to ever prove anything, then?"

"Peirce says that 'every hypothesis that merits attention should be subjected to severe, but fair, examination.' Even after such an examination, though, it should still only be held as a provisional truth, not as an absolute."

"But why?"

"Because, for one thing, every hypothesis has an if-then quality to it, meaning that its truth is defined by what you can learn about it given your present context, tools, and knowledge. You never know when new information might arise that could change the situation."

I could tell I was being too vague for him, so I offered an example. "Just think about how quantum mechanics and Einstein's special theory of relativity changed Newton's laws of motion into Newton's laws of the motion of large bodies on earth. Newton's laws were not wrong. They just were not the absolutely final word on the subject, as most people used to believe."

"That makes sense. I understand that."

"The whole point of this seventeen-line sentence is that Peirce believes that philosophy should take a lesson from the natural sciences where 'a radically false step is rarely taken'."

"Would that be because, in the real world, if something does not prove out to be true, you would not use it?"

"Yes. Peirce adds that, in science, even the most faulty theories that become generally accepted are true in the sense that their 'main experiential predictions' work."

"How could you know this in philosophy? How would you know whether something works or not when you are just dealing with ideas?"

"Think back to what we said earlier about blueprints," I suggested. "This statement operates along that same idea. Up until Peirce, you could not know whether an idea worked or not because philosophy was making its own rules separate from the laws of experience."

"Ontologically?"

"Yes," I agreed, with a quick wink to acknowledge his expanded vocabulary. "In philosophy, language is both the primary tool for and the result of inquiry. Peirce even wrote in another essay that pragmatism is 'merely a method of ascertaining the meanings of hard words and abstract concepts.' If something is just a pointless porcupine, if it changes nothing as a result being true, then Peirce contended that there is no point in mucking around in it."

Hal laughed at this. He shares with me a strong distaste for pointless porcupines, our name for arguments about irrelevancies such as, "how many angels can dance on the head of a pin?"

"Then, with the issues left, the ones that do matter, Peirce is saying that we should approach these in the same way we should approach a scientific experiment."

"How would you do this with philosophical ideas?"

"With language. Philosophy can be made scientific by using language as a tool for discovering and proving concepts. Peirce gave us a valuable gift by making language into a tool that we can use to better explain and understand ideas. His work in language and meaning also shows us how to take well-formed ideas and construct solutions with them."

"What kinds of ideas and solutions?"

"For one thing, we can use Peirce's methods to improve education. With Peirce's language-based system, we can provide educators with a common language and a common understanding of the skills that underlie the development of good reasoning abilities. Without these underlying skills, you cannot do much of anything with knowledge, except store it up and regurgitate it. Peirce's theory of pragmatism can be used to revolutionize education."

"What else can you use it for besides education?"

"Peirce's concepts about language reside at the foundation of both linguistics and computer programming. His contention that we should be as precise with defining the terms of ideas as we are with the terms of scientific experiments led to the language-based logic we now use for computer languages. Today we can teach people how to use language more effectively because of Peirce's efforts at making philosophy more scientific."

"So by cleaning up language, he made philosophy pragmatic, or useful. That sounds reasonable enough."

"Then this is a good place to stop for today."

"What will tomorrow bring?"

"More of the same," I warned him. "For the next few days, Peirce will be laying out the justification for his theory of pragmatism."

"Tomorrow then!"

Three
THE NAME GAME—DAY TWO

"One thing about Peirce's writing," I said, as I perused the first sentence of the section for that day, "is that it never improved over time."

"Bad, huh?"

"Yesterday we made our way through one seventeen-line-long sentence."

"And today?"

"Nineteen lines long."

"Wow! That must be a world's record."

I was not sure if I heard amazement or dismay in Hal's voice, but I continued anyway. "Peirce claims that the sciences that have done the best job with naming things are the taxonomic sciences."

"Do you mean the ones that stuff dead animals and hang them on walls?"

It took me a moment to understand what he meant.

"Do you mean 'taxidermy'?"

He nodded.

I thought a moment here before deciding whether to go into an extensive explanation of the term 'taxonomy.' The meaning of this word is significant in the development of Peirce's theory of signs which eventually resulted in the development of an entire category of study, semiotics. Semiotics includes the fields of semantics and linguistics. I decided that I had better explain this and headed for Greek root words as the best place to start.

"The words 'taxonomy' and 'taxidermy' mean entirely different things, but they share a root word and that could tend to confuse things."

"Tax?" Hal offered.

"Almost. They share the root word 'taxis'."

"Taxes?" Hal said, looking even more confused, "like income taxes?"

"No. The root word is 't-a-x-i-s.' It means arrangement or order."

"How can stuffing dead animals mean arrangement or order?"

"The suffix of that word is 'dermy.' 'Derma' is a Greek word for skin."

"Like dermatology?"

"Yes, so taxidermy means order or arrangement of skin."

"As in stuffing the skin of dead animals!" Hal finished triumphantly.

"Yes!"

"So then, what does the word 'taxonomy' mean? Or, I guess I want to know what does 'o-no-my' mean?"

"The first 'o' is just a typical ending of the first part of a compound word of Greek origin, so all we need to know is the meaning of 'nomy'."

"And that meaning is?"

"Having to do with laws, customs, distribution, or management."

"And taxonomy means?"

"One sense of the word means the arrangement of laws, customs, distribution, or management. Another sense means the laws, or rules, of arrangement. This second sense is closer to what Peirce means."

"Now, what were you saying about Peirce and taxonomy?"

"I said that Peirce claims that the sciences that have done the best job in naming things are the taxonomic sciences."

"So," Hal said thoughtfully, "those would be the sciences having to do with the arrangement of laws, custom, distribution, or management?"

"The specific meaning of the word 'taxonomy' is the classification of things in relation to general laws or principles. The word 'classification' implies an arrangement of things based on rules for distributing them among the categories."

"Is a taxonomy the same thing as a classification?"

"Yes. As you know, we teach three basic ways of classifying in Engaged Intelligence training. In a general sense, they are all taxonomic classifications. However, the specific taxonomy that Peirce is referring to here classifies according to categorical relationships. Categorical relationships reflect similarities and differences among selected qualities of things."

"Qualities? Are these the same qualities as for Engaged Intelligence?"

"Yes. Qualities are aspects such as, color, size, shape, sound, feelings, number, substance, or function. They are the aspects of things that enable us to differentiate one thing from another."

"I see that."

"Most people think of classification as sorting things into kinds, or types, of something. For example, they do not think of structural relationships as classifications. Structural relationships are often expressed as blueprints and diagrams, so they look significantly different from categorical classifications. As you know, structural classifications reflect the part to whole relationships of how things fit together. Structural classifications are used for designing or analyzing structures, like bodies and buildings."

"But structural classifications use qualities, too."

"Yes they do. Structural relationships rely mostly on qualities which differentiate spatial relationships. They use qualities like 'above,' 'below,' 'next to,' 'inside.' Qualities of size, substance, and direction also apply here."

"I guess operations would be even more difficult for people to recognize as classifications."

"Yes. Operational classifications, which produce systems analyses, are the third way of classifying things. Operations rely upon qualities of time, such as 'before,' 'after,' and 'during'. People may miss the classification aspect of complex operations since we usually need to use a mix-and-match approach to perform them."

"Mix-and-match?"

"Yes. For a complex systems analysis, you need to classify in terms of all three sorts of classifications. You must classify by categories, structures, and operations in order to effectively perform a complex analysis."

"Let me see if I understand you," he said, collecting his thoughts. "Peirce feels that the sciences which have done the best job naming things are those sciences which classify things in relation to general laws or principles."

I nodded.

"What science does not?"

"Philosophy, for one. That was the science Peirce was most interested in reforming."

"Philosophy is not a science, is it?"

"Peirce would have argued that philosophy is second only to mathematics as a science of discovery. According to Peirce, mathematics studies what is and is not logically possible, without bothering with whether it does, or even can, actually exist. The job of philosophy is discovering what is true, based on what can be inferred from common experience. In this sense, philosophy underlies all of science, because it is the study of the concepts with which we approach the world. That makes philosophy the main tool with which we should approach scientific study. Peirce's argument here is that the science of philosophy should be held to the same standards as chemistry, mineralogy, botany, and zoology."

"Are those the same as the taxonomic sciences?"

"Yes. Peirce is pointing out that these sciences have an accepted and universally understood language for grouping things into 'kinds of this or that,' or 'parts of this or that,' or 'stages and phases of this or that'."

"Let me see if I understand this. The sciences doing the best job naming things are those which arrange things into categories and sub-categories?"

"Yes."

"It sounds like he means just the 'hard sciences.'"

I nodded in agreement and continued.

"Peirce has just pointed out the success of taxonomic sciences at overcoming the difficulties of terminology, the 'name games' as you call them. He argued that this success conclusively demonstrates the effectiveness of scientific terminology for removing ambiguity and misunderstandings. Next, he contends that the only way you can get past the problem in other fields...."

"Which problem?"

"The problem of misinterpretations about what something means due to different beliefs and preferences."

"Oh."

"Peirce argues here that the only way to avoid misunderstandings in other fields is to apply the techniques of scientific classification to those fields. This would avoid the confusions that arise in those other fields, such as philosophy, due to individual habits and preferences."

"I see that."

"Next, Peirce claims that the only way to make language mean what it is intended to mean is to make the underlying rules of explanatory language...."

"Explanatory as opposed to what?" Hal interrupted again.

"Explanatory is my word. I use it to mean language which functions to explain things, as opposed to language used to produce art, like poetic language. Peirce claims that the only way to make language mean what it is intended to mean is to make the rules of language in general follow the same requirements as the terminology of scientific taxonomies."

"How does he propose to do this?"

"That is not an easy answer for me to give you at this point. What Peirce says here is that the 'underlying canons of terminology'...."

"Canons?"

"The rules or doctrines upon which the terminology is based. Peirce proposes that these underlying 'canons of terminology,' the rules by which things are named, should be such that they 'shall gain the support of moral principle and of every man's sense of decency'."

"What does he mean by 'moral principle' and 'decency'?"

"Peirce believed that reasoning is a species of conduct and therefore subject to praise or blame. In philosophy, matters of conduct subject to praise or blame belong to the category of ethics. Peirce is proposing here that the rules of language should be such that words and their meanings could be examined and agreed upon. Then, once agreed upon, these should be adhered to as a matter of ethical principle."

"What does that have to do with morals and decency? Does he mean that certain words should not be used?"

"No, that is not what he means. Peirce is proposing that the language of philosophy should be held to the same standards as scientific language."

"That is reasonable enough, but I still do not see what that has to do with morals and decency."

"Just as we have standards for performing scientific research, Peirce believes that we should also have standards for philosophical inquiry. Such standards are called 'norms.' Peirce holds that reasoning and logic are ethical issues because they both have to do with the way something is done."

"That still does not make any sense to me."

"The norms that Peirce proposes for scientific and philosophical reasoning have to do with the way in which an inquiry is done. Either you follow standards, or you do not. Whether you choose to follow standards or choose not to follow them, you are making a choice of how to conduct yourself. Everything having to do with choices in human conduct belongs in the category of ethics. A major aspect of Peirce's theory is that all reasoning is a species of conduct and must thus be informed and supported by universal ethical principles, just as all conduct should be."

"What does the name of something have to do with conduct?"

"The act of naming requires a choice of conduct. If you use or select a particular name for something, that means you also could have chosen some other name. Peirce is proposing standards for naming philosophical terms. Just as no one would violate the standards for scientific terminology, so too, no one should violate standards of philosophical terminology. Both the following of standards and the violating of standards are choices of conduct and, therefore, a matter of ethical concern."

"It still sounds strange to me that names have to do with conduct, but I think I understand what he means. You can continue."

"I am going to go over what I just read before we go on," I said, feeling the need of a running start into the next part of Peirce's sentence.

"Fine with me."

"First, Peirce writes that the taxonomic sciences have done the best job with terminology. Secondly, he says that other fields should use the same methods as science for developing terminology. His idea is that these other fields can then be held to the same moral and ethical standards as science."

"And is there a thirdly?"

"Yes, there is a thirdly," I teased. "Remember, this is a nineteen-line long sentence we are discussing. So far, we are only up to line ten."

Hal sighed.

"Third is that anyone who introduces a new conception into philosophy should have to invent acceptable terms to express it. Once the terms are invented, then other philosophers have to accept those terms and not tinker with them to make them mean other things."

"That is only fair."

"Peirce claims that tinkering with someone else's terms and changing their original meaning is not only a gross discourtesy to the person who came up with the original terms, but it is also an injury to philosophy."

"How so?"

"Let me see," I began, trying to think of an example. "I can think of one case that fits, one that bothered Peirce a great deal. He was irritated that the theory of evolution developed by Charles Darwin had been twisted into a belief system called 'Social Darwinism'."

"Social Darwinism?"

"Yes. There were people in the nineteenth and early twentieth century who took Darwin's term 'survival of the fittest,' which Darwin meant in a biological sense. They combined a generalized misinterpretation of Darwin with pieces of other doctrines, and then applied the mixture to social issues."

"And this was bad?"

"Yes, it was bad. Conclusions drawn in part from Social Darwinism gave Hitler his pseudo-scientific basis for exterminating Jews. The fittest were, in that case, those of Aryan descent. Social Darwinism gave predatory American capitalists justification for ignoring the social effects of their greed-based actions. The fittest were, and still are, those who can make the most money."

"Either one of those could have given philosophy a bad name."

"I agree. Back in Peirce's day, and throughout history, philosophers were tinkering with each other's terminologies. Peirce has even more to say about this. 'Furthermore...once a conception has been supplied with suitable and sufficient words for its expression, no other technical terms denoting the same things, considered in the same relations, should be countenanced'."

"Countenanced?"

"That is a nineteenth century way of saying 'put up with.' Peirce means that, in addition to not tinkering with someone's original words and making them mean something else, we should also refuse to put up with people who make up new terminology for the same concepts."

"But that is what we are doing here," Hal protested, adding, "making up new terminology, I mean."

"No. We are clarifying and defining, trying to make a better way to understand what Peirce means by his terms. We are not trying to make his words mean something else or trying to come up with new words to replace his. I am just explaining what he means."

"Oh," Hal said, apparently satisfied.

"We are finished with the sentence. Shall I try to sum it all up now?"

"Do you mean everything or just this sentence?"

"Just this sentence."

"Sure."

"First, Peirce says that the taxonomic sciences have done the best job with terminology. Secondly, he says that other fields should use the same methods as science for developing terminology, so they can be held to the same moral and ethical standards as science."

I paused here as I phrased this last part.

"Thirdly," I continued, "Peirce states that people should not tinker with other people's terminologies by making the words mean something other than they were intended to mean. Nor should anyone make up different words for describing the same concept."

"And is that all?"

"Yes, all nineteen lines of it. Peirce begins this next sentence by saying, should this suggestion find favor...."

"Which suggestion?" Hal asked, interrupting.

"His suggestion that philosophy should adopt the same rigorous rules for naming things as the taxonomic sciences."

"Oh, yes. I remember that."

"Next, Peirce says that, 'should this suggestion find favor, it might be deemed necessary for philosophers as a group to come together and devise canons,' meaning laws or rules, 'to define the naming process in philosophy'."

"I see that."

"Peirce says, just as is done in chemistry, 'it might be wise to assign fixed meanings to certain prefixes and suffixes'."

Hal raised an eyebrow as I said this, and I knew exactly what I needed to explain. Sometimes I forget that not everyone experienced a Catholic school education and its relentless emphasis on Latin and Greek prefixes and suffixes.

"You are wondering about the terms 'prefix' and 'suffix.' Am I correct?"

He nodded.

"A prefix is hooked onto the beginning of a word to alter its meaning in some way. A suffix is added to the end of the word."

I could see he had vaguely heard about this somewhere.

"Now, let me see. We were at the place where Peirce says, 'just as is done in chemistry, it might be wise to assign fixed meanings to certain prefixes and suffixes'."

"What does that mean?"

"Peirce means that meanings are fixed according to the subject matter for which they are used. Words take on different meanings when they are used in different contexts. A scientific term, however, can mean only one thing when used scientifically."

"Can you give an example?"

"Sure. The word 'gravity' is a good example. In the context of science, gravity refers to a general law, or principle, having to do with the force of gravitational pull. But the word 'gravity' has several other meanings also."

"I can think of at least one other meaning," Hal offered, "as in, 'she did not understand the gravity of the situation'."

"Yes. All meanings of the word 'gravity' come from the same Latin root '*gravitas*,' meaning heavy."

"Are you saying that the word 'gravity' means only one thing in science, even though the word has other meanings as well?"

"That is what I am saying. Peirce proposes that, just as in the sciences, it might be wise to assign fixed meanings to certain prefixes and suffixes in philosophy. Then he gives some examples. He suggests that the prefix 'prope'...."

"Meaning?"

"Think of words like 'propel,' 'propeller,' and 'propellant.'"

"To go forward?"

"Not necessarily forward, but outward for sure, away from the point of origin. Peirce suggests that the prefix 'prope' indicate 'a broad and rather indefinite extension of the meaning of the term to which it was prefixed.' Then he says that the name of a doctrine would naturally end in the suffix 'ism'."

"Why naturally?"

"Because that is what 'ism' means. It is a suffix applied to Greek root words to make them denote actions or practices."

"Such as?"

"Such as 'criticism' or 'barbarism.' This suffix is also used to denote doctrines or principles, such as 'Protestantism,' 'Judaism,' 'communism'...."

"And 'pragmatism'?"

"And 'pragmatism,'" I agreed. "Next, Peirce proposes the suffix 'ic-ism' to mark a more strictly defined acceptance of a particular doctrine."

"That sounds picky to me."

"He means to be picky," I said emphatically. "Peirce's point here is that we should be precise when we use language. We are at a good place to stop now. We can begin here tomorrow."

"And tomorrow?"

"Name game, day three."

"This is a long game."

"It was for Peirce, too. He played it his whole life."

"Until tomorrow, then."

Four
THE NAME GAME—DAY THREE

"We are going to be able to go along more quickly today," I said to Hal as we settled in for that morning's conversation. "Compared to what we have just been through, this will be much easier."

Hal took another sip of coffee and settled comfortably into his chair. I could see that he was ready for me to begin.

"Peirce says that, 'just as in biology no account is taken of terms antedating Linnaeus,' so too in philosophy it might be found best not to go back to anything developed before scholastic terminology."

"What does he mean?"

"I guess we should deal with Linnaeus first. He was an eighteenth-century Swedish botanist. Linnaeus developed a method for classifying plants and animals that became the norm. We still use Linnaeus's taxonomy today for grouping living things into a general category, which Linnaeus called 'genus,' and then into more specific sub-categories, which he called 'species'."

"I vaguely remember that from high school biology. I guess what I need is a rephrasing of that whole sentence."

"Let me see if I can do that for you. Peirce is saying two things in this sentence. His first point is that, in biology no one would pay much attention to biological classification systems that existed before Linnaeus. The reason for this is that the method Linnaeus devised is superior to all that came before."

"And Peirce's second point?"

"The second point runs into the first. Just as no one would think of giving credence to a biological classification system that existed before Linnaeus's taxonomic system, so too in philosophy it might be found best not to go back to anything developed before scholastic terminology."

"Uh, scholastic terminology?"

I should never be amazed at how much background a person needs in order to understand Peirce. Not only is his sentence structure difficult to decipher, you also need to know something about the references that he mentions in passing. I often find myself coming up against odd references in Peirce's writings that lead me down historical pathways. Scholasticism was one of those references that I had tracked down a few years before, only to discover that it housed something vital to Peirce's concept of reality.

"Scholasticism was the dominant philosophical approach in Europe in medieval times. It began around the eleventh century and prevailed in the Western world until the humanists arose during the Renaissance. Humanism, which broke the religious limitations on knowledge, prepared the way for Descartes, who lived from 1596 to 1650."

"Descartes," Hal said thoughtfully. "'I think, therefore I am'?"

"The same. Peirce was not at all fond of Descartes or the Cartesian theory of knowledge. He much preferred the scholastic version, although it had a church-based history to it. Peirce was definitely not fond of the Catholic Church."

"Why not? I thought you said Peirce believed in God."

"I did say that, but Peirce also felt that religion should not be able to dictate what science could and could not do. Historically, the Catholic Church was known for keeping a tight lid on scientific inquiry. Just think of Galileo."

"Oh, good point. So, in what way was the scholastic version of knowledge church-based?"

"In the sense that scholasticism was the philosophy taught in monasteries and church schools. Scholasticism combined religious doctrine with philosophical and logical work based on Aristotle and somewhat on Plato, as well. Peirce just ignored the doctrine parts and used the knowledge parts."

"Then, what is the difference between Descartes and the Scholastics?"

"One difference that presented a big problem for Peirce was the position that Descartes had on doubt and certainty. Descartes claimed that all reasoning should be based on absolute starting points from which you reason deductively. According to Descartes, you begin your reasoning journey from an *a priori,* or fixed, absolute. Peirce believed that you should begin your reasoning journey from wherever you are, not from some arbitrary fixed point or absolute. Pure reason, of the sort that Descartes proposed, leaves no room for responding to anomalies and using them as a springboard for inquiring into supposed absolutes."

"Why was that a problem?"

"Because whenever our beliefs interact with experience, they do so in the real world. If the final authority for truth ignores experience and resides in the mind alone, you have to ignore anomalies that occur in experience. Anomalies are aberrations that let you know you might be missing something. If you are only permitted to reason deductively from an absolute starting point, you must ignore anomalies that occur in experience but which do not belong within the system you are addressing deductively. These anomalies might be clues that you are causing unforeseen consequences to another part of a system. They might also be clues leading you toward a new hypothesis. Deducting from absolute starting points leaves out the most important stage of the scientific method as far as Peirce was concerned."

"What stage is that?"

"The discovery stage. If you are a true Cartesian, once you decide upon that absolute starting point, you are stuck with following your deductions, regardless of the consequences. Most consider Descartes to be the father of modern philosophy. He laid the foundation for the kind of science that I so despise. I hold his followers personally responsible for the techno-sociological mess we are in today."

Hal gave me a perfunctory nod here. I knew he did not want to hear another rant from me at this point.

"According to Descartes, or at least according to the way he has been interpreted," I continued, "you are supposed to doubt everything in your experience, except the fact that you doubt and are, therefore, thinking. You are only supposed to believe something after you can prove its existence through logic and reason. The reasoning mind is the sole arbiter of what is or is not true. Descartes claimed that the point of certainty resides within the reasoning function of individual minds, not in society, nature, or even in experience. That is where 'I think, therefore I am' comes from. No body and no experience is implied in that statement, only mind."

"Ah! That must be where pointless porcupines come from!"

"No, pointless porcupines are vague and unproveable matters that make absolutely no difference one way or another. Descartes said we should focus on individual porcupine points. We should then act as if the porcupine, itself, were meaningless."

"And the Scholastics?"

"Scholasticism embraces a broader range of applications than the narrow definition of knowledge that Descartes allowed. Scholasticism includes all human activities, including those in the arts. Peirce especially liked the work of one scholastic philosopher, John Duns Scotus, who wrote during the late thirteenth century. Duns Scotus claimed that everything that exists has two natures. One is a measurable quantitative nature, a 'whatness.' The other is a unique qualitative nature, a 'thisness.' The whatness of something can be defined and classified based on qualities it shares in common with others in its class. Thisness consists of the qualities that set a thing apart from every other thing in the universe. Thisness is a qualitative essence that makes a thing unique, and capable of being discerned from among all others."

"Are you saying that the Scholastics relied on experience but Descartes did not?"

"Not exactly. Descartes did not completely exclude experience. He included the experience of his own thinking, for example. Also, the Scholastics did not rely on experience alone. They just did not exclude sensory experiences or common sense from the reasoning process. Peirce often described his pragmatism as being 'critical common-sense-ism' because it is a method of applying reason to reality."

"Critical-common-sense-ism," Hal repeated. "That is a mouthful!"

"You are right about that! However, you already know what it is. The Davis Non-verbal Assessment identifies the degree to which a person has, or lacks, the ability for applying critical common-sense."

"Oh, I see that."

"Now, back to the Scholastics. They had been out of favor in the secular philosophical world for centuries when Peirce took up with them. The humanists used to ridicule followers of Duns Scotus for being foolish. The term 'dunce' was originally a derogatory term applied to followers of the scholasticism of Duns Scotus."

"Then, did Peirce like Duns Scotus because of common sense?"

"He liked him for several reasons. For example, Peirce had an interest in Duns Scotus because he worked with the concept of universals."

"What are universals?"

"Universals are general laws that can be demonstrated by means of a number of examples."

"Like gravity?"

"Yes, gravity is a good example. Science deals mainly with finding and applying universals. Duns Scotus was interested in universals from a realist perspective. This means he considered universals from the perspective of the way things are and are destined to become. His perspective was opposed to the nominalist perspective, which says that we just make up concepts by naming them. The nominalist says that principles, like justice, goodness, or the laws of nature are not pre-existing. They come about within contexts where you identify, or name, them. Peirce argued that concepts exist whether we ever discover them or not. That was one reason why scholastic realism appealed to Peirce. However, Duns Scotus's treatment of qualitative essences probably appealed to him most."

"And qualitative essences are?"

"They are the 'thisnesses' that we just talked about, the 'being-ness' of things. Qualitative essences exist independent of our perception of them. They already exist whether we ever come to know that they exist or not. And," I added, "implied in this pre-existing qualitative 'isness' is the assumption that a reality exists outside of what a human mind can construct through reasoning."

"That would be obvious."

"Not everybody would agree with you on that. This 'isness' that Duns Scotus, and later Peirce, addressed exists before anyone's experience of it. That was a fundamental point to Peirce. His conception of reality was founded on the belief that qualitative essences exist independent of anyone's experience of them."

"Why would that matter one way or the other?"

"Because Peirce used this idea of qualitative essences to explain the nature of reality. This 'isness' applies to everything, including everything within the realm of possibilities. Peirce contended that qualitative potential exists independent of anyone's knowledge of it. This realm of quality, which is also value and possibility, is as real as the realm of actuality where actual events occur. Peirce felt it necessary to distinguish between reality and actuality."

"Why?"

"Because something can be real, but not actually exist. A phenomenon which appears may or may not be actual. Even mere possibilities can appear to us. Peirce emphasized that, while reality consists of both actual events and potentialities, general laws and principles are what organize these to comprise reality. The purpose of science, according to Peirce, is to discover these general laws and principles so that we can shape our future behaviors to get in line with them. We do this discovering by means of observation and interpretation. We do all of our interpreting through the lens of purpose. Purpose is a tool for directing us toward discovering the possibilities, qualities, and potentialities inherent in things, events, and even mere appearances."

"Unlike Descartes, then?"

"Yes, unlike Descartes and others as well." I thought for a moment about bringing up Comte and positivism at this point. However, I realized that I had wandered off into another historical alley and needed to return to the topic at hand. "Now, back to this essay. Let me sum up this sentence we have been discussing and then go on to the next one."

"That would help," he said gratefully.

"Peirce was saying that, just as no one would pay much attention to biological classification systems prior to Linnaeus, so too in philosophy we should avoid using terminology that predates the Scholastics."

"I see that now."

"Next, Peirce brings up another issue. He says that every time a philosopher has given a general name instead of his own name to a philosophy, that name always ends up meaning something broader than the philosopher originally intended. For example, he says that 'Kantianism,' 'Benthamism,' 'Comteanism,' 'Spencerianism'...."

"Those are 'isms' I have never heard before."

"He just means the specific philosophies proposed by specific philosophers like Kant, Bentham, Comte, and Spencer. They are all philosophers with whom Peirce agreed in one way or another."

"Oh."

"Peirce is saying here that, when the philosopher's name is used as the name of the specific philosophical system he created, then the meaning of that name stays close to the original philosopher's intent. However, when a philosophy is given a more general name, the meaning tends to eventually stray away from its original meaning."

"What do you mean by a general name?"

"Peirce lists several, 'transcendentalism,' 'utilitarianism,' 'positivism,' 'evolutionism,' and 'synthetic philosophy.' He feels that all of these ended up with a broader application than their original developers intended."

With this statement, I had finished that paragraph and debated with myself over whether to go on. The next paragraph tied in so closely with the end of the last one that I felt I should continue. We had already come near to our time allotment for that day, so I gave Hal the option of stopping here or continuing into the next sentence.

"Oh, continue, definitely. I am enjoying this."

"This next paragraph is the final one in the name game," I promised.

"Go for it!"

"Peirce begins by saying that, for years, he has been waiting in vain for a good time to propose his notions of the ethics of terminology."

"That ethics connection to terminology still eludes me."

"Think of it," I suggested, "as the ethics of not tinkering with someone else's terminology and of not making up new terminology to indicate the same concepts someone else has already defined."

"That is simple enough."

"Good. Now, after waiting years to propose his notions about the ethics of terminology, Peirce has decided to just drag these notions in 'over head and shoulders' and plop them down here in this essay. He says that he has no specific proposal to offer in doing this. He is mostly satisfied with the way word usage has developed without having any canons or resolutions of a congress."

"But?" Hal interrupted.

"But what?"

"There is a 'but,' or a 'however,' in there somewhere," he said teasingly. "I can feel it coming."

I laughed. "You happen to be right, but it does not come in yet. Peirce has more setting up to do before we get to his 'however'."

Hal shrugged. I could tell he was enjoying this.

"Peirce comments that his word 'pragmatism' has gained recognition in a generalized sense. This supports his contention that pragmatism has the 'power of growth and vitality'."

"By 'growth and vitality,' does he mean fit and healthy?"

"Yes, or flourishing. Next, Peirce says that William James, the American psychologist, first picked up the word, 'pragmatism.' James started using the term when he saw that his concept of radical empiricism matched Peirce's definition of pragmatism, but from a different point of view."

"What is radical empiricism?"

"We are not going to discuss that here. That is a series all on its own."

"I would enjoy hearing about it, though."

"I am sure you would. Maybe another time," I offered, then continued. "In addition to James, Peirce mentions Ferdinand C. S. Schiller, a British philosopher whom Peirce calls 'an admirably clear and brilliant thinker'."

"Did he say William James was clear and brilliant too?"

"No. Peirce had warm personal feelings toward James, but I do not think he would ever have called James either clear or brilliant. They approached things from different directions. But we should not go into that here either."

Hal nodded at this, and I continued.

"Peirce then mentions two of Schiller's works. He says that Schiller was looking around for a more attractive name than 'anthropomorphism,' which he used in his first article. He used the term 'pragmatism' in his second paper. Peirce says that the way in which Schiller applied this term was in generic agreement with his own doctrine. That is, Schiller's use of the term 'pragmatism' was in general agreement with Peirce's own doctrine of pragmatism. Then Peirce mentions that Schiller found a more appropriate name for his own theory but that he still used the term 'pragmatism' when discussing these ideas in a broader sense."

I paused here to see if Hal had any questions but his expression encouraged me to continue.

"Peirce comments that, in regards to James's and Schiller's use of the word 'pragmatism,' so far all went happily."

"But?" Hal interjected playfully.

"Yes! This is it!" I said laughing at his teasing. "The big 'however'."

"Which is?"

"Which is 'that some literary journals had gotten hold of this perfectly good word and abused it in the merciless way that words have to expect when they fall into literary clutches'." I read this last part exactly as Peirce had written it. "The phrase, 'falling into literary clutches,' has a nineteenth century ring to it."

"It sure does. It sounds melodramatic. I can almost see villains tying the word 'pragmatism' down onto iron tracks in the path of an oncoming train."

I love how he joins into the spirit of things!

"Next, Peirce criticizes the British, whose manners, he says, have sometimes grown into scolding at the word 'pragmatism' as being ill-chosen. 'Ill-chosen' is Peirce's word, by the way."

"That sounds nineteenth century also," Hal commented, then asked. "Where is his criticism of the British?"

"The British only think his word is ill-chosen, Peirce says scornfully, because they are misusing the word 'pragmatism.' They are using it in a way Peirce meant to exclude."

"The old ethics of tinkering with someone else's terminology problem," Hal said wryly.

"Yes. Peirce felt that pragmatism, this term of his own creation, was being used to include things he did not mean for it to include. He decided that it was time to 'kiss his child goodbye and relinquish it to its higher destiny'."

"And that higher destiny was?"

"To stand for a general grouping of philosophical concepts that could all be considered pragmatism, just not his specific brand of pragmatism."

"And what did he use for his own personal brand?"

"Pragmatic-ism."

"Oh, I see where that came from. It is from the 'isms' and the picky 'ic-isms,'" Hal said, deliberately pronouncing these two suffixes in such an odd way that I could not help laughing.

"Yes. Peirce even said that his word 'pragmaticism' was 'ugly enough to be safe from kidnappers'."

"I am sure he was right about that. It is an ugly name!"

"Yes it is. And that is the end of the name game!"

"Whew! That was a real chunk. How many pages have we covered?"

"Do you mean how many pages have we covered in Peirce's essay?"

"Yes."

"Let me see," I said, counting back the pages, "about three and a half."

"Out of how many total?"

I counted the remaining pages.

"The essay is close to sixteen pages long."

"Then we are one-quarter of the way through!" Hal exclaimed victoriously. "And so far I understand every word you have said."

"We will see how well you do on the exam," I teased. "Tomorrow, we will finally begin learning what pragmatism is."

"I am ready!" He said, pushing up a sleeve of his polo shirt and flexing his biceps for me.

"I hope so. Tomorrow we begin to delve into some of Peirce's most difficult concepts."

"I can handle it," he assured me confidently. "We have been lifting heavy weights for the past four days, and I am still here."

I had to admit that we had covered some difficult terminology and that he was still enthusiastic about continuing. The next session would probably be fun as well.

Five
BEFORE BELIEF AND DOUBT

That morning I could see that Hal was ready to do heavy lifting, as he called it. He rushed us through breakfast and suggested we finish our coffee out in the cottage. The cottage houses my office, where we were having our daily conversations. I had relegated us to a single time and a single spot for these discussions because I did not want them to wander into a variety of topics, as most of our conversations do.

"In the first part of this next paragraph, Peirce says that, although he has gotten something out of what other pragmatists have written, he still thinks that there is 'a decisive advantage in his original conception of this doctrine.' Peirce felt he had laid out this doctrine in an essay he published twenty-five years earlier."

"Then how come we are not discussing that essay?"

"The earlier essay 'How to Make Our Ideas Clear' is much more difficult to understand than this one. I decided that this essay would be a better place to start, since it is easier to follow and gives an overview of Peirce's philosophy."

"If that other essay is harder to understand than this one...," Hal said shaking his head unbelievingly. He did not bother to finish the statement.

"Peirce says," I continued, acknowledging Hal's comment with a nod, "that you can deduce every truth that comes from the other forms of pragmatism just by following his original form of this theory. At the same time, you avoid the errors into which the other pragmatists have fallen."

"That must be the nineteenth-century way of saying, 'I am right and they are wrong'."

"There is more. Peirce also contends that his original view is 'a more compact and unitary conception' than the others. Its main merit is that 'it more readily connects itself with a critical proof of its truth'."

"Does he mean his theory is easier to prove than the others?"

"That is what he is saying. However, this 'critical proof' part has a special meaning that we will deal with later. He emphasizes this point here:"

Quite in accord with the logical order of investigation, it usually happens that one first forms a hypothesis that seems more and more reasonable the further one examines into it, but that only a good deal later gets crowned with an adequate proof.

I read this directly from the text, so Hal knew I was quoting Peirce here. I paused to give him a chance to ask for clarification. When he failed to pose a question, I wondered whether I should mention the term "abduction" yet. Abduction is Peirce's theory of the logic of discovery, to which this sentence alludes. I decided that introducing the term at this point might lead us astray.

"Peirce lets us know that he has had the pragmatist theory under consideration for many years longer than most other pragmatists. For this reason, he says, anyone should only expect that he would have given more attention to the issue of proving the theory."

"But, of course," Hal said, in a pseudo-Parisian dialect.

"Peirce was trying to say in a nice way that 'you other pragmatists are way off base, and I am standing on home plate. However, I have been in the game longer than you have, so you are not to blame for being stuck out there in left field'."

Hal laughed at my mixed-up metaphor, one reflecting the entire scope of my baseball knowledge. At least I stuck to the same sport.

"Peirce says that, as he tries here to explain pragmatism, he wants you to excuse him for sticking to the form of pragmatism he knows best."

"That is a reasonable request."

"Peirce explains that, in this present article, there will only be enough room 'to explain what this doctrine really consists in'."

"Which doctrine?"

"Peirce's conception of pragmatism or, I should say, pragmaticism. He makes a parenthetical statement here in which he predicts that pragmatism is going 'to probably play a pretty prominent part in the philosophical discussions of the next coming years'."

"And did he predict rightly?"

"For American philosophy he did. The *Encyclopedia Britannica* describes Peirce as the greatest American philosopher. I believe that Peirce will eventually take his place among the great philosophers of all time. As I said earlier, Peirce's theory could revolutionize education and, as a result, society as a whole. If we were to use his theory of right reasoning to develop a populace capable of making good decisions, we would go a long way toward solving our social and environmental problems. The key is providing education that results in real learning and provides people with the capability to make reasoned judgments and to continue learning throughout their lifetimes. Peirce's pragmaticism gives us insights into those core basics of reasoning necessary for real learning to take place."

He accepted my enthusiastic response to his question with an agreeable shrug. I led us back into the essay.

"Peirce next offers to write a second article for *The Monist*, the periodical for which this essay was written. He suggests that interested readers would find his proposed second article even more interesting than this one. In the second article, he would have his readers assume pragmaticism is true. Then he would give samples of various applications of pragmaticism for solving many kinds of problems." I could see by his expression that Hal was following this train of thought, so I continued. "Then Peirce proposes that, after that second article, readers might take an interest in a proof that the doctrine of prag-maticism is true. He adds here that this proof of his leaves no reasonable doubt concerning the subject and is the one contribution of value that he has to make to philosophy."

"I thought you said that Peirce did not believe that we can ever know for sure that we have reached the absolute truth."

"I did."

"Then, why does he say here that he has 'proof' that his doctrine is true?"

"When Peirce uses words like 'true' and 'proof,' he has a special mean-ing for them. In 1898, Peirce gave a series of lectures, which he titled 'Rea-soning and the Logic of Things.' In the fourth lecture he offers a good de-scription of this issue of truth." I found my copy of the book, *Reasoning and the Logic of Things* and read from it:

> [W]hether the word truth has two meanings or not, I certainly do think that *holding for true* is of two kinds; the one is that practical holding for true which alone is entitled to the name of Belief, while the other is that acceptance of a proposition which in the intention of pure science re-mains always provisional.[3]

"When Peirce says that he has a 'proof' of his doctrine, he means that he can demonstrate, in a scientific way, that it is worthy of being called 'true' in this provisional sense of pure science."

"Did he ever write an article about this proof of his?"

"Not exactly. But I suspect you are going to be surprised when you find out what this unfinished part is. I am sure that you will recognize its connec-tion to Relational Thinking Styles. Sadly for Peirce, though, he never pub-lished this proof, so we do not know for sure yet that he completed it."

"I guess it would have been sad for Peirce, especially since he thought that it was his one contribution of value to philosophy."

"But it was not his only contribution," I assured Hal. "Peirce says next that proving pragmatism would 'involve the establishment of synechism,' which he also called his doctrine of continuity."

"Can you give me an explanation?"

"If it can be brief. Let me see. Peirce's doctrine of continuity refers to the interconnectedness of one discovery to another. You cannot throw in some in-explicable ultimate as the proof of your contention."

"Such as?"

"Such as 'because God wants it that way.' Or 'because that is what some prior authority claimed was true.' Peirce believed that you cannot use inexpli-cable ultimates or the authority of people who use inexplicable ultimates as proof of your contention."

"Would inexplicable ultimates be like ontological assumptions?"

I love how Hal remembers things and ties them back in to one another! He is a good example of continuity in action.

"Yes, they would work in the same way. Peirce wrote several things explaining his doctrine of continuity. Some of these explanations were collected in one chapter of a Peirce anthology edited by Justus Buchler. He titled the chapter, 'Synechism, Fallibilism and Evolution.' Maybe we will discuss that some day."

"That is a formidable title! The only two words that make any sense to me at all are the words 'and' and 'evolution'."

"Next paragraph," I said, hoping to bring us back to the topic.

"I am ready."

"This paragraph will be less difficult because we will not have to deal with so much nineteenth-century language. Peirce says that a definition of pragmatism requires the forthcoming long commentary because just giving a bare-bones definition would not be enough. He also wants us to know that the explanation he is about to give will not mention one or two other doctrines upon which pragmaticism is based. He tells us that Schiller mentioned these, but he does not want to discuss Schiller because he does not want to mingle different propositions."

"Is that all?"

"Yes. Except for saying that he is now going to state his own preliminary propositions."

"That was quick."

"It was," I agreed. "Peirce begins this next paragraph by saying that the main problem in trying to make a listing of these preliminary propositions is that no formal list of them has ever been made."

"Does that mean that Peirce has never made a list of them?"

"It means that neither he nor any of the other pragmatists had made a list of them. Peirce states that these preliminary propositions might all be included under the vague maxim to 'dismiss make-believes'."

"'Dismiss make-believes?' That is an odd statement."

"He explains what he means."

"I figured he would," Hal said wryly. "That does not mean he is going to make sense to me."

"Peirce will be much easier to understand from now on," I promised. "I think you are going to be pleasantly surprised."

"Then surprise me."

"Peirce points out that different philosophers with diverse philosophies propose that philosophy has to start from one state of mind or another. Then he adds that these states of minds do not actually exist."

"What are these states of mind?"

"One is a state of mind in which you begin by doubting everything."

"But that is what you should do to keep an open mind."

"No, that would be 'make-believe,' according to Peirce. Nobody doubts everything. You cannot possibly doubt everything and function in the world."

"I suppose that is probably true," Hal agreed tentatively, "if you want to be literal about it."

"This non-existent state of mind is the state of mind in which there is only one thing you cannot doubt."

"What is that one thing?"

"You cannot doubt that you doubt and are, therefore, thinking. The state of mind that Peirce is describing here is the one proposed by Descartes."

"Then, that must be why Descartes did not say 'I smell, therefore I am'."

I smiled at his clever comment, then continued.

"The method Descartes proposed is called 'radical doubt.' The only thing you cannot doubt is that you doubt. As I said before, Descartes held that a reasoning mind is the sole arbiter of what is true. He claimed that the point of certainty resides within the reasoning function of individual minds, not in society, nature, or even experience. Peirce says that this non-existent state of mind that Descartes proposed is 'the state of mind in which there is only one thing you cannot doubt, as if doubting were as easy as lying'."

"What does he mean by that?"

"He means that, since we truly doubt so few things, real doubting is more difficult than lying. Peirce is mocking the Cartesian concept of radical doubt, saying that it was little more than lying."

"Why is doubting harder than lying?"

"He is coming to that," I assured him. "Next, Peirce mentions another state of mind he considers impossible, the state of mind that says we should begin 'by observing the first impressions of sense'."

"What is the problem with that one?"

"Peirce claims that no such state exists. He contends that our precepts, which are the categories or rules we use as a basis for noticing our sensory impressions, result from 'cognitive elaboration'."

"Cognitive elaboration?"

"Let me see," I said, searching for words. "Cognitive elaboration means that our minds are so full of what we already know that we cannot possibly observe first impressions of anything."

"Do you think that is true?"

"This is about what Peirce thought," I reminded him. "And, yes, except under rare and rigorous conditions, I think he is probably correct."

Hal nodded thoughtfully.

"Quiz time!" I announced abruptly.

"I am ready," Hal said.

"Then, here goes. What are the states of mind that Peirce says are impossible to start from when doing philosophy?"

"Let me see. The first impossible state of mind is doubting everything," he said confidently, then faltered. "I am not sure how to say the other one."

"The second impossible state to begin from is 'by observing the first impressions of our senses'."

"Ah!" he said, "Because of 'cognitive elaboration'."

"Yes, good!"

"Then if you are not supposed to start out from either one of those states of mind," Hal wondered, "what state of mind should you start out from?"

"Peirce says there is only one place you can begin," I answered. "'In truth,' says Peirce, 'there is but one state of mind from which you can set out, namely, the state of mind in which you actually find yourself at the time you do set out'."

"That last sentence makes too much sense. It does not even sound like a philosopher wrote it. It sounds too normal to say that 'the only place you can set out from is from wherever you are'."

"That is word for word what Peirce wrote," I assured him. "I told you he was going to surprise you as we go further into the theory."

Hal shook his head in near amazement. I could see he was still surprised at the clarity of that last statement.

"Peirce then says that this state from which you must start out is one in which you are already carrying around an immense pile of cognition. That is to say, you are carrying around previously thought thoughts and previously acquired information. You could not possibly rid yourself of all of this prior knowledge, even if you wanted to. And who knows, Peirce adds, even if you could rid yourself of all of this prior cognition, maybe you would not be able to learn anything at all without having that prior knowledge in place."

"He is still making sense."

"Good. Now Peirce starts to become indignant here. I am going to quote him directly. Interrupt me if you have questions."

"When have I not?"

"'Do you call it doubting,' Peirce says, 'to write on a piece of paper that you doubt? If so, doubt has nothing to do with any serious business. But do not make believe, if pedantry has not....'"

"Question! What is that word you just said?"

I checked back in the text. "Do you mean 'pedantry'?"

"Yes. What does it mean? Is it the same thing as 'pedagogue'?"

"No. The word 'pedagogue' means teacher. Pedagogy is a philosophical specialty having to do with education. The word 'pedant' means a person who stresses trivial details of learning. Pedantry is the kind of teaching that involves instruction in trivial details, while pedagogy is the study of teaching in general. My entire approach to Peirce is pedagogical," I added, "meaning that I have come to understand his philosophy from a teacher's perspective. But I would never, ever want to be called a pedant."

"I will never, ever call you a pedant," he agreed with mock solemnity. "Thank you," I said with equal solemnity. "Here is what he said next:"

Do you call it doubting to write down on a piece of paper that you doubt? If so, doubt has nothing to do with any serious business. Do not make believe; if pedantry [the pursuit of trivial details] has not eaten all the reality out of you, then you must realize that there is much that we do not doubt. Anything that you do not at all doubt, you must, and do, regard as infallible, absolute truth. Here breaks in Mr. Make Believe: "What! Do you mean to say that one is to believe what is not true, or that what a man does not doubt is *ipso facto* true?" No, but unless he can make a thing white and black at once, he has to regard what he does not doubt as absolutely true.

"*Ipso facto*," I added, "means 'therefore by default' true."

"Is this what he was getting at earlier, when we talked about Descartes? Is this about how hard it is to doubt?"

"Yes."

"And are those Peirce's own words? They are so easy to understand! They make so much sense!"

I had read this passage with such dramatic emphasis that I could understand why Hal thought they were my own. Peirce makes this point well, however, and his words do make sense. It is a shame that so few people can get far enough into Peirce's writing to discover what he has to say.

"They are Peirce's words *verbatim*," I assured him. "Next, Peirce writes, 'suppose you,' meaning the reader, 'are that man'."

"Which man?"

"The one who has to regard what he does not doubt as absolutely true."

"I will suppose that," Hal agreed amiably.

"Then Peirce has you argue with him."

But you tell me "there are scores of things I do not doubt. I cannot really persuade myself that there is not one of them about which I am mistaken." You are adducing one of your make-believe facts, which, even if it were established, would only go to show that doubt has a limen, that is, is only called into being by a certain finite stimulus. You only puzzle yourself by talking of this metaphysical "truth" and metaphysical "falsity," that you know nothing about. All you have any dealings with are your doubts and beliefs, with the course of life that forces new beliefs upon you and gives you power to doubt old beliefs.

"That sounds like what you said before."

"What did I say before?"

"The thing about doubts and beliefs."

"Oh, yes," I said, remembering. "This is what I wanted to explain about belief and doubt interacting with experience. Peirce introduces some fundamental concepts here." I repeated Peirce's last sentence before continuing.

All you have any dealings with are your doubts and beliefs, with the course of life that forces new beliefs upon and gives you power to doubt old beliefs. If your terms "truth" and "falsity" are taken in such senses as to be definable in terms of doubt and belief and the course of experience…well and good: in that case you are only talking about doubt and belief.

I stopped here to do some explaining. I had left out a parenthetical statement that I felt would have muddied up the sentence. Now it was time for me to clarify this statement.

"What Peirce is saying here is both simple and profound. This is what I was getting at when I said that differing styles of thinking and learning consist of differing ways in which our beliefs interact with experience. Peirce says that all that we have any dealings with are the interactions of our beliefs and our doubts during the course of our lives."

"I guess I fail to get the simple part," Hal commented wryly.

"The simple part is that we are always dealing only with beliefs or doubts as we interact with experience."

"What do you mean?"

"I mean, and Peirce meant, that in all of our interactions with experience, both mental and physical, everything that we ever deal with involves only two kinds of choices. One choice is to apply our existing beliefs to a situation. The other kind is to attempt to resolve whatever doubts we may have about a particular matter so that we can apply a new belief. We are always doing one of these two things."

"Always?"

"Always," I affirmed. "I left out part of the last statement. I want to go back to it now."

"That is fine with me."

"I am referring to the sentence that begins 'if your terms 'truth' and 'falsity' are taken in such senses as to be definable in terms of doubt and belief and the course of experience…'." I quoted this much from the essay and then continued. "Peirce inserted a phrase that clarified what he meant by this. In essence, he was saying that if you defined the word 'truth' to mean 'what a belief would be if it were to head toward absolute fixity,' then that is 'well and good.' He means that you can use the word 'truth' if what you mean by truth is that you are heading in the direction of absolute truth."

"That sounds picky to me."

"Peirce intended for it to be picky. This statement is on the same order of the one we talked about earlier, about 'holding for true' in a 'provisional' sense. A good scientist, according to Peirce, would be dealing with truth in this way. Peirce is being specific about what he is willing to call truth. Remember he is not fond of ontologically derived truths."

"Because they would be make-believes?"

"Yes. And, in addition, Peirce is not willing to say truth does not exist."

"What is he saying, then?"

"We should continue. He offers a contrast in the next sentence."

"Good!"

"I am going to quote again," I warned.

But if by truth and falsity you mean something not definable in terms of doubt and belief in any way, then you are talking of entities of whose existence you can know nothing, and which Ockham's razor would clean shave off.

"Ockham's razor?"

"Ockham's razor is a logical precept that says you should keep to the simplest and most logical explanation. When possible, take the simplest explanation that answers the question and still covers all the bases."

"That makes sense to me. What is Peirce's point about this?"

"He is trying to say that if you are thinking of truth and falsity in terms of being unchanging, everlasting absolutes instead of beliefs and doubts, then you are going to have problems down the road. Do you remember earlier when I mentioned Peirce's doctrine of continuity?"

"I think so. Continuity had to do with not using something that cannot be explained as the basis for explaining something else."

"Yes. This statement is tied into what I said earlier about Peirce's doctrine of continuity. He had a big problem with absolutes in general and inexplicable ultimates in particular."

"I can understand rejecting inexplicable absolutes, but not all absolutes." Hal said, apparently bewildered. "Does that mean Peirce believed that there is no such thing as truth then? No reality?"

"Good question. Some people have mistakenly interpreted Peirce to mean that. However, that is not what he meant. He believed that there is such a thing as an absolute truth, but that we should not start out thinking we already know what it is. Nor should we ever believe, at any point, that we have the absolute truth about something."

"Why not? I can understand why we should not start by assuming we already know the truth about something, but why not believe that we eventually will?"

"Because those are just two sides of the same coin for Peirce, functionally speaking, that is. When and how do we make the decision that we have found an absolute truth? And what do we do with that truth when the opportunity to learn something new comes along?"

"As with the Hubbell telescope and astronomy?"

"Yes, that telescope is opening up the possibility of new hypotheses in the field of astronomy," I agreed. "Next, Peirce makes a suggestion for getting around this absolute truth problem. 'Your problems would be greatly simplified, if, instead of saying that you want to know the Truth, you were simply to say that you want to attain a state of belief unassailable by doubt'."

"That sure sounds like picky wording to me," Hal said dubiously.

"He explains next what he means by the word 'belief.' Maybe that will help broaden the picture for you:"

Belief is not a momentary mode of consciousness; it is a habit of mind essentially enduring for some time, and mostly, at least, unconscious; and like other habits, it is, (until it meets with some surprise that begins its dissolution) perfectly self-satisfied. Doubt is of an altogether contrary genus. It is not a habit, but the privation of a habit. Now the privation of a habit, in order to be anything at all, must be a condition of erratic activity that in some way must get superseded by a habit.

"That is a lot to digest!" Hal said when I finished reading this. "Especially the last part, about doubt."

"Maybe we should finish for now and take it up again tomorrow."

"Tomorrow is Saturday," Hal reminded me.

"I am willing to discuss this on Saturday if you are."

"That sounds fine to me! I am enjoying this."

We agreed then to save our deep exploration of this issue of belief and doubt for the next day.

Six

BELIEF, DOUBT,
CRITICAL SELF, AND SIGNS

Essay lines 240-294

We started late this morning because neither of us wanted to give up our regular Saturday morning ritual. This ritual consists of a leisurely breakfast at the Wild Coho Café while we read the weekend edition of the *Seattle Times*. When we finally settled into the cottage for our discussion, I decided that I needed to go back over Peirce's last statement about belief and doubt before continuing.

"I want to go back to that last quotation I read to you yesterday."

"Fine with me."

"Peirce was writing here about belief and doubt," I reminded him.

Belief is not a momentary mode of consciousness; it is a habit of mind essentially enduring for some time, and mostly, at least, unconscious; and like other habits, it is (until it meets with some surprise that begins its dissolution) perfectly self-satisfied. Doubt is of an altogether contrary genus. It is not a habit, but the privation of a habit. Now the privation of a habit, in order to be anything at all, must be a condition of erratic activity that in some way must get superseded by a habit.

"What does 'privation' mean?"

"It means essentially the same thing as deprivation. It means the lack of something. Doubt is the lack of a habit."

"Does he mean beliefs and doubts as for religious or political issues?"

"Not just for those. Habit has time connected to it. All of reality is the result of habit in Peirce's sense of this word. So beliefs and doubts have to do with the continuance and the interruption of habit. In another essay, Peirce explained his use of 'belief' and 'doubt' to 'designate the starting point of any discussion, no matter how small or how great, and the resolution of it'." [4]

"The whole belief and doubt thing sounds just like binary code to me."

"Binary code is an excellent metaphor for what Peirce means! Imagine that the number one stands for beliefs and zero stands for doubts."

"All beliefs and all doubts, no matter what they are about?"

"Yes. Peirce is saying that all we have for interacting with experience are our beliefs and our doubts, our ones and our zeros. At any point we have two choices. We can apply our beliefs, which like any habits are perfectly 'self satisfied' until they are interrupted. Or else, we can doubt what we already know for some reason. Because doubt is an erratic activity, it must be overcome by a habit before we can continue. When we encounter a doubt, we attempt to resolve it. Once the doubt is resolved, we will have formed a new belief. Only then can we continue."

"And is that what you mean when you say that thinking and learning styles are the ways in which our beliefs interact with experience?"

"Just that! Relational Thinking Styles describes the mental habits which different people use to apply beliefs and settle doubts."

"And is that what Peirce means?"

"No. Peirce is going to describe how we 'should' go about settling doubt and applying beliefs. His pragmatism lays out norms, or standards, for the way we should reason if we are to reason like an experimentalist. The Relational Thinking Styles model describes our everyday habits of reasoning as they relate to Peirce's standards."

"And are Peirce's standards the same thing as right reasoning?"

"Yes."

"And is that why we started this whole thing?"

"Yes," I agreed again. "But there is more to this issue of belief and doubt. Peirce says 'now the privation of a habit, in order to be anything at all, must be a condition of erratic activity that in some way must get superseded by a habit.' The phrase 'in some way' holds the key words here."

"Why are they key words?"

"Because this is what Peirce's theory is all about. He addresses how doubt should be settled versus how people tend to habitually settle it. Peirce called the 'should' method *logica docens*, meaning that it is a method derived from formal training and used in a deliberate manner. He called the 'habitual' methods, the ways people habitually apply beliefs and settle doubts, *logica utens*. *Logica utens* are everyday reasoning habits that we use automatically."

"Does that make Relational Thinking Styles the same as *logica utens*?"

"Yes. And in critical thinking classes, we teach the basic skills for performing Peirce's formal logical method, *logica docens*."

"But we call our classes 'Engaged Intelligence'."

"Engaged Intelligence is a training program in critical thinking based upon Peirce's concept of *logica docens*."

"Docens sounds a lot like the word 'docent.' It reminds me of when we trained as docents for the art museum."

"Both words come from the same root and have the same general meaning as well. A docent is someone who is trained to lecture about a particular subject matter, but who is not part of the staff or faculty at an institution. *Logica docens* is a specific and deliberate method to use for inquiring into a topic, but is not a part of that topic."

"That makes sense."

"Now, Peirce explains more about his meaning of the terms 'belief' and 'doubt.' He says that anyone reading this is surely a rational person. Not one of us would question the fact that, in addition to having habits, we also have at least some self-control over our future actions. In other words, we can decide to change or alter our habits to some degree if we so desire."

"I would agree that we can change our habits, but it is not easy to do."

"Good point. By the way, Peirce does not mean the 'you create your own reality' type of control of the future. He does not mean that you can control outcomes by just imagining or affirming what you want to happen. 'On the contrary' says Peirce, 'a process of self-preparation allows a person to take action when the occasion for it shall arise'."

"That is like saying that 'the Lord helps those who help themselves'."

"I guess you could say that, but there is more here. Peirce claims that this self-preparation 'will impart to action one fixed character, which a person applies with little or no feelings of self-reproach at the time something is done.' But afterwards, while thinking things over, that person may say 'I should have done this or that instead.' Peirce says that this reflection then becomes part of the activity of self-preparation for the next occasion."

"Is that just a way of saying that we learn from experience?"

"Yes, but Peirce is talking about the formation of habit here. He says the more that an action is repeated, the more a tendency exists for that action to become fixed in character. Eventually, you reach a point at which you possess an entire absence of self-reproach."

"And is that bad?"

"It might be bad, or it might be good. It depends upon the habit and the situation. Whether good or bad, the more closely you approach this entire absence of self-reproach, the less room you have for self-control. Peirce says, where no self-control is possible, there will be no self-reproach."

"Is he talking about conscience here?"

"He is talking about everything we think and do and, in particular, everything that has to do with reasoning. Remember, Peirce counts reasoning as an aspect of ethical behavior. So yes, he is talking about conscience, as well as everything else we think about and do."

"This sounds like a unified field theory of mind."

"I suppose it could be. Maybe it is more like a unified field theory of habit, though. This tendency for an action to become increasingly fixed in character is the way all habits are formed. Peirce says that, at the point that a habit becomes so ingrained that self-reproach is entirely absent, you cannot possibly think or do otherwise."

"What if you are wrong?"

"You are likely to be wrong if you leave out the 'self-reflection' and 'self-reproach' parts as you are forming the habits. If you leave out those self-correcting activities, you have not engaged your intelligence in the process of fixing a belief into a habit. You have just thoughtlessly moved into a state of absolute certainty about something. If you fail to engage your intelligence in the way Peirce is proposing here, you can end up with deeply ingrained bad habits and completely mistaken beliefs that you continue to apply inappropriately because you absolutely believe you are correct."

"That must be what direct thinkers do. Just as the bumper sticker says, they are 'often wrong, but never in doubt'."

"Good insight! Some people use the term 'linear' for the mental habit that we call 'direct thinking.' However, regardless of what you call it, people who habitually use this method for reasoning do not self-correct. They become experts at doing whatever they already know how to do, without regard to the quality or effectiveness of their results. We all operate this way for some things, even if we do not habitually reason in this way. We need our habits. Forming good mental and physical habits is an important part of learning. The more good habits we have mastered, the more we are able to learn and reason well in the future. This comment of Peirce's about self-reflection and self-reproach has major implications for learning theory."

"What do you mean?"

"I mean that, if correct skills are not ingrained when they are first learned, then incorrect skills will become ingrained. People learn how to be incompetent as well as how to be competent. The longer someone practices a skill incorrectly, the more ingrained that incorrect skill becomes. This includes thinking skills. We are always in the act of reinforcing old habits or establishing new ones, regardless of whether these habits are good or bad. Every typing teacher and tennis coach knows this. It is much more difficult to undo deeply ingrained bad habits than it is to instill correct habits from the start. This holds true for habits of character, as well as for learning skills."

"That seems obvious."

"It may seem obvious to you, but this intuitively obvious phenomenon is not obvious to everyone. Otherwise, we would be training teachers as if they were going to be Olympic coaches, paying them like CEOs, and holding them accountable for the results they produce."

"Is this habit issue where Peirce's pragmatism connects with education?"

"Yes, it is one place. However, everything in Peirce's pragmatism concerns reasoning, so everything in his theory connects to education. This issue of habit formation is vital to Peirce's theory of how truth is determined. In another essay, 'The Fixation of Belief,' he explains four different methods that people use for coming to believe that something is true. This essay we are discussing now focuses upon one of those methods, the one describing how people 'should' come to decide what is true. When you use 'self-reflection' and 'self-correction' in combination with repetition, your repeated actions will tend toward the perfection of a particular trait. When that trait finally reaches perfection, self-reproach is entirely absent. The closer you are to this absence of self-reproach, the less room you have for self-control. When the habit is so strong that you no longer have any self-control, you have lost the capacity for self-reproach. You have perfected the trait."

"But you also lose the capacity for self-reproach when you absolutely believe you are right, even if you are completely wrong," he countered. "Would you use the word 'perfected' in that case?"

"I suppose you could say that someone had perfected doing something incorrectly," I conceded. "However, for rational people, the two behaviors, self-control and self-reproach, operate together. Peirce would not consider your thinking to be rational if you did not engage your powers for self-control and self-reproach. He believed that 'these phenomena seem to be the fundamental characteristics that distinguish a rational being'."

"Which phenomena?"

"The phenomena concerning our capabilities for self-reproach and self-control with the eventual absence of self-reproach due to repetition of habit. Peirce even proposes that 'blame in every case appears to be a modification of the primary feeling of self-reproach.' He says this modification is often accomplished by a 'transference or projection' of that primary feeling of self-reproach onto others."

"That sounds Freudian to me."

"It is not Freudian," I assured him. "The words 'transference' and 'projection' both had meanings well before Freud used them. Peirce was using already well established meanings of these terms."

"Is Peirce saying that we blame others because we have stopped blaming ourselves?"

"No."

Hal's question made me realize that I had inadvertently led us into a psychological topic here, one with which I did not want to deal. "Peirce is saying," I explained, "that a fundamental characteristic of rational beings exists which allows us to self-correct. Because we have that characteristic, we expect that other rational beings can also self-correct. Peirce says, 'accordingly, we never blame anybody for what has been beyond his power of previous self-control'."

"Such as?"

"Such as, we would not put a four-year-old in jail for stealing a diamond tiara, because a child of that age can not be expected to be rational. We do, however, jail twenty-year-old cat burglars, since they would be expected to know better."

"And would an insanity defense be the same thing?"

"It would, and so would blaming someone for not being able to do something which that person has never been able to do before. Peirce then says that 'thinking is a species of conduct which is largely subject to self-control'."

After reading this last statement, I decided I had better do some explaining before continuing. "In philosophy, everything that has to do with conduct belongs in the category of ethics. Peirce is the first philosopher to propose that rational thought is a species of conduct and therefore subject to praise or blame, like all other conduct. This refers back to what we discussed the other day about the ethics of terminology, and about norms and standards."

"Is he referring to morals here?"

"Not just to morals in the religious sense but to all conduct. He means all conduct, everything that we do that is subject to self-control."

"That is quite a statement."

"Yes it is. Peirce even says that 'logical self-control is a perfect mirror of ethical self-control.' Then he adds that instead of thinking of ethics and logic as mirrors of one another you could put logical self-control as a species under the genus of ethical self-control."

"Let me see," Hal said, thinking aloud, "genus means general, and species means specific. That means that ethical self-control would be the general category and logical self-control would be a kind of ethical self-control?"

"Excellent thinking!" I responded enthusiastically. I love it when people pull concepts forward and apply them to the making of new connections. "Next, Peirce follows up his statements about not blaming someone for something they cannot control and about thinking being a species of conduct. 'In accordance with this, what you cannot in the least help believing is not, justly speaking, wrong belief. In other words, for you, it is absolute truth'."

"Does that make it true then? Does someone only need to believe something is true for it to be true?"

"No. What Peirce is claiming is that truth has a functional use apart from whether it turns out to be true or not. The reason for this is because what we believe to be true functions the same for us whether what we believe to be true ultimately turns out to be true or not."

"What do you mean by functional use?"

"I mean that the habit of mind that Peirce calls belief, which the rest of us might think of as truths, beliefs, habits, facts, and so on, all provide a basis from which to take action. Peirce is not saying that something is absolutely true because you absolutely believe it is true. He is saying that what you absolutely believe to be true functions for you as if it were true, since you cannot help believing that it is true. Since you cannot help but believe that something is true, then you cannot help but take action based on that belief when the occasion arises."

"That makes sense."

"Peirce concedes that, come tomorrow, you might completely disbelieve something that you cannot help but believe today. Then he suggests that we need to draw a distinction between two sorts of things that we believe we cannot do."

But then there is a certain distinction between things you "cannot" do, merely in the sense that nothing stimulates you to the great effort and endeavors that would be required, and things you cannot do because in their own nature they are insusceptible of being put into practice.

"That is reasonable."

"Next, Peirce says, 'In every stage of your excogitations'...."

"That is quite a word!"

"I consider it a nineteenth-century gem. The word 'excogitations' just means intense and careful studying in order to grasp something fully," I explained, then began the sentence again. 'In every stage of your excogitations, there is something of which you can only say, I cannot think otherwise and your experience-based hypothesis is that the impossibility of thinking otherwise is of the second kind'."

"I forget. What is the second kind?"

"The second is the 'impossibility of thinking otherwise' that comes from believing that something is incapable of being put into practice."

"Is he saying that, no matter where you are in thinking about something, you are going to think some things are absolutely true because you cannot possibly think otherwise?"

"Yes."

"Even at the beginning? Even when we know hardly anything about the subject?"

"Maybe especially at the beginning, depending upon how someone reaches certainty. In every case we have beliefs that we cannot do certain things because they are impossible to do. We have many more of these beliefs than you might imagine. This is what Peirce is referring to when he says that 'doubting is more difficult than lying'."

"Hmm," he began, forming his next question carefully. "So, when people absolutely believe that something cannot be done because of their beliefs, they are going to assume that it cannot be done because it is not possible? Are they going to think this even if the real reason is because they are ignorant or too lazy to dig into the matter?"

"Probably."

"Surely some things are impossible! I mean, surely some things are not worth bothering with in the first place because they are impossible."

"That is like asking if some things are absolutely true or false. Peirce would say yes, but that we are fallible. We cannot ever be completely sure that we know what is absolutely true or false."

"Would that be like believing that it was impossible for man to ever fly?"

"Exactly. And like believing that man could never land on the moon," I added. "Good experimentalists do not believe in words like 'always' or 'never.' They do not close themselves off from the possibility of re-opening a question for further investigation. Good experimentalists would not state, even after much research, that a given proposition is absolutely, finally, and forever true. Instead, they will 'hold something for true' and be willing to test it out repeatedly if necessary. Once a proposition has been thoroughly tested, then a good experimentalist is justified in saying, with a high degree of probability, whether the odds are in favor of the proposition being true."

"That sounds a lot like the way I play blackjack."

"And the way you do everything else as well. Peirce next wants to clarify what he means by the term 'thought.' He does not want you to think he means the term in a narrow sense, like something that people only do 'in silence and darkness.' He means for thought to cover all rational life, 'so that an experiment shall be an operation of thought'."

"Then, that is why the Davis Non-verbal Assessment works!" Hal interrupted suddenly. "It is an operation of thought! Wow! You were right, everything is here to connect with the non-verbal assessment."

"I am glad you have made that connection, but we are dealing only with Peirce at the moment."

"I know we are," he said. "You can go on. I promise to refrain from future outbursts."

"I like your outbursts. I just do not want us to lose our train of thought here," I explained. "Peirce wants us to consider thought as applying to all rational life, not just to what goes on in ivory towers. That means that anything we think about with intent and anything that we do with intent constitutes what Peirce defines as thinking."

"Why did you say 'with intent'?"

"Because all rational thought comes through the lens of purpose. The word 'rational' pre-supposes intent, or purpose."

"Why does 'rational' pre-suppose intent?"

"Because," I said, perhaps a little too impatiently, "if no intent is involved, all you have is an accident, or a dream, or something of that nature. You cannot have rational thought without an intention of some sort."

"Is a thought automatically rational, as long as you have an intention?"

"No. You can have irrational intentions as well as irrational thoughts," I said, still feeling impatient. "Peirce's pragmaticism deals with the meanings of rational thoughts, which include rational intentions and purposes."

"Oh, I see now," Hal said, apparently missing my impatient tone.

"Good. Now, I want us to go back to this idea that Peirce intends for thought to cover all rational life. In the next sentence, he brings up the point that 'the action of self-control tends toward that ultimate state of habit, where there is no more room left for self-control'."

"Does that mean that the thinking is no longer subject to blame then?"

"Good question," I said, my momentary irritation now gone. "Yes. Peirce says that, in the case of thought, this ultimate state of habit is the state of 'fixed belief' or 'perfect knowledge'."

"'Perfect knowledge' sounds like it might be an absolute to me," Hal said suspiciously. "I suppose Peirce will have something to say about these states."

"Good supposing! What he says next is that we should know and remember two all-important things."

"And these all-important things are?"

The first is that a person is not absolutely an individual. His thoughts are what he is "saying to himself," that is, is saying to that other self that is just coming into life in the flow of time. When one reasons, it is that critical self that one is trying to persuade; and all thought whatsoever is a sign, and is mostly of the nature of language.

I stopped here in case Hal had questions. He had none. This meant one of two things to me: either he understood the passage so well that he did not need to ask questions, or else he did not understand it well enough to ask questions. Considering the passage, I decided his silence must be due to a lack of understanding and offered an unsolicited explanation.

"Peirce proposes here that we are made up of more than one self," I began. Hal nodded so I continued. "He wants us to know that one of these selves is always just coming into being as time flows along."

"How does he mean that? Does he mean a separate personality?"

"No. By 'critical self,' Peirce means a non-habit-driven self that says to the habit-driven self, 'Hey! Wait a minute, why are you doing that?' or 'Why do you think that is true or false?'"

"Does everyone have this critical self?"

"Everyone who is capable of rational thought does, at least to some degree. The degree to which a person has this critical self operating is the degree to which that person is capable of rational thought." I paused for a moment, trying to decide how I wanted to address this next issue. "Now, the part here where Peirce mentions that 'all thought whatsoever is a sign and is mostly of the nature of language'...."

"Yes?"

"Sign theory is connected to the rest of Peirce's pragmaticism, but he does not go into it in this essay. I am just bringing your attention to the word 'sign' because you should not think that it is a throwaway line. Engaged Intelligence classes are primarily based upon Peirce's sign theory."

"If his sign theory matters so much why did he not write about it here?"

"I am not sure. Maybe because he felt it was too complicated."

"Is it too complicated to deal with here?"

"It is complex, but not all that complicated, at least not in the way we use it for Engaged Intelligence training. Would you like for me to give a brief explanation of Peirce's sign theory?"

"Yes."

"It might keep us here a while longer than usual."

"That would be fine with me. I would rather not have to wait until Monday to hear about it."

"By the word 'sign,' Peirce means a significator. A significator is something that represents, points to, or stands in place of something else. In general terms, this is what Peirce means when he says that 'all thought whatsoever is a sign and is mostly of the nature of language'."

"All thought is a sign? Does all thought signify something else?"

"Yes."

"What does it signify?"

"Whatever is thought about. All thinking is done by means of signs. You cannot think of nothing. Once you have something to think about, you are dealing with a sign of some sort."

"I guess I am going to need a definition of what Peirce means by the word 'sign' for that to make any sense."

"We will get to that," I assured him. "Besides stating that all thought whatsoever is a sign, Peirce also believed that all thought is mostly of the nature of language."

"Do you agree that all thought is mostly language?"

"No, I do not agree with Peirce on that. However, I understand why that may appear to be true for some people. You can see why it would have appeared that way for Peirce, who did all of his thinking by means of words and other symbols, such as numbers. Other people, such as artists and auto mechanics, do not need to use language when they are thinking. I do not disagree with Peirce that all thought is a sign, though. I disagree that thought is mostly in the nature of language. It is obvious that all thought is a sign."

"Not to me."

"This might help. Peirce held that there were three basic ways for something to be a sign: as an icon, an index, and a symbol."

"I think I know what symbols are, but not the other two."

"Do you know what the word 'icon' means?"

"I think it has something to do with Russian art," he said, "and with computer screens, as well."

"Icon means an image. In the context of Russian religious art, the word refers to a religious image. In the context of computers, an icon is a miniature image on computer screens that represents a function, like 'copy' or 'delete'."

"But that could not have been what Peirce was referring to."

"You are right. He was referring to 'icon' in general terms as an imitation or representation of something."

"Such as?"

"Such as copies of an actual or imagined thing, like a picture or a statue. Icons are of two main sorts, projections and likenesses. Projections are direct copies. They have a point-for-point connection to the original thing."

"Would a projection be like an image from a movie projector?"

"Yes, or a still camera, or from a building projecting its shadow onto the ground or onto other buildings. Projections can also come in the form of a recording, say of music, speech, or a movie or television show. A projection is an icon that is a point-for-point copy of something. A scaled map, for example, is a projection of the territory it represents. An icon that is a projection could also be a sculpture or a painting that looks just like its subject. Also, a photocopy is a projection. Icons as projective imitations come in many forms."

"What about the other kind?"

"Do you mean likenesses?"

"Yes."

"A likeness is an imitation in a more general sense. Mickey Mouse is a likeness of a mouse. The Hammering Man statue in front of the Seattle Art Museum represents the likeness of a man with a hammer."

"Meaning that Mickey and the Hammering Man have general features of a mouse and a man?"

"Exactly! All of the pictures in the international sign code are likenesses. Just think of the man and woman figures they use on restroom doors. These likenesses are still iconic, in the sense that they are imitations of something, but they are not point-for-point projections of a specific thing. In other words, they are not replications of a specific person."

"What if someone makes a duplicate copy of Hammering Man? What is the copy then, a projection or a likeness?"

"A copy of Hammering Man would be a projection of a likeness, but I do not want to go into that. I only agreed to take this side trip into signs if I could make it a short detour."

"Then I suppose I will have to settle for a short detour."

I could tell he had at least a dozen questions, but I felt that we needed to forge ahead. The study of Peirce's sign theory can be a lifetime vocation.

"That is the short version of icons. Can you sum it up?"

"Sure. An icon represents something by imitating it. One way to imitate is by being just like it, a photograph for example. The other way is by resembling something in the sense that a cartoon does."

"Good! Peirce called the next kind of sign an index. Do you have an idea why he might have used the word 'index'?"

"Maybe I would if you gave me an example."

"Here is a hint," I offered. "Rain clouds are an indication of rain."

"Indication?"

"The word 'indication' is part of the hint."

"Does indication mean the same thing as index?"

"That is your only clue," I said, refusing to be any more specific.

"Rain clouds are pointing to what will happen in the future. Does the word 'index' have to do with the future?"

"It can. An indication, or an index, as Peirce called it, has to do with pointing to something else. An index in a book tells you the location of certain terms in that book. A sign that is an index points toward information that you are going to locate somewhere else in time or space. And space does not only mean physical space," I added. "Signs occur in the mental realm as well."

"So an icon represents something else, and an index is an indication of something else."

"Yes. A sign acting as an index requires us to think about what something means in a different way than icons do. We imply or infer meaning from indications. Say someone has the sniffles. We could say that the sniffles are an indication of a cold."

"But they could be allergies," Hal argued.

"I did not say that the inferences made from an index are necessarily correct. When you move out of the territory of icons and into the realm of indicies, you move deeper into ambiguity."

"Ambiguity?"

"Meaning that a sign can be interpreted in more than one way. Ambiguity is more likely to occur when you move away from signs that imitate into signs that indicate, or point to, something. Indicies are signs that indicate, or point to, something else. The word 'indices' is the plural form of index, by the way. Because of their function as indicators, indicies are potentially more ambiguous than icons. Symbols, the third kind of signs Peirce identifies, are the most ambiguous type of signs. They are, by their nature, ambiguous."

"By symbol, do you mean like the flag as a symbol of the country?"

"Yes, the flag is an example of a public symbol. We rely on all sorts of symbols, both public and private. A piece of string tied around your finger to remind you to call home before you leave work could be a symbol, a private symbol. Most symbols are public, though."

"Meaning?"

"Meaning that a symbol stands for some thing, or some concept, that has been generally agreed upon."

"Like what?"

"Maybe it would be easier for you to think about symbols if you consider that our entire conversation is being conducted by means of symbols."

"How so?" my favorite engineer inquired.

"All words are symbols. Symbols stand in the place of other things, but without an obvious representational connection to them."

"You say words are symbols and that symbols are the most ambiguous of the types of signs, but I am understanding what you are saying."

"That is because you know the language and you know me. Words and numbers are symbols that stand for things, qualities, and concepts. Words do not look anything like what they represent. The word 'apple' does not look or sound anything like an apple, does it?"

"No," he said, still not trusting this definition.

"Unless you know what the word 'apple' means, you cannot know if it functions as a representation, an indicator, or a symbol of something else. You have to already know the meaning of a symbol to know what it represents."

"I suppose that is true," he said, still tentative.

"Just think of physical symbols, like a crucifix and the Star of David. Neither of them has a natural relationship to what they stand for, like icons and indices do."

"But a crucifix is a representation of a cross."

"Yes, but its main purpose is to symbolize the Christian faith. A crucifix is a physical symbol. The meaning of a cross comes from what it symbolizes, not what it resembles."

"Are you saying then that representations are literal, but indices and symbols are not?"

"I would not put it that way. I would say signs that imitate something else are less likely to be interpreted ambiguously than are signs operating either indices or symbols. But any of these can be meant and interpreted in a literal way, or not."

"Can you give me an example of ambiguity?"

"Sure. Suppose a little boy in a Boy Scout uniform comes into a room."

"How is that ambiguous? It just means that he is a Boy Scout."

"Does it? How do you know that?"

"Because he is wearing a Boy Scout uniform."

"That does not necessarily mean he is a Boy Scout. It could be his brother's old uniform."

"I guess that could be true."

"It could even be his costume for a school play. Or, he could be coming back from a Boy Scout meeting during which he was drummed out of scouting for stealing the dues."

"That all sounds silly to me."

"What does?"

"The little brother, the costume, the drumming-out thing. It just sounds silly. It is obvious that the most logical assumption is that the boy is a member of the Boy Scouts. If you were in the room, you would surely know."

"You might or might not know. The point is that you would have to have more information to know what that boy in the uniform means. The boy's meaning is ambiguous. All that you can say for sure is that a little boy is wearing a Boy Scout uniform. Without more information, you cannot know if he is a Boy Scout in good standing, a wearer of hand-me-downs, or an actor in costume."

"What does this have to do with signs?"

"I was referring to ambiguity here. That boy in the scouting uniform is a sign. Depending upon the situation and how he is interpreted, he can be any type of sign. All signs must be interpreted. They do not mean anything in and of themselves. Anything open to interpretation is ambiguous. That is why Engaged Intelligence training focuses so much upon building better interpretation skills. Ambiguity is at the root of nearly every problem that has to do with human communication and understanding."

"How does knowing about icons and such help you to interpret things?"

"For one thing, when you know what kind of sign you are dealing with for a particular situation, you can begin to see what you might need to know in order to correctly interpret that sign. Or, knowing what kind of sign you are using may help you to clarify your meaning for others."

"Oh," he said then, "is that because of ambiguity?"

"Yes. Now, I said earlier that signs used as indices or symbols are likely to be more ambiguous in their meanings than are icons. This does not mean that icons are not at all ambiguous. That boy wearing the scouting uniform could have been interpreted in several ways. All of these ways could have been true at the same time, or not. For example, that boy could be interpreted as an icon, a point-for-point representation of a typical Boy Scout. His presence could have been taken as an index, his uniform indicating that a scout meeting might be about to take place. He could also have been interpreted as a symbol, such as young manhood at its best."

"Are you saying that it all depends upon how the boy is interpreted? That sure leaves things up in the air!"

"That is a main point in Peirce's theory of signs and their meanings. How do we extinguish enough ambiguity to make our ideas clear enough for others to understand? How do we go about saying what we mean to say? How do we use language as a precision instrument so that others can correctly interpret our meanings? How do we go about determining the meanings that others attempt to communicate to us? How is it that anything ever means anything?"

"Good questions. What are the answers?"

"Peirce proposed that our framing and interpretation of a context, sometimes called a 'sign situation,' enables, or even produces, meaning. We do this framing and interpreting based upon our purpose. We form our purposes based upon the way in which we value. A goal, or purpose, is a value in action. Much of what Peirce discusses in the rest of this essay is an example of what he was trying to do with language. He wanted to make language work as a tool for developing and for communicating about logical functions. Maybe later we will talk more about other elements of sign situations. Sign situations involve signs as they relate to context and matrix. But this is all I want to say now about Peirce's theory of signs."

"I guess this will have to do then."

"Would you like to be done for today? Monday we can begin again and put ourselves back on track."

"That is fine with me," he said agreeably.

Seven
EXPOSITION OF PRAGMATICISM

Essay lines 290-341

"Last time we veered off topic, so we need to go back a few lines today."

"I am not afraid of a little hard work," he said in a mockingly gruff and manly manner. "Bring it on!"

"We went off topic when I said that Peirce had two important things for us to know. I am going to repeat the first one:"

> The first is that a person is not absolutely an individual. His thoughts are what he is "saying to himself," that is, is saying to that other self that is just coming into life in the flow of time. When one reasons, it is that critical self that one is trying to persuade: and all thought whatsoever is a sign, and is mostly of the nature of language.

"I could tell as you re-read this passage that our discussion of signs did lead us away from a discussion of 'critical self,' but how could I possibly have known what he meant by the word 'sign' if you had not explained it?"

"You could not have known. That lapse in information may be one reason why people find it so difficult to read Peirce's essays. Peirce often threw in a word or concept, which he had defined elsewhere in a special way, without referring to his prior definition. Since he published little of what he wrote during his lifetime, you can see why even philosophers in his own era had a difficult time understanding what he meant."

"Yes, I can see that."

"The first important thing Peirce wants us to remember is that we all have a critical self," I reminded him. "Next Peirce tells us the second thing:"

> The second thing to remember is that the man's circle of society, (however widely or narrowly this phrase may be understood), is a loosely compacted person in some respects of higher rank than the person of an individual organism.

"Does he mean that a group of people is like one person?"

"Yes. He means that the group with whom you are connected is like a loosely compacted person. Peirce claims that this group-self is in some ways of higher rank than a single individual."

"Does he mean that a group is smarter than an individual?"

"Peirce means a group in the sense of a community of seekers where knowledge can be shared and can evolve because of this sharing. I suspect he is setting the stage for his idea that truth is that which all rational people, having thoroughly examined the issue at hand, would agree upon."

"What he wants me to keep in mind, then, is that both inside and outside I am not a single individual. Is that right?"

"Yes. He says these two things make it possible for you to tell the difference between absolute truth and what you do not doubt."

"By the phrase 'these two things' does he mean because I am more than one person inside my head and also part of a group?"

"Yes."

"Then the rest of that statement does not make any sense at all."

"Which statement?"

"The part that says I can tell the difference between what is absolute truth and what I do not doubt. That does not make any sense. Just before this, Peirce said that I should never say that I have the absolute truth."

"Good point. However, Peirce clarifies this sentence by saying that this 'ability for you to distinguish between absolute truth and what you do not doubt is only true in the abstract and in a Pickwickian sense'."

"What does he mean by a 'Pickwickian sense'?"

"He is making an allusion to *The Pickwick Papers*, by Charles Dickens. The term comes from an incident in the first chapter of the book when Mr. Pickwick accuses another character, Mr. Bottom, of acting in a 'vile and calumnious manner.' Mr. Bottom then calls Mr. Pickwick 'a humbug.' It turns out that both men hold each other in high esteem. So, when harsh words are used in a Pickwickian sense, they are not supposed to be taken as having the force of implication that they would usually have."

"What does Peirce mean by 'Pickwickian sense' in that sentence?"

"He means that the supposed ability to distinguish between what is absolute truth and what you do not doubt does not have the clarity of distinction that you might think it would have. Do you remember back when Peirce said that what you absolutely believe to be true functions for you as if it were true, since it is impossible for you to believe otherwise?"

"Yes."

"This is along those same lines. The differences between the absolute truth and what you do not doubt are not all that significant."

"That still comes across as an odd thing to say."

"I know what you mean. It is a difficult distinction to grasp. In the next paragraph, Peirce begins what he calls 'the exposition of pragmaticism itself'."

"Ah, pragmaticism! His own special word."

"Peirce says, 'Let us now hasten to the exposition of pragmaticism itself.' He proposes here that we imagine that somebody just like you is asking questions of a pragmaticist."

"Wait a minute!" Hal interrupted. "Exactly what does Peirce say that makes you think he means someone just like me?"

"He says 'somebody to whom the doctrine is new but of rather preternatural perspicacity'."

"And that means somebody just like me?"

"Just like you. Do you agree that the doctrine is new to you?"

"Yes, but...."

"And," I interrupted, "the term 'preternatural perspicacity' means having almost supernatural powers of mental perception and understanding."

"Oh, in that case, I guess he does mean just like me," Hal agreed, playfully polishing up several non-existent medals on his chest.

"Peirce says he is not going to provide any dramatic flair to this little dialogue. He says it will be a cross between a dialogue and a catechism, but much more like a catechism."

"What is a catechism?"

Catechism? I was amazed. I thought everybody knew what a catechism is. I keep forgetting how many of my general assumptions carry over from my twelve-year experience in parochial schools.

"A catechism," I began, trying to think of a meaningful comparison, "is like the frequently asked questions section on a web-site. The purpose of a catechism is to instruct people, usually little people, in the basic principles of a religion using a question and answer format."

"Do you mean like a dialogue?"

"No. Catechisms are known for being dry. They are meant to be used for reference or to be memorized. Dialogues are more freewheeling, like our discussion here."

"Is Peirce expecting me to memorize what he writes here?"

"No," I assured him. "Peirce is just letting us know, in his quaint nineteenth-century way, that we should not expect much in the way of entertainment from what he is about to present."

"As if there were a chance we would," he commented wryly.

"Ready?"

Hal nodded.

"Here goes. See if you can hold your questions until I finish."

Questioner: I am astounded at your definition of your pragmatism, because only last year I was assured by a person above all suspicion of warping the truth—himself a pragmatist—that your doctrine precisely was "that a conception is to be tested by its practical effects." You must surely, then, have entirely changed your definition recently.

Pragmatist: If you will turn to Vols. VI and VII of the *Revue Philosophique* or to the *Popular Science Monthly* for November 1877 and January 1878, you will be able to judge for yourself whether the interpretation you mention was not then clearly excluded. The exact wording of the English enunciation, (changing only the first person into the second), was, "Consider what effects that might conceivably have practical bearing [that] you conceive the object of your conception to have. Then your conception of those effects is the WHOLE of your conception of the object."

Questioner: Well, what reason have you for asserting that this is so?

Pragmatist: That is what I specially desire to tell you. But the question had better be postponed until you clearly understand what those reasons profess to prove.

Questioner: What then, is the *raison d'être* of the doctrine? What advantage is expected from it?

Pragmatist: It will serve to show that almost every proposition of ontological metaphysics is either meaningless gibberish—one word being defined by other words, and they still by others, without any real conception ever being reached—or else is downright absurd; so that all such rubbish being swept away, what will remain of philosophy will be a series of problems capable of investigation by observational methods of the true sciences—the truth about which can be reached without those interminable misunderstandings and disputes which have made the highest of the positive sciences a mere amusement for idle intellects, a sort of chess—idle pleasure its purpose, and reading out of a book its method. In this regard, pragmaticism is a species of prope-positivism.

"Uh, honey?" Hal said when I stopped to catch a breath.

"Yes?"

"I have to interrupt. I know you want me to wait until the end, but this is just too much to take all at once."

I knew he was right. I needed to go back and reinterpret this for him, but how far back was the question.

"Where do you think I started to lose you?"

"I started getting lost when Peirce started to explain his *raison d'être*. At first, I thought he was just going to rant and rave, but I could not follow along well enough to know for sure what he was talking about."

"Then, I will go back to the *raison d'être*. Do you understand what Peirce meant when he said that 'almost every proposition of ontological metaphysics is meaningless gibberish'?"

"I think I know what metaphysics means and I know Peirce did not like ontologically derived...stuff," Hal finished lamely, unable to find a suitable word to accompany ontologically derived. "But no, I have to say that I do not understand what he means."

"When Peirce writes that the propositions are meaningless gibberish, he follows up this claim by saying that these propositions are 'made up of words that define each other with no conception being reached.' Or else, claimed Peirce, 'the conception that is reached is absurd.' This would be like stating that the purpose of life is to find happiness. Then you define happiness as the state of being cheerful. You could probably substitute any one word for the other in these sorts of cases and go round in circles for years without ever defining the meaning of happiness. For certain, you would not have settled the question as to whether the purpose of life is to find happiness."

"I understand that now." Then he added with mock formality, "Proceed!"

"Next, Peirce says that, 'with all such rubbish swept away'…."

"Which rubbish?"

"He means the meaningless gibberish of ontological metaphysics," I answered. "'So that all such rubbish being swept away, what will remain of philosophy will be a series of problems capable of investigation by the observational methods of the true sciences'."

"By 'true sciences' does he mean the taxonomic sciences?"

"Yes, and operational sciences like mathematics and physics, as well. Peirce then says that once this rubbish is swept away and the problems of philosophy are limited to those capable of scientific investigation, we can finally start getting at the truth. He means that we can consider these problems without the endless misunderstandings and disputes that have made the study of philosophy into a mere amusement for idle intellects. The way Peirce sees things is that philosophy should be respected as the highest of the positive sciences. He feels that the study of philosophy has been reduced to 'nothing more than a game of chess…idle pleasure its purpose, and reading out of a book, its method'."

"It sounds to me like Peirce is describing people who like to play with pointless porcupines."

"I agree with you on that. 'In this regard,' Peirce wrote, 'pragmaticism is a species of prope-positivism'." I stopped here to offer him the opportunity to define this word. "Would you like to try figuring out what he means by the term 'prope-positivism'?"

"Sure."

"Do you remember the prefix 'prope' from before?"

"I think so. It means to go forward, as in propeller and propel."

"Or outwards. Do you remember what Peirce said about the meaning of 'prope' when it is used as a prefix in philosophy?"

"No. What did he say?"

I found the passage we had read earlier. "Peirce wrote that 'the prefix 'prope' should mark a broad and rather indefinite extension of the meaning of the term to which it was prefixed'."

"I vaguely remember that now."

"And what do you think he means by the word 'positivism'?"

"I remember that 'ism' refers to a doctrine of some sort," he reasoned, "and positive is the opposite of negative, but it is also the opposite of unsure. I guess I do not know what positivism is."

"I am not sure what the root meaning of positivism is either," I admitted. "In philosophy, the term 'positivism' was first associated with Auguste Comte. Comte held that the highest form of knowledge is simple description."

"Simple description? How could he think that? What about applications? What about inventions and such?"

"Comte lived in France between 1798 and 1855. Those were unstable times. The French Revolution ended in 1799, when Comte was just a year old. The people of France had rebelled against a decadent monarchy. Comte, in turn, rebelled against the decadent philosophies of his day. He abhorred philosophers who made up doctrines that paid no attention to the laws of nature or social realities. Comte was disgusted by the convoluted philosophical theories of his day, theories as over-blown and over-decorated as the decadent monarchy had been. You could say he was sick and tired of pointless porcupines."

"Just like Peirce?"

"On that issue, yes."

"I can see how Comte would have thought that simple description was the highest form of knowledge. But I would expect more than that from Peirce. You need to do more than describe things to know what they mean."

"That is an insightful comment! Adding in the 'prope' part will help you to solve that problem."

"Maybe I can put this together myself. Positivism is the doctrine that simple description is the highest form of knowledge, and 'prope' means to go outward. Peirce says that, in philosophy, 'prope' should mean a broad and indefinite extension of the meaning of something." Hal thought for a moment. "Prope-positivism must mean a broad and indefinite extension of simple description. But that does not make any sense to me."

"Think back to the meaning of prefix 'prope' again. Think of 'prope' as carrying simple description outward or forward."

"Could it mean forward in time?"

"Yes," I said encouragingly, "and in other ways as well."

"Like toward a conclusion?"

"That would be one outward direction, but that kind of conclusion-based outwardness would be more like another kind of positivism. Peirce means that his species of prope-positivism pointed toward describing consequences and describing the meaning that resides in consequences."

"Which kind of positivism is the conclusion type?"

"The kind that Bertrand Russell preached, for one."

"Knowing that you are not a fan of Russell, I realize there must be a catch here," Hal said, in a decidedly understated comment. "If Russell was a prope-positivist and Peirce was also one, then what is the difference?"

"Both kinds of prope-positivism stressed the importance of language and scientific method. Remember when I said earlier that Russell believed that if you cannot measure it, count it, or prove it with existing methods and tools then it does not matter?"

"I vaguely remember you saying that."

"That is the difference," I said conclusively.

Hal looked confused by my statement. "What is the difference?"

"The difference is the idea of a conclusion, of having absolutes and once-and-for-alls," I said. "Russell's philosophy of science ignored the importance of those things that could not be measured. He discounted them as not real and, therefore, not worth attention. Wait a minute," I said, getting up to find a book on my reference shelf. "I want to read you something from *Wittgenstein's Vienna.*"

"Who is Wittgenstein?"

"You do not need to know who he is to grasp the point I am going to make," I said. "This excerpt is about what the philosopher, Paul Engelmann, said about Russell's positivism."

Positivism holds, and this is its essence, that what we can speak about is all that really matters in human life. Whereas Wittgenstein passionately believes that all that really matters in life is precisely what, in his view, we must be silent about.[5]

"Russell interpreted Wittgenstein through his own positivist eyes and thought if we cannot speak of something, it must not be real and, therefore, must not matter."

"What about Peirce? How is his kind of positivism different?"

"Peirce's brand of prope-positivism allows for realities that are general concepts, including values, potentials, and possibilities. Peirce holds that even things you cannot touch, such as general concepts, purposes, and values, are real things. Just because you cannot speak of something does not mean that it is not real. For Peirce, any subject is real as long as it possesses qualities sufficient to characterize it, whether or not anyone ever knows what those qualities are. His concept of reality holds that something can be true even if it has never occurred and even if it is an idea no one has previously thought."

"What does he mean by qualities?"

"He means the same thing that we mean in Engaged Intelligence training. Qualities are the properties or aspects of things, like color, size, and density, that make them similar to and different from one another."

"How about an example?"

"Do you remember Duns Scotus and the terms 'thisness' and 'whatness'?" When he nodded, I continued. "Qualities, which are sometimes called 'properties' or 'characteristics,' are aspects of things. Things cannot exist separate from the qualities that make them what they are. I know the 'whatness' of an object because of the qualities which that object shares with others of the same sort. For example, I know what an apple is because of the qualities

it shares with other apples, but not with oranges. I also know what fruit is because of the qualities that apples, oranges, and grapes have in common with
each other, but not with broccoli or rutabagas. On the other hand, I know the
'thisness' of a particular object by the qualities that distinguish it from all
other things that exist. Thus I know that a specific apple is unique in all the
universe because it has at least one quality that differentiates it from all other
things, including all other apples."

"What quality would that be?"

"I can think of two qualities that differentiate that apple from all others,"
I said, pointing to the apple sitting on top of my computer monitor, the one
intended for my morning snack. "One quality is location. That apple is there
and not in the fruit bowl on the kitchen table. Another quality is time. That apple is right there, right now, and no other thing in the universe is in exactly that
place at that time."

"Then location and time are qualities of that apple?"

"Sure, and that apple has many other qualities as well. Everything that
exists or might possibly exist has at least one quality that differentiates it from
all other things, in addition to having qualities in common with other things."

"Then does everyone notice the same qualities? For example, everyone
knows what an apple is and what that means."

"No. Everyone does not notice the same qualities. We notice qualities
based upon how we do our looking and why. We also bring whatever biases
we might have along with us whenever we qualify among options to create or
discover relationships."

"Relationships?"

"Relationships come from making connections between things. Peirce
believed that all actual and all potential relationships already exist and that we
are discovering these when we inquire into some matter. I am not so sure I
agree with him on that, but that is another matter. In any case, we make relationships by relating the qualities of things to one another for some purpose. In
doing this, we use or construct general categories. General categories allow us
to make sense of things, to make sense of the world. However, they can limit
us as well."

"How can categories limit?"

"Remember Tom, from Tucson, who used to comment that one person or
another suffered from 'hardening of the categories'?"

"I remember, but I have to admit I never understood what that meant."

"Do you remember back when Peirce said that all thought is a sign?"

He nodded.

"A sign stands for a relationship. We learn what signs mean from our
parents, from schooling, from culture, from experience, from all sorts of
places. These relationships and their meanings eventually become habits for
us. Habits provide us with the foundation we need for operating in the world.

Because of learned habits, we do not have to think about how to read, or what a stop sign means, or how to ride a bike, or whether something is an apple or not. As we gain experience, we do most of our relationship-making habitually, based upon what we already know. We only suffer from 'hardening of the categories' when we become mindlessly stuck in a rut and do not have the mental flexibility to think our way out of it."

"Such as?"

"Such as insisting an apple can only mean a fruit," I suggested, "and not also a symbol of temptation or...."

"Of temptation?" he interrupted. "Like in the Garden of Eden?"

"Sure. People who approach meaning literally do not grasp that language is inherently ambiguous, that it functions metaphorically. This greatly limits their mental flexibility and capacities for understanding. They suffer from 'hardening of the categories'."

"This is not just about apples, is it?"

"No. Practically all language was initially constructed metaphorically. We are so used to the meaning of signs in our own language that this metaphorical connection may be easier to recognize in other languages than it is in our own. In French, for example, the word for apple is *la pomme*, and the word for potato is *la pomme de terre*."

"What does that mean?"

"*La pomme* means 'apple.' *La pomme de terre* means 'apple of the earth' when it is taken as a literal translation," I said. "But, for anyone who speaks French, *la pomme de terre* is simply a sign in the form of a symbol, which stands for the thing 'potato.' As I said before, most people fail to notice the metaphorical aspects of their own language. Most people just think that words mean what they mean."

"What does this have to do with Peirce's positivism?"

"It has more to do with his theory about signs and general categories, which his version of prope-positivism is based upon. Peirce contended that we must use language of one sort or another to differentiate among the qualities of things. Qualities are the properties of a relationship. We use qualities to construct our categories and to differentiate among them. We examine a relationship that exists, or might exist, among things by comparing and contrasting qualities."

"Can you explain that?"

"In the case of the French word for potato, for example, someone once made a relationship between certain qualities that potatoes have in common with apples, as well as qualities that are different between them. A metaphor, 'the apple of the earth,' came from these relationships among these qualities. The metaphor eventually became the sign for the entire category, potatoes."

"Oh, I see that."

"In science, and for everything else as well, we differentiate among the qualities of things guided by some purpose, goal, or value. For Peirce, a directing purpose is just as real as the things that we discover when we follow that purpose. He proposed that purposes and goals also have qualities that make them real, even if most people never bother to think about what these are. Peirce even contended that developing good purposes is the most vital aspect of his theory. His version of prope-positivism aims at describing the logical methods by which we develop worthy goals and purposes."

"So Peirce believed there was a logic for making goals?"

"For constructing worthy goals," I said, emphasizing the word "worthy." "He called it 'abduction.' Abduction is the logic of discovery, the logic of forming good hypotheses. I call it the logic of valuing, of deciding what matters. We also call this 'multi-relational thinking' in Dottie Davis's theory of Relational Thinking Styles."

He nodded thoughtfully at this. "Then what is the difference between the positivism of Russell and the positivism of Peirce?"

"The difference is that Russell set out to measure and prove what could logically be proven to be true or false, without spending time formulating hypotheses or worrying about consequences. For him, getting a hypothesis is like setting a goal. You just pick something you want to find out and then spend your time finding it out. Russell's version of scientific method focused mainly on decisions of how best to answer questions. Peirce, however, set out to identify the way we should be formulating our questions."

"What does that have to do with the meaning being in the results?"

"Peirce's version of prope-positivism propels the meaning of a thing into the consequences that it produces upon a whole system. So, Peirce's method of formulating hypotheses takes into account web-like relationships among things within the larger system. In this sense, Peirce's logic of discovery is the same as the pattern of reasoning someone would use for making unique metaphorical and analogous relationships. The logic of discovery lays out how to discover and examine a potential purpose in terms of its qualities, values, and wide-ranging potentialities, including potential consequences. Using his methods, we can examine potential consequences in a global, systems-wide way. For Peirce, this method of formulating a purpose is the key stage for performing good scientific method."

"What are the other stages?"

"They are the stages of the scientific method we all learned in school. One is stating a hypothesis and setting up the methods for testing it. The other is using those methods to test out the proposition."

"So, are you saying that, for Peirce, the scientific method has three stages instead of two?"

"Yes. However, Peirce's description of this first stage in scientific method is the part of his theory that he apparently never completed. He thought that it would be his greatest contribution."

"If Peirce failed to complete that part, then how would the doctrine he proposed be any better than the one Russell had?"

"Peirce opened up a new way of exploring questions. He created a way of understanding ideas that allows us to go past the limits of our immediate senses and existing logical tools. He also opened a doorway that allows us to consider ethics and aesthetics as integral parts of good research."

"By 'aesthetics' do you mean art?"

"Not exactly, but we can deal with that a little later." I posed a question to pull us on track. "Do you understand what 'positivism' means?"

"It means that you deal in what can be described."

"And do you think you understand the difference between the two versions of prope-positivism, the difference between Peirce and Russell?"

"I think so. Let me see if I can say it." He took a moment to gather his thoughts. "Russell focused on proving something true or false. While Peirce said that hypothesizing matters as much as everything else and that the meaning of something is in the consequences it produces. This means that, if your hypothesis is no good, your consequences will be no good."

"Uh, not quite," I said tentatively. "You could have a perfectly awful hypothesis and still have good consequences. Everything we do produces consequences. A hypothesis does not create consequences. The belief in a hypothesis causes us to act in one way or another. That action based on the hypothesis produces consequences. A bad hypothesis, say one that is completely incorrect, might not have any effect at all on what happens or it may cause us to act in a beneficial way."

"What do you mean?"

"Peirce's pragmaticism proposes that the meaning of a hypothesis, or a proposition, resides in the sum of the consequences that affect human conduct when you implement that proposal. That does not mean that the consequences are going to be good or bad. It only means that the consequences are subject to self-control. By self-control, Peirce means human beings can change their conduct before taking action on something."

Knowing we would be coming back to this issue at a later point, I decided to let him digest this for a while and continued into the essay.

"I took us off on a side trip here to discuss positivism. Let me do a quick summary. Then we can see if we want to go on now or not."

"Sure."

"Here goes," I said. "Peirce says that his doctrine would show that 'almost every proposition of ontological metaphysics is meaningless gibberish or downright absurd.' Then he follows this statement by saying that, when he is finished sweeping all of the rubbish away, 'all that will be left are a series of problems capable of investigation by using the methods of the true sciences.' No longer will philosophy be the subject of idle dilettantes, who play at philosophy as if it were a game of chess. No longer will philosophers spend their time haggling over endless misunderstandings and disputes, dragging this highest of the positive sciences into a game for fools. 'In this regard,' says Peirce, 'pragmaticism is a species of prope-positivism'."

"I heard that this time!"

"Heard what?"

"I heard Peirce call philosophy 'the highest of the positive sciences.' I had not heard that before, the word 'positive.' Or else, if I heard it, I must have thought 'optimistic,' or 'not negative'."

"Great!" I was encouraged by Hal's increasing comprehension. "Do you know what Peirce means when he says that philosophy 'should be the highest of the positive sciences'?"

He thought for a moment then said, "I guess not."

"He is referring back to positivism in general. Remember that Comte, the first positivist, believed that simple description is the goal of science."

"I remember that. I also think I understand prope-positivism."

"Peirce is saying that philosophy should be the highest of all the true sciences, but it is not, because of the game-players. He wants philosophy to undergo the same scrutiny as the other sciences so that philosophy can take its rightful place as king of the positive sciences."

"Oh, now I remember. This has to do with the taxonomy thing. So, by cleaning out the rubbish and installing his pragmaticism, Peirce was going to set philosophy on its throne?"

Hal said this with a peculiar tone is his voice. I was not sure if he was teasing me or lightly mocking Peirce for his grandiosity.

"I suppose you could say that. In any case, it is too late to take on the next section today. We can hasten to more of this exposition tomorrow."

"That sounds like a good plan to me."

Eight
COMPONENTS OF AN EXPERIMENT

Essay lines 341-398

"Do you remember where we left off?" I asked Hal as we settled in that day.

"I remember that Peirce was cleaning out ontological rubbish," Hal recalled, "and getting ready to set pragmaticism on its throne."

"Good memory! That is just what he was doing. Today we can start with the next part of the paragraph. Now, this is the pragmatist speaking."

> But what distinguishes [pragmaticism] from other species is, first, its retention of a purified philosophy; secondly its full acceptance of the main body of our instinctive beliefs; and thirdly, its strenuous insistence upon the truth of scholastic realism (or a close approximation to that, well stated by the late Dr. Francis Ellingwood Abbot in the Introduction to his *Scientific Theism*).

"I am assuming an explanation is on the way," Hal said hopefully when I paused for a breath at the end of that long sentence.

"We can begin by individually discussing each of Peirce's three points."

"Good. Maybe that will help me to remember."

"The first difference between pragmaticism and other species of prope-positivism is that 'it retains a purified philosophy'."

"Because he has swept away all the gibberish?"

"Yes. And, because after sweeping away the gibberish, pragmaticism 'retains only those problems capable of investigation by observational methods of the true sciences'."

"I see that," Hal said. "What is the second point?"

"The second difference is pragmaticism's 'full acceptance of the main body of our instinctive beliefs'."

"What does he mean by that?"

"He means that pragmaticism does not expect us to leave out what we know, or can know, by means of our senses and through experience," I told him. "This is the 'starting out from wherever you are' idea."

"Oh, then he must mean common sense."

"'Critical common sense,'" I reminded him, "common sense that uses reason also."

"And the third difference?"

"The third difference, Peirce says, is pragmaticism's 'strenuous insistence upon the truth of scholastic realism'."

"Duns Scotus again?"

"Yes. Or, as Peirce said, 'a close approximation' to scholastic realism. He mentions that the conception he is proposing was well stated in Dr. Francis Ellingwood Abbot's introduction to *Scientific Theism*."

"And who was the good doctor?"

"He was a contemporary of Peirce, an American, and a liberal theologian. As I mentioned before, Peirce was not comfortable with the kind of realism which holds that what we know is all that exists. Scholastic realism is a higher power realism, one that grants the possibility of a force, law, or guiding principle of existence. Peirce called this force 'agapacism,' or 'evolutionary love.' This force mattered a great deal to Peirce, but most scholars are a little bit embarrassed by this aspect of his theory."

"I can see why. It is unscientific to throw in something mushy like that."

"This concept was not at all mushy the way Peirce conceived it," I quickly retorted, adding more kindly, "but I do not want to go into that now. Are you ready for more?"

Hal nodded agreeably.

"Because of Peirce's scholastic realism, he believed that his doctrine differed greatly from others. Here is what he said:"

So instead of merely jeering at metaphysics, like other prope-positivists, whether by long-drawn-out parodies or otherwise, the pragmaticist extracts from it a precious essence, which will serve to give life and light to cosmology and physics. At the same time, moral applications of the doctrine are positive and potent; and there are many other uses of it not easily classed. On another occasion, instances may be given to show that it really has these effects.

"Is he saying that he does not make fun of religion like other positivists?"

"Peirce is referring to all of metaphysics, not just religion. Peirce says that, instead of making fun of metaphysics like other prope-positivists, like other describers of experience who go forward with what they observe, a pragmaticist extracts from metaphysics a 'precious essence'."

"What would that essence be?"

"He does not say here. He does say that this precious essence extracted from metaphysics 'will serve to give life and light to cosmology and physics'."

"What is cosmology?"

"Cosmology is a branch of philosophy that seeks to understand the origin and structure of the universe. If you consider cosmology along with ontology and metaphysics, you will find that they deal with many of the same issues."

"Would that mean that Peirce's pragmaticism extracts the essence of metaphysics and uses it to guide the study of the origin and structure of the universe?"

"Yes. Peirce claims that, because he extracts this 'precious essence' from metaphysics, he is, unlike the other positivists, able to say that his pragmaticism has 'moral applications that are positive and potent.' For this same reason, he can also say that there are other uses of his theory that are not easily classified into one category or another."

"Such as?"

"Such as the whole field of semantics, for one thing. Semantics is the study of meaning in language. No such field of study existed at the time Peirce wrote this essay. The authors of the 1923 book, *The Meaning of Meaning*, used Peirce's concepts as the basis for their book about semantics. Their book, in turn, was the primary reference that Albert Upton used when he developed his system, *Design for Thinking*, and its accompanying workbook. I began using that workbook years ago for teaching critical thinking."

"And *Design for Thinking* is what you used for developing Engaged Intelligence training. Right?"

"That and Dottie's non-verbal model of reasoning habits. Some Peirce experts think these sources are too simplistic. Back in 1996, Jaime Nubiola, a philosopher from Spain, wrote an article in which he mentioned that many people consider Ogden, one of the authors of *The Meaning of Meaning*, as an inferior source for interpreting Peirce."

"But not you?"

"No, not me. One person's idea of simplistic can be another person's idea of a good place to get started. There is not much point in starting off from a place where no one can understand you. I consider it a big mistake to correlate 'easy to understand' with simplistic and inferior. Even materials that appear simple can bring about complex understandings. The Engaged Intelligence course provides a good example of this. Considering the results we have produced by using that system, I do not think that Ogden was simplistic. Besides, a true experimentalist will test an idea and make assessments based on the results it produces, not on pre-conceived notions or mere appearances."

"Would Peirce have liked that book?"

"Probably not," I admitted. "From what I have read about his personality, he would not have had much patience for the beginning levels of anything. Besides, as you can tell, Peirce was not aiming at a general audience."

"Then, who was he aiming at?"

"Peirce's theory was about philosophy. He was aiming his writing at philosophers because he wanted them to start treating philosophy like a scientific study. His theory is also about how to reason more effectively in science, in education, and in every other case as well. The main reason that so few people have realized this is probably because Peirce's writings are difficult to read." I noticed then that we had gone off course again. "Now, back to the paragraph. Peirce says here that, finally, he will offer examples that show that his theory works in the ways he says it does, but he is not going to do that in this essay."

"Letting himself off the hook, huh?"

I nodded and then continued on to the next section of this dialogue.

"Now we are back to someone just like you asking another question."

"And what do I ask?"

Questioner: I hardly need to be convinced that your doctrine would wipe out metaphysics. Is it not as obvious that it must wipe out every proposition of science and everything that bears on the conduct of life? For you say that the only meaning that, for you, any assertion bears is that a certain experiment has resulted in a certain way: Nothing else but an experiment enters into the meaning. Tell me, then, how can an experiment, in itself, reveal anything more than that something once happened to an individual object and that subsequently some other individual event occurred?

"What is the question?"

"The questioner believes that, if pragmaticism were to be taken seriously, it would wipe out every other consideration in life other than the results of experiments. He wants to know how an experiment can demonstrate anything other than isolated events."

"Oh. Good question. What does Peirce have to say?"

"Plenty, I can assure you. I am going to paraphrase this next part a little bit," I told him. Then I read a slightly altered version of Peirce's response:

Pragmatist: That question brings us right into the purpose of this explanation, which is to correct any misapprehensions of pragmaticism. You speak of an experiment in itself, emphasizing "in itself." You evidently think of each experiment as isolated from every other. It probably has not occurred to you, for example, that every connected series of experiments constitutes a single collective experiment.

"What does he mean by a 'collective experiment'?"

"He means that pragmatism does not deal in single, isolated experiments. Any series of related experiments that an individual performs and any series of interrelated experiments that differing people perform are all part of a 'collective experiment.' Just remember what he said earlier about the little critical self inside your head being another self who helps to keep you on alert. Also remember that he said that the circle of a person's society is like a loosely compacted person. If you think about those two things, this statement might make more sense to you. Later, we are going to talk more about Peirce's doctrine of continuity. That should help too."

"I will keep them both in mind."

"Peirce then explains the purpose of his essay:"

That question brings us right into the purpose of this explanation, which is to correct any misapprehensions of pragmaticism. You speak of an experiment in itself, emphasizing "in itself." You evidently think of each experiment as isolated from every other. It probably has not occurred to you, for example, that every connected series of experiments constitutes a single collective experiment. What are the essential ingredients of an experiment? First, of course, you need an experimenter of flesh and blood. Secondly, you need a verifiable hypothesis. A verifiable hypothesis is a proposition relating to the physical and mental universe of the experimenter, or to some well-known part of it. In order for a hypothesis to be verifiable, it must be one that is capable of affirming or denying some experimental possibility or impossibility. The third indispensable ingredient of an experiment is a sincere doubt in the experimenter's mind as to the truth of that hypothesis.

Hal interrupted me at this point. "You lost me on that last part."

"The part about a 'verifiable hypothesis'?"

"Yes."

"He is saying that a verifiable hypothesis is a proposition capable of being tested, one which relates to the physical or mental universe surrounding the experimenter. This universe is the context to which a hypothesis relates. This context resides in a larger universe, which some call the 'matrix'."

"What do you mean by matrix?"

"The matrix is like an ocean of possibilities which might alter the meaning of a sign by altering the meaning of its context. When Peirce refers to 'a person's universe or to some well-known part of it,' we could say he means that the proposition relates to a particular context, a particular situation, that exists within this larger universe, or matrix. The matrix is where value and purpose reside."

"Then, Peirce is saying that you can make your proposition about the bigger picture or about a specific issue within the bigger picture?"

"In a sense. Your proposition must be tied into a context for a purpose. You derive your purpose out of the possibilities which exist within the matrix. Later Peirce will propose a particular method for deriving a purpose out of the matrix. For now, you only need to know that a 'verifiable hypothesis' must be capable of being tested and must be connected to something within your physical or mental universes. A pragmatist's hypothesis does not just come out of thin air. Now, I want to go over that last statement."

What are the essential ingredients of an experiment? First, of course, an experimenter of flesh and blood. Secondly, a verifiable hypothesis. This is a proposition relating to the universe environing the experimenter, or to some well-known part of it and affirming or denying of this only some experimental possibility or impossibility.

"What does he mean by affirming or denying?"

"He means that a verifiable hypothesis is one capable of being proven or disproved."

"Oh, that makes sense."

"Would you like to rephrase the first two essential ingredients before we go on?" I offered. "It might help you to remember them."

"I am not sure that I can."

"Just give it a try."

"The first one is easy. You have to have someone to do the experiment."

"Right."

"The second one is...," he paused. "The second one is that the thing you are trying to prove or disprove has to be something that relates to the experimenter's universe."

"Good," I said encouragingly. "And?"

"And it has to be something that can be proven or disproved by an experiment!" He finished this last part triumphantly.

"Great! I should add here that, for Peirce, an experiment does not have to be something that you are actually able to perform at the present time. It has to be capable of eventually being tested, which is why he says, 'experimental possibility or impossibility'."

"I think I understand what he means by that. You only have to consider recent discoveries in outer space to understand that. Just look at all the theories scientists will be able to prove and disprove now that they have the Hubble telescope!"

"Good point. Next, Peirce gives us the third ingredient. He says that 'the third indispensable ingredient of an experiment is a sincere doubt in the experimenter's mind as to the truth of that hypothesis'."

"Why would he have to write that down? Why would anyone bother to do an experiment about something you already know is true or false?"

"Do you remember 'dismiss all make-believes'?" I reminded him. "Peirce is referring to the Cartesian pretense of doubting everything."

"Oh, I see."

"Do you see how these three ingredients might connect to learning?"

"I can see that the experimenter could be the student. I imagine that the something to prove or disprove would be whatever the student is supposed to be learning. And I would assume that students would have genuine doubt, otherwise they would not be students."

"Good point. Unfortunately, few students, and even fewer teachers, have genuine doubt, at least not in the sense that Peirce means. Peirce believed that genuine doubt causes the will to learn. He contended that even teachers must have genuine doubt if they are to inspire learning. Doubt, in the case of both students and teachers, is openness to real learning as opposed to just adding in more information, or thinking that you already have all of the answers. Peirce believed that American teachers in his day were so strongly attached to what they were teaching that they entirely missed the point of education, which is learning. The problem with educational institutions in his time was that they were set up for teaching, instead of learning."

"But that was nearly a hundred years ago."

"Yes," I agreed, adding, "and things have not changed all that much, believe me. Genuine doubt is the only point at which you can engage your intelligence. Otherwise, you are only collecting data or reciting what you know. Engaging intelligence means giving up absolutes and certainties long enough to engage your curiosity in whatever ideas and tasks are at hand. That goes for teachers as well as students."

Hal rolled his eyes at this description. I am sure he was recalling struggles we had with some of our own children concerning this matter.

"Peirce then continues with more explanation of one of these three ingredients. Here is what he says:"

Passing over several ingredients on which we need not dwell, the purpose, the plan, and the resolve, we come to the act of choice by which the experimenter singles out certain identifiable objects to be operated upon. The next is the external (or quasi-external) act by which he modifies those objects. Next, comes the subsequent reaction of the world upon the experimenter in a perception; and finally, his recognition of the teaching of the experiment.

"Are you going to break this down into smaller pieces for me?"

"As always."

Although this day's passage had, up to this point, been fairly easy to understand, we were soon going to be doing some more heavy lifting—as Hal called it. We had begun to address complex concepts. I decided that I would need to proceed at a much slower pace.

"I want to go back to the first part of that last passage from the essay:"

Passing over several ingredients on which we need not dwell, the purpose, the plan, and the resolve, we come to the act of choice by which the experimenter singles out certain identifiable objects to be operated upon.

"I remember that."

"I want you to know that the three ingredients that Peirce skips over, 'purpose,' 'plan,' and 'resolve,' are major aspects of his whole theory."

"Then why does he skip over them?"

"Because he is trying to make the point that pragmaticism is not proposing single, isolated experiments. He is concentrating on what he sees as the essential elements of performing an experiment so he can show how these elements lead to proving his premise that pragmaticism is not dealing in isolated events."

"Oh."

"The next thing that he mentions, 'the act of choice by which the experimenter singles out certain identifiable objects to be operated upon,' also matters a great deal. This is a big issue for Peirce, one that relates in a larger sense to his logic of discovery. How should we go about deciding what to pay attention to?"

"That makes sense."

"The next thing concerns whatever the experimenter does to those objects, whatever action he takes to modify the objects. Peirce refers to this action as being external or quasi-external, meaning that it could also be a mental as well as a physical modification."

"Is Peirce saying that you can do experiments in your mind, without doing them in the physical world?"

"In a sense. Peirce did much of his own experimenting mentally, without performing physical experiments. He also worked ideas out in diagram form."

"On diagrams? How can you experiment on diagrams? Do you mean as in engineering?"

"Sure. Diagrams are a means of thinking things through. Peirce produced what may be the first diagram of an electrical circuit. However, his diagrams are much more than engineering diagrams. One type is called existential graphs. He created these in an attempt to describe reasoning processes in all aspects of mental activities. From what I can tell, at least some of them are similar to the graphical diagramming methods we teach in Engaged Intelligence."

"So," Hal said—this time he was keeping me on track, "Peirce was saying you can modify something mentally as well as physically?"

"Yes. But if you try to do everything mentally, then the next part is a little more of a problem."

"Why is that?"

"'The subsequent reaction of the world upon the experimenter in a perception,'" I quoted. "If you have done everything inside your head, you will have nothing but what is inside your head to provide you with a reaction to what you have done, to keep you grounded in reality."

"Unless you write it all down or diagram it all out as Peirce did?"

"Yes, or represent it in some other way. Next, Peirce says that an experiment involves an action on the part of the experimenter and a subsequent reaction coming from the external world. Finally, Peirce says, there must be a point at which the experimenter 'recognizes the teaching of the experiment.' At that point, the experimenter makes an interpretation of the results leading to a decision about what these results mean. Action, reaction, and interpretation are central concepts in Peirce's theory of meaning."

"Action, reaction, interpretation. That sounds a lot like belief interacting with experience."

"It sure does," I agreed. "Now here is Peirce's next statement. 'While the two chief parts of the event itself are the action and the reaction, yet the unity of essence of the experiment lies in its purpose and plan, the ingredients passed over in the enumeration'."

"If the purpose and plan are so vital, why did he pass them over?"

"Maybe because the purpose and plan part are so essential to his theory of pragmaticism that he waits to address these later on, once you have had a little more background," I suggested. "Peirce was never able to explain to his own satisfaction how purposes should be formed, though this is an essential part of his theory. He does make a good case for their importance though."

"Is that the unfinished part of his theory you talked about earlier?"

"Yes. The unfinished part of his theory concerns the logical method by which worthy purposes are discovered and formed. He felt this logical method was the key to his theory, but was never able to explain how the method is performed, at least not in a way that people can understand. Experts are still struggling over this aspect of Peirce's work. Fortunately, this method of forming purposes is one of the things we are able to demonstrate by using Dottie's non-verbal model."

"Does the non-verbal model do what Peirce could not do?"

"Yes. One pattern of reasoning that Dottie's model demonstrates is the non-verbal equivalent of what Peirce means by 'formation of purpose'."

"Hmm."

"When Peirce says that the 'unity of essence of the experiment lies in its purpose and plan,' he means the hypothesis and the proposed method for testing it out."

"I think that action should be an aspect of interpretation," Hal proposed. "Since the experimenter is doing the action, interpretation would be involved in that."

"No. An action is taken based on a belief. Interpretation can only occur before and after action. When we receive a response from whatever action we take, what Peirce calls a 'reaction,' then our minds interpret that reaction to decide what it means. We can only change our behavior in advance of doing something. We take action based on a belief. We get back a reaction. We interpret the reaction in light of our action. That is an experimental loop."

"Not just scientists operate that way," Hal argued. "Some non-verbal reasoning patterns work that same way, too."

"Yes. The non-verbal reasoning patterns described in the Relational Thinking Styles model reflect the 'habitual' ways in which someone tends to make those interpretations before taking action and when interpreting the response from that action. Peirce is attempting to lay the groundwork here for showing how the interpreting 'should be done' in those cases when it needs to be done deliberately."

"I see that."

"So, action, reaction, and interpretation are all connected to one another in an interactive way," I summarized. "Shall we go on?"

Hal nodded in agreement.

"Remember now, this is Peirce speaking to his Questioner."

Another thing: in representing the pragmaticist as making rational meaning to consist in an experiment (which you speak of as an event in the past), you strikingly fail to catch his attitude of mind. Indeed, it is not in an experiment, but in experimental phenomena, that rational meaning is said to consist.

"What does he mean here?"

"Peirce is criticizing the person who is just like you for implying that an experiment is an event in the past tense," I said in a mock scolding tone that Peirce might have used. "He is saying you just do not get it because you fail to catch an experimenter's 'attitude of mind'."

"Which is?"

"Which is 'that meaning consists not in the experiment, but in experimental phenomena'."

"And what are 'experimental phenomena'?"

"Here is what Peirce says:"

When an experimentalist speaks of a phenomenon, such as "Hall's phenomenon," "Zeeman's phenomenon," and its modification, "Michelson's phenomenon," or "the chess-board phenomenon," he does not mean any particular event that did happen to somebody in the dead past, but what surely will happen to everybody in the living future who shall fulfill certain conditions.

"Translation, please."

"Before I translate that, you should know that you do not have to know any of those examples, such as 'Hall's phenomenon,' to understand his point."

"That is a relief! I would probably not understand them anyway."

"They are just examples. See if the sentence makes more sense to you once I have taken them out."

When an experimentalist speaks of a phenomenon...he does not mean any particular event that did happen to somebody in the dead past, but what surely will happen to everybody in the living future who shall fulfill certain conditions.

I looked over to see if this edited version made sense to him.

"Would gravity be an example of what he is saying here?" Hal asked. "Does he mean the difference between saying, 'what goes up must come down,' instead of 'when I threw the ball up into the air, it came back down'?"

"Yes, you are right! 'What goes up must come down' refers to a general principle, a generalization of a phenomenon having to do with gravity. What Peirce means here is that experimentalists aim to predict repeated occurrences of a phenomenon. They hypothesize what will probably occur under a particular set of conditions. Then they aim to demonstrate whether their prediction occurs. Here is what he says about phenomena:"

The phenomenon consists in the fact that when an experimentalist shall come to act according to a certain scheme that he has in mind, then will something else happen, and shatter the doubts of skeptics, like the celestial fire upon the altar of Elijah.

"This is what Peirce means when he says that 'meaning consists not in the experiment, but in experimental phenomena'."

"I still do not understand that."

"By 'experimental phenomena,' Peirce means that by doing something according to a particular method or plan, the experimentalist deliberately brings about certain consequences."

"What are 'experimental phenomena'?"

"The best way I can say this is that experimental phenomena are the consequences that result from the application of a method," I offered this phrase tentatively, wishing I could think of a better one.

"Are you saying that experimental phenomena are methods?"

"They are what occurs because of the way in which the experiment is performed. Experimental phenomena are consequences that occur because of methods, because of the way that the experimenting is done."

"Surely that is true of anything a person does. Surely consequences occur because of the way that anything is done. This is what the non-verbal reasoning processes in Relational Thinking Styles demonstrate."

"Oh, you are right. I left out a word. I should have said that experimental phenomena are consequences that occur because of the way that the experimenting is 'deliberately' done."

"Then, deliberateness is what separates the experimentalist who Peirce is describing from people who use their everyday reasoning habits?"

"Yes. Peirce is referring to the way that a pragmaticist would deliberately go about forming and testing a hypothesis to produce good results."

"And the everyday reasoning habits are not deliberate?"

"They are not deliberate because they are habits. Remember *logica docens* and *logica utens*?"

"The trained and un-trained logic?"

"Yes. *Logica utens* are mental habit patterns that we use for making most of our decisions. Because these patterns are habitual, *logica utens* is usually outside of our powers of self-control. As long as thinking patterns remain habits, they will remain outside conscious control and, therefore, non-deliberate."

"What if they could be controlled?"

"If they could be controlled, then people could be expected to use particular reasoning methods appropriately as a situation requires. This is exactly what Peirce meant by *logica docens*, deliberate self-control of reasoning. This is the whole point of Engaged Intelligence training as well."

"So *logica docens* is knowing how to use each of the reasoning habits?"

"Yes. Though, Peirce's concept of *logica docens* includes knowing when to use each, as well as how to use each."

"What does this have to do with experimental phenomena?"

"Experimental phenomena are consequences produced by deliberately doing something in a particular way to bring about a particular outcome. We produce outcomes from the way in which we do things, whether we do so deliberately, or not. Because pragmaticists pay attention to experimental phenomena, they are able to make judgments all along the way. These judgments lead them to make adjustments as needed to develop and refine a hypothesis, adjust conditions, plan for contingencies, and so on."

"Is Peirce just describing what a pragmaticist does?"

"Peirce is describing what every experimentalist 'should do' according to the pragmaticist doctrine. Whenever we are being deliberate in a particular way during each stage of an inquiry, we are behaving as an experimentalist. When we know what those ways are and deliberately select a particular reasoning method because it is the appropriate one to use at a particular stage, we are being a pragmaticist."

"What do you mean by a particular stage?"

"Experimental phenomena never just occur out of thin air. Every experiment has three stages. Hypothesizing is the stage for determining what might be so and formulating this determination into a proposition. The planning stage involves deciding upon and planning for experiments to determine whether the hypothesis is true or not. Actual experimenting occurs in the testing stage. The pragmaticist who Peirce describes would be moving in and out of those three stages as is necessary for interpreting what those phenomena mean and then deciding what to do next. A pragmaticist would not just follow some rote plan all the way through to the end."

"And is that the same as deliberately changing future conduct?"

"Yes! We have just covered a lot of material. Shall we call it a day?"

"Sounds good to me."

I was glad he was still interested in our discussions. Tomorrow promised to be even more challenging. We would be dealing in depth with concepts we had only touched on this day.

Nine
PROPOSITIONS

"Today, we will be covering complex material that relates to what we discussed yesterday," I began. "Maybe we should review what we talked about yesterday before we go on."

"That is fine with me," he said, with what I took as a note of gratitude.

"Yesterday, we ended up with a definition of experimental phenomena. Do you want to give it a try?"

"It is pretty early in the morning," Hal said. "But, hey, what the heck, I can try anyway." He stared at that spot on the wall that usually holds all of his answers. "Experimental phenomena are what you get from doing something in a particular, deliberate way."

"Good!" I was encouraged by his overnight retention of this concept. He, too, appeared pleased to have remembered this and ready to continue. "Next," I continued, "Peirce goes back to the issue of single experiments and emphasizes the pragmaticist view on the subject:"

And do not overlook the fact that the pragmaticist maxim says nothing of single experiments or of single experimental phenomena (for what is conditionally true *in futuro* can hardly be singular), but only speaks of general kinds of experimental phenomena. Its adherent does not shrink from speaking of general objects as real, since whatever is true represents a real. Now the laws of nature are true.

"That last sentence does not go with the rest."

"Do you mean the sentence, 'now the laws of nature are true'?"

He nodded.

"Maybe I should go back and re-state the first part before we tackle that statement."

"Fine with me."

"I am going to begin with his parenthetical statement, 'for what is conditionally true *in futuro* can hardly be singular.' Does this make sense?"

"I think so,"

"Can you put it into your own words or give me an example?"

"Maybe I can. I think it means that if you are able to say that 'so and so' will happen under 'such and such' conditions, then, it means that this event is going to occur in the future anytime those conditions are met. That means it cannot possibly be singular!"

"Because?" I asked, hoping to elicit a general statement.

"Because, if something is going to happen every time a particular set of conditions are met, then it is not a single event," Hal said confidently. "It has to be at least potentially multiple, or plural, just as Peirce says."

"You win the prize!" I said enthusiastically. "Now the rest of the sentence, the part after that *in futuro* aside, says that pragmaticism only speaks of general kinds of experimental phenomena."

"Meaning?"

"Meaning just what we talked about before. Pragmaticism is not dealing with single experiments or with single experimental phenomena. A proposition predicts what will happen in the future under certain conditions. And, what is conditionally true *in futuro*...," I said, leaving this sentence up in the air for him to finish.

"Has to be plural!" Hal said triumphantly.

"Yes! Now, in order to describe something that is general, you have to have a way of talking about all of the things which that general object describes. You do not want to have to name each thing in the group every time you want to talk about it."

"Is that like being able to say 'our children,'" he offered, "instead of having to name each one of them every time we refer to them?"

"Yes. The word 'children' stands for a general category, and the phrase 'our children' is still general, although it is more specific. David, Amy, Greg, Tonya, and Andrea are the children whom we classify as ours. They are what philosophers call 'reals'."

"What are 'reals'?"

"Most philosophers say reals are the immediate objects of what is true."

"Meaning?"

"Meaning that, if it is true that our five children exist, then each of the five who are our children are 'reals.' Each of those children is an immediate object of that which is true."

"You said 'most philosophers.' Does Peirce disagree with this?"

"No, but Peirce contends that general objects are also real since 'whatever is true represents a real'."

"General objects?"

"By the term 'general object,' he means something that covers a whole group of things, for example, a category like 'our children.' According to Peirce, the category of 'our children' is as much a real thing as each of the specific children that it stands for, because 'whatever is true represents a real'."

"Does he mean because it represents a real, it is a real?"

"Yes. He is saying that, because a general object, such as a general principle or a category, represents a real, that general object is also a real. That general object is as much a real as the things or events it represents."

"It just sounds like a matter of definition to me."

"In a sense it is," I agreed, then decided I should explain what I meant by this. "We talked about the word 'real' before when we discussed how, for Peirce, something can be real but not actually exist. Real means anything that has sufficient qualities for identifying it, whether it 'actually' exists or not and regardless of whether anyone ever knows about these qualities. In this way, values and purposes can be real, although you cannot touch values or purposes. If something is 'actual,' on the other hand, that means that it is a brute fact of existence. Actualities have an actual existence because they act and react against other actualities. An actuality is something that, at some point, either has, had, or will have an actual occurrence in time and space."

"Why would Peirce fool with qualities if they do not actually exist?"

"Because general things like values, purposes, laws of nature, and mental categories, guide the formation of what we call reality, even though they can never actually occur at a specific time or in actual space."

"Why can they never occur?"

"Because they are general objects. A particular expression of a value or a purpose can actually occur, but not the general values and purposes which guide that expression. Generals are much more than just general words like 'our children.' Peirce contended that general laws, categories, and systems are reals because they are true. If they are true, they are real because whatever is true represents a real."

"How do we know they are true?"

"We know that some generals are true because they have been established as true by means of experiment. They have been shown to be true based upon action-reaction-interpretation loops that eventually validate a hypothesis and lead us to a general law or rule. However, Peirce also says that, even if no one ever discovers a particular law or principle, it is still real. For example, if no one had ever managed to figure out that the earth orbits the sun, it would still be true."

"That makes perfect sense to me."

"Peirce is saying that we have to accept that general categories are real because they are true and 'whatever is true represents a real,'" I summarized. "Then Peirce says that someone who is a pragmaticist, as he is, 'does not shrink from speaking of general objects as real.' At that point, he adds, 'now the laws of nature are true'."

"Meaning that they are also real. I see that now. How, though, can a law be an object?"

"One of the great contributions of Peirce's theory to language is that, by defining the laws of nature as reals, Peirce demonstrated the reality of operational reals, as well as categorical ones. These operational reals, including the purposes directing them, are also capable of being described and analyzed by means of signs. Purposes and processes are objects, just like things you can touch. This means that a producing system is real. It also means that the purpose for producing it and the values that drove the formation of that purpose are real as well. Peirce considered this concept of the reality of purpose and its formation the most essential aspect of his pragmaticism."

"Is Peirce saying that values and purposes are real and that categories and producing systems are real too?"

"Yes. He is saying that anything that is true and that stands for something else is a real thing. That is like saying that a general object, like the word 'fruit' which stands for all kinds of different fruit, is just as much a real thing as a particular apple or a particular orange. The reason it is just as real is because the general concept 'fruit' represents a real, like an apple or an orange, and other individual pieces of fruit as well. Peirce would also say that a formula, a recipe, even mental possibilities are reals. They are reals even if they are never discovered or developed, because they have properties. They have these properties whether anyone ever notices them or not."

"So, operations are reals, and the laws of nature are operations," Hal said thoughtfully. "They are real because they are true and because they stand for something real. But what do they stand for?"

"They stand for the phenomena that they describe. Many of them stand in place of phenomena for which we know the meaning, because the meaning has been experimentally derived."

"Oh. That makes sense to me now."

I continued anyway, just to make sure. "Peirce means that the laws of gravity are just as real as the falling of a particular apple from a particular branch of a particular tree."

"I understand that too."

"Now, let me see if I can sum it up for you. When Peirce says 'now the laws of nature are true,' he means that since operations can be true, and because the laws of nature are operations as well as true, the laws of nature are also reals. This means that the laws of gravity are as real as a particular apple falling from a particular tree. That leads us right into the following paragraph. 'The rational meaning of every proposition lies in the future. How so? The meaning of a proposition is itself is a proposition'."

"I do not understand that."

"Maybe we should go back to the first sentence. He said that 'the rational meaning of every proposition lies in the future.' Does that make sense?"

"The sentence sounds like a sentence, but I do not know what it means."

"Do you remember what Peirce means by the term 'rational'?"

"No," he admitted reluctantly.

"Back when Peirce was stating his definition of thought, he wrote that he considered thought as covering all rational life, 'so that an experiment shall be an operation of thought'."

"I remember that now!" Hal said, brightening up.

"So, your rational life is any situation for which you use reasoning skills. Your rational life includes any situation where you have to figure something out. Rational thought is used for any situation in which you exercise your reasoning skills."

"I remember all of that now. You can go on."

"A proposition is a proposed operation being offered for consideration, like a proposal to do or make something."

"Is a proposition an operation?"

"Always. At least, a proposition has to include an operation, otherwise there would be no need to propose something. If it did not include an operation, whatever it proposes would already have been done. An operation is a structure unfolding through time and space. A proposal is a plan. A plan is a prediction of how a structure will unfold and what the consequences of its unfolding will be. A structure can be a thing or an idea. In other words, it can be a physical structure, like a body or a building. Or, it can be a mental structure, like an idea, a formula, or a plan. An unfolding structure can even be a sequence of movements involving structures with no physical outcome, like a dance or a golf game. So, when Peirce says that the rational meaning of any proposition lies in the future...."

"He means," Hal said, interrupting me excitedly, "that a proposition is an operation and that you cannot know for sure what the effects of an operation are going to be until you do it!"

"Right! Since you are dealing with a proposition, that means you have not done it yet. Therefore, what a proposition means in terms of its effects has to be in the future."

"Wow! That was great!"

"What was great?"

"It was great fun figuring out that one sentence 'the rational meaning of every proposition lies in the future'."

"Now, we can take on that next sentence, the one that says, 'the meaning of a proposition is, itself, a proposition'."

"I am ready if you are."

"We should read over more of the paragraph first to give us a running start," I suggested, then read from Peirce's text. "'The rational meaning of every proposition lies in the future. How so? The meaning of a proposition is itself a proposition. Indeed, it is no other than the proposition of which it is the meaning, it is a translation of it'."

"Is Peirce saying that the meaning of a proposition is a proposition because it is an translation of the original proposition?"

"Yes."

"Then, is Shannon's blackberry pie the meaning of her recipe?"

Shannon, our daughter-in-law, is an excellent baker. She has won several blue ribbons at county and state fairs for her baking skills.

"Yes. Just think about Shannon's recipe as a proposition for the operation that results in blackberry pies. Then think of a particular pie as a translation of that proposition."

"When Peirce says that the form that is the meaning of the proposition is also a proposition, would that mean that one of Shannon's pies is also a proposition just like the recipe?"

"Yes. Each pie is a translation of the proposition, an expression of the recipe. What else could the recipe mean?"

"The recipe meaning the pie is not the problem for me. The problem comes from thinking about it the other way around."

"Are you having trouble with the idea that the pie proposes the recipe?"

He nodded.

"If there is a pie, then there must have been some method for making it. Do you agree with that?"

"Sure."

"Then the existence of that pie means that a particular recipe, or method, was used to make it. The pie's existence tells us that a particular set of conditions was met which resulted in that pie. Thus, that pie is a proposition that can be taken to mean that a recipe, a particular method of making blackberry pies, exists."

"Where is the proposition part?"

"The proposition is the part that says that, since the blackberry pie exists, it must have resulted from following a particular recipe. Its existence is a proposition that informs us that a method exists by which it was made. This is how we discover and validate propositions in the first place."

"What do you mean?"

"We notice something, a phenomenon, and then develop a hypothesis to explain its cause. A hypothesis is a proposition about the conditions and actions which probably caused a particular phenomenon. The phenomenon, itself, is a proposition that something caused it to occur and will cause it again under the same conditions. I should probably mention here that Peirce made a distinction between 'facts' and 'occurrences.' He said that a fact is a part of the real universe that can be represented in a proposition. The existence of a particular blackberry pie and a method for making it is a fact. Occurrences, however, are a slice of the whole universe of everything that is and we can never know everything about that slice." [6]

"Why not?"

"Because we are human beings and, therefore, fallible. We can never know everything. Peirce said that a fact is like a principle of chemistry which we extract from the universe of everything that is. In its real existence, that fact is 'inseparably combined with an infinite swarm of circumstances' which have no part of the fact itself. Propositions are the way that we establish facts by explaining and verifying whatever it is that we can know about some thing or some event under certain conditions. However, no proposition can completely define an occurrence, since an occurrence is a slice of the entire universe, or, we would say, a slice of the matrix within which everything swims."

"Oh, I think I see that."

"Do you see that Shannon's recipe is proposed by the existence of a particular pie?" When he nodded, I continued. "That pie is, itself, a proposition that there must be a set of general rules, in this case a recipe, from which other pies can be produced. Otherwise, that pie could not exist. Here is what Peirce wrote next."

But, of the myriads of forms into which a proposition may be translated, what is that one which is to be called its very meaning? It is, according to the pragmaticist, that form in which the proposition becomes applicable to human conduct, not in these or those special circumstances, nor when one entertains this or that special design, but that form which is most directly applicable to self-control under every situation and to every purpose.

"What does he mean here about 'conduct' and 'self-control'?"

"You have nothing to experiment with if there is no way to deliberately change the conditions and affect the outcome. To have a verifiable hypothesis, you must be able to manipulate conditions in some way that will affect the outcome. Otherwise, how can you test your hypothesis to see if it means anything or not?"

"Is that why science uses control groups?"

"Yes. Control groups are one way of manipulating conditions in an experiment. When scientists compile two groups of specimens, they are seeking to control the conditions of an experiment. When they do something to one group but not to the other, they are testing a proposition. Experimental phenomena are the data that come out of the experiment. This data shows a difference between what occurred in the control group and what occurred in the experimental group due to whatever the scientist did. The results of the experiment are consequences which occur due to the deliberate, self-controlled conduct of the scientist upon the experimental group."

"Must you have a control group to do experiments?"

"No, you do not have to have control groups. As I said, control groups are just one way of manipulating conditions. However, you must be able to alter an outcome by altering behavior if you are to experiment. If there is nothing you can do to affect an outcome one way or another, how can there be any experimenting?"

"Then miracles and the whims of Mother Nature must not count."

"They definitely do not count! You have to pick the meaning of your proposition from the form of it which is directly applicable to self-control under every situation and to every purpose for which that proposition is meant to apply. So the meaning of Shannon's blackberry pie recipe has to come from whatever is in that recipe that is subject to self-control."

"Which would be all of it."

"No," I countered. "Shannon has no control over some things, such as how much rain the wild blackberries receive during summer. That affects their size and sweetness."

"But she could add more sugar if she needed to."

"True. And the act of deciding to add more sugar would be a proposition. She would have to see if she could, indeed, increase the sweetness to just the right degree."

"Oh, now I see what you mean. She would be thinking it out ahead of time, making it a proposal."

"Good!" I said, then began reading again from the essay. "'This is why [the pragmaticist] locates the meaning in future time, because future conduct is the only conduct that is subject to self-control'."

"What about the present?" Hal interrupted. "Surely we can exert self-control in the present?"

"Not one bit! For one thing, the present is an infinitesimal piece of time. You cannot make a decision in the present and take action in the present, because not enough time exists for you to do both."

"By the present, then, you are not referring to 'today' as opposed to 'yesterday' or 'tomorrow'."

"Correct. Peirce is referring to 'right now' when he speaks of the present. We have no self-control over the present moment because self-control requires a deliberate decision, one that has to be made before an action is taken. In the present time 'all you have are your beliefs and doubts,' as Peirce would say. Once you take action, you are acting on a belief."

"What if the action you are taking is testing out something you doubt?"

"In that case, you have made a guess based on what your critical self is causing you to doubt. When you act, you act on that guess as if it were true. The 'as if' functions the same way as believing something is true. The self-control, the deliberate modification of conduct, still happens prior to your taking action."

"So future conduct is the only conduct that I can control," Hal said to himself thoughtfully. "That is a big concept for such a short sentence, but I think I understand it now."

"Good. Now, here is what Peirce says next:"

But in order that that form of the proposition which is to be taken as its meaning should be applicable to every situation and to every purpose upon which the proposition has any bearing, it must be simply the general description of all the experimental phenomena which the assertion of the proposition virtually predicts.

"I do not understand what he means here."

"He is trying to say that, for the meaning of a proposition to be a translation of that proposition, you have to describe all of the experimental phenomena that the proposition predicts."

"What if the proposition does not predict anything?"

"Then it would not be a proposition. The whole point of any proposition is to predict experimental phenomena that will happen in the future. This is why a proposition has to include an operation. Peirce is arguing that a proposition needs to apply to every situation and for every purpose upon which it has any bearing. To do this, the proposition must be the general description of all the experimental phenomena that the proposition predicts."

"Are experimental phenomena the only things a proposition predicts?"

"Yes. Experimental phenomena are facts. They are expressions of the form of the proposition each time it is applied."

"Then, Peirce must be saying that in order for the proposition to mean what it says it means, the proposition must result in what it says it is going to result in."

"Yes," I agreed. Then I thought of another example. "Suppose Shannon thought of a way she might alter her recipe in order to make better blackberry pies. She would then propose to herself deliberate changes in her recipe. The changes to that recipe would be a proposal, which she uses to guide her conduct while making a pie with those changes. The meaning of her proposed improvements to her blackberry pie recipe resides in the pie she makes when including those deliberate changes. The meaning also resides in whatever future pies she makes using those same deliberate changes."

"I see that."

"Good. Now, take this statement of Peirce's again:"

But in order that that form of the proposition which is to be taken as its meaning should be applicable to every situation and to every purpose upon which the proposition has any bearing, it must be simply the general description of all the experimental phenomena which the assertion of the proposition virtually predicts.

"This," I added by way of explanation, "says much the same thing as what Peirce wrote earlier in the essay."

"What is that?"

"He wrote that all there is to the meaning of something is whatever you can imagine to be all of the possible experimental phenomena implied in proving or disproving that concept."

"I would think that some things might be impossible to prove."

"Of course some things are impossible to prove. But remember, Peirce's pragmaticism only concerns itself with matters that are subject to rational self-control. If the concept is impossible to prove, then it is not subject to rational self-control. If something is not subject to rational self-control, then Peirce did not consider it a topic worthy of pragmatic concern."

"Oh. What does Peirce mean by 'the form that the meaning takes'?"

"The 'form of a proposition which is to be taken as its meaning' could be a blackberry pie resulting from following a recipe. Or, it could be a reduction of new cancer cases in a group of people who are given high doses of vitamin C. The form the meaning takes could be a new office building that was constructed based on a particular set of plans. Peirce is referring to the particular expressions of a proposition which are subject to self-control, expressions which can be rationally altered in some way. You have to be able to rationally alter these expressions, via self-control, under every situation and for every purpose that the proposition addresses, not just for special circumstances."

"That sounds to me that he is saying that nothing means anything unless it means everything. Surely he could not mean that!"

"No, that is not at all what he meant. Peirce is preparing here to talk more about generals. Remember that he is still explaining to the Questioner why pragmaticism does not concern itself with single events. Peirce's pragmaticism is concerned with general laws and principles. For something to be a general law or principle, you must be able to consistently apply self-control to your behaviors based on that principle. You must be able to apply this self-control under every situation and for every purpose to which the principle applies."

"I still do not understand what he means."

"Think of it this way," I suggested. "Suppose Shannon wants to create and then prove a general proposition about making blackberry pies. She first has to imagine all of the possible experimental phenomena implied in proving or disproving that concept. These might include phenomena concerning qualities of taste, texture, color, cooking time, and other such characteristics."

"That could be a lot of phenomena."

"Yes, it sure could. Then, once she had imagined all of the possible experimental phenomena that are implied in proving or disproving her concept or, in Shannon's case, her recipe, she would have the complete definition of the concept that her recipe proposes. In order for Shannon to prove that her blackberry pie recipe is a valid proposition, she would need to use it to consistently produce the kind and quality of pies that her recipe proposes. She would test out the validity of her proposal by following the conditions laid out in that recipe to produce what she says she will produce."

"I understand that."

"For Shannon's blackberry pie recipe to become a general law or principle concerning the production of blackberry pies, she would have to be able to consistently apply self-control to the making of these pies. That self-control would have to do with those factors that affect the proposed experimental phenomena that result from the production of her pies."

"And those experimental phenomena would be the pies. Is that right?"

"Yes. She would have to be able to apply this self-control under every situation and for every purpose that she proposes these pies are to be made. This means that her recipe might have to take into account such things as differing purposes of the pie baking, say cooking one or two pies at home as opposed to producing a quantity of pies for a commercial venture. She might have to consider oven types and temperatures, geographic altitudes, and humidity differences. She might need to lay out the criteria for picking, or selecting from, differing grades of berries and different flours. She might need to take into account the effects of weather and develop exact methods for figuring out how much sugar to use for each batch of berries, and so on."

"In other words she needs degrees in physics and chemistry."

"At least. What I am getting at with this example is that all of those factors are capable of being affected by self-control. If she knew how, Shannon could adjust for every one of these factors, though she might ruin quite a few pies in the process."

"That would be quite a chore."

"True experimentalism usually is a chore. Eventually, if she were to continue to consider all of those factors, plus other factors that come up, she would eventually have a general proposition for making blackberry pies. These other factors could include aesthetic and ethical issues that we have not even touched upon."

"What would ethical issues have to do with a pie?"

"Everything we deliberately do touches upon ethical issues. Remember, all of human conduct belongs to the category of ethics. In Shannon's case, since she is a vegetarian because of animal rights issues, some parts of this ethical component happen to be very obvious."

"How are they obvious?"

"For one thing, she would never use lard in a pie crust. Nor would she use butter that came from a dairy that has not been certified as humane."

"Oh, I see what you mean."

"In any case, at the end of all this, Shannon would have a general proposal. In this proposal, both the proposition, which is the recipe, and the form of its meaning, which is the blackberry pie, are the same. Following such a recipe will produce what it is supposed to produce under every situation and for every purpose for which it is meant to be applied."

"Would Shannon's recipe become a general proposal, then?"

"A recipe already is a general proposal. It stands for many individual instances of something. In Shannon's case, it stands for individual blackberry pies, both actual and potential. What I just described refers to what she would need to do if she were to alter her recipe and produce a new general proposition for blackberry pie making under different conditions. The fact that her recipe exists means that she, and a whole line of other pie-bakers stretching back to whomever made the first piecrust, have already collectively done this. These pie-makers, like Peirce's experimentalists, are part of a larger self. They comprise a community of pie-makers past, present, and future. Just as Shannon does not have to reinvent the wheel every time she sets out to bake something, scientists do not start all over every time they set up an experiment. Peirce felt that one of the most admirable traits of scientists is that they freely share knowledge with one another. Scientists and pie-bakers build upon what others have done and upon what they already know whenever they do something. Peirce wanted philosophers to do this as well."

"What do you do about things that are not possible to experiment upon? What about things that are not subject to deliberate self-controlled conduct?"

"What do you think?" I asked, figuring he could probably come up with some good examples without any help.

"Maybe things that are impossible to experiment on would be the same sorts of things as the Serenity Prayer covers?" he suggested, reciting the prayer to me from memory. "'Lord, grant me the serenity to accept the things I cannot change, the courage to change the things I can, and the wisdom to know the difference'."

"Now there is a good thought! Maybe the Serenity Prayer could be the motto of Peirce's pragmaticism."

"A motto?"

"Sure. The goal of an experimentalist is to gain the wisdom to know the difference between the things that can and cannot be changed. Peirce contended that too many people, even so-called scientists, close off their minds as to what is and is not possible, without bothering to think things through."

"People still do that today."

"Sure. For some people, that little critical self inside the head goes on alert the minute something new comes along. For other people, the critical self just keeps on snoozing. Those people just keep on doing what they already know how to do and believing what they already believe, while expecting their pre-conceived beliefs to continue working for them regardless of the results they actually produce."

"That is the definition of crazy."

"What is?"

"Doing what you have always done but expecting different results."

"That is also the definition of belief mindlessly applied in place of good reasoning. Now, we should probably call it a day."

When Hal starts quoting maxims and clichés, I consider it a sign that he is growing weary of philosophical talk.

"Tomorrow then."

He responded so quickly to my suggestion, that I knew that my assessment had been correct.

Ten
EXPERIMENTAL PHENOMENA

Essay lines 405-451

"Do you remember where we left off yesterday?" I asked as we began the next morning.

"Shannon's blackberry pies," he replied confidently.

"And what was the point of her blackberry pies?"

"The point was experimental phenomena and propositions. Or, maybe I should say that the point was that the meaning of her blackberry pie recipe is located in the future time when she makes a pie using that recipe."

"Good!"

"And," he continued without prompting, "the pie, itself, is a translation of the recipe she used. So, the existence of the pie is also a proposition because it proposes a recipe."

"Yes, that is right. Now, let me see if I can restate this so that it sounds a little more 'Peircean.'

The rational meaning of every proposition resides in the future, because a proposition is a proposal, or a plan, about something that has not yet been done. Results, or experimental phenomena, that you get from putting a proposition into action are a translation of the proposition. As a translation of the proposition, the result, which provides the meaning of the proposition, is itself a proposition. Because the results of propositions can be replicated, the result of a proposition is itself a proposition, proposing that the same result will occur in the future when that proposition is acted upon again. The form of the proposition which is to be taken as its meaning must be applicable to human conduct in every situation and for every purpose for which the proposition has any bearing. This form is the general description of all the experimental phenomena that the proposition virtually predicts.

Does that make sense to you?"

"It sure does!" Hal sounded a little surprised that it made sense.

"Right after Peirce says that 'a proposition must be simply the general description of all the experimental phenomena which the proposition predicts,' he tells us why:"

For an experimental phenomenon is the fact asserted by the proposition that action of a certain description will have a certain kind of experimental result; and experimental results are the only results that can affect human conduct.

I paused here. Although I thought that he was following me, I could not be sure. I waited for him to form a question or a comment.

"I understand all of that," he said after a moment, "and I hear what he is saying, but I think that it is extreme to say that experimental results are the only results that can affect human conduct. It sounds to me like he is painting with a broad brush."

"Maybe we should go on. This next part may answer your question."

No doubt, some unchanging idea may come to influence a man more than it had done; but only because some experience equivalent to an experiment has brought its truth home to him more intimately than before. Whenever a man acts purposively, he acts under a belief in some experimental phenomenon. Consequently, the sum of the experimental phenomena that a proposition implies makes up its entire bearing upon human conduct.

"Oh! I see what is happening here. Peirce is not just talking about scientific experiments now, is he? He is talking about all purposeful activity, everything that we do for a purpose!"

"Which is most of what we do when we are not sleeping."

"Then is he laying out the basis for the non-verbal reasoning patterns?"

"Yes. Peirce is saying that, whenever we take purposeful action, we are putting some belief into action. That is what he has been saying all along. Dottie's non-verbal theory of Relational Thinking Styles makes this same claim. What is different in this sentence is that Peirce is saying that, whenever someone acts purposefully, that person acts under a belief in an experimental phenomenon. That is, indeed, the foundation of the non-verbal model."

"Does he mean then, that no other kind of belief exists except for the belief in an experimental phenomenon?"

"That is exactly what he means. Notice that Peirce is referring to taking purposeful action."

"Then, what does Peirce mean by 'purposeful'?"

"He means that an aim, a goal, or an intention of some sort is involved."

"What does Peirce exclude from the category of purposeful?"

"Any behavior that does not involve the person having a purpose, or a goal, or an intention of some sort."

"I suppose unconscious behaviors like sleeping and hallucinations would fall in that category of lacking purpose."

"I suppose they would be excluded, though sometimes people try to induce hallucinations, so that could be purposeful. Almost everything we do is goal-directed, even if the goal is immediate and transitory."

"What about playing around? Playing around is not purposeful."

"Oh, but it is!" I countered. "A purpose does not have to be distinct or earthshaking. When you act purposefully, you have an intention that you are aiming to fulfill at some point in the future, just as you would if you were forming a hypothesis or making plans to test it. When you take action, you are doing so based on a belief that if you do X, then you will get your intended Y as a result, just as you would do in an experiment. This holds true for play, as well as for everything else."

"If people act purposively in all sorts of different ways, for all sorts of different purposes," he argued, "then they would not always be acting like a pragmaticist, would they? Does Peirce mean that, even when someone is not acting as a pragmaticist, the person is still operating on a belief in an experimental phenomenon?"

"Yes. The belief here is that, 'if I do X, then phenomenon Y will occur.' That is a general proposition about an experimental phenomenon."

"Is it still a proposition even if someone does not act like a pragmaticist?"

"Sure. All purposeful thought is like a general proposition. The experimental phenomenon is what you believe will be the consequence of doing X. Everything you set out to do is based upon a general proposition, a belief in some experimental phenomenon. We have to have a belief in an outcome to take any purposeful action. Just having a purpose means you have an outcome in mind."

"What about people who are not experimentalists?"

"'Believing in an experimental phenomena' is not the same as being right about them. Believing in a future outcome does not mean that people automatically get what they believe they will get. As you know, many people repeatedly apply the same beliefs, regardless of whether these produce the outcomes they want. Such people do not pay much attention to the reaction or interpretation part of the action, reaction, and interpretation loop. Either they do not recognize that what they do, or fail to do, produces consequences, or else they do not know how to interpret these consequences correctly. Even today, you will find that non-experimentalists think that the meaning of something is contained in whatever belief they have, not in the consequences that result from applying that belief."

"When do they do the experimenting?"

"Maybe never."

"Then how can they have a belief in an experimental phenomenon?"

Since he had now asked nearly the same question three times, I figured that we must have hit on a difficult concept. I decided to diverge a little from this essay and use some concepts from Peirce's essay "Fixation of Belief" to see if I could explain this better.

"Believing in an experimental phenomenon," I explained again, "is not the same thing as experimenting. It just means that you have a belief that if you do X, then you will get Y as a result. It does not mean that your belief is correct, nor does it mean that your belief has arrived by means of experimentation. You could have taken that belief from any number of places. The belief may have come to you from traditions of culture or from habits you developed over the course of your life and have never examined. We all have beliefs that were formed in this way. Some people rely almost entirely upon unexamined habits for their beliefs. Beliefs also come from accepting a doctrine or the teachings of an authority, such as your parents, teachers, religion, or government, without question. Beliefs also come from accepting basic principles as true without keeping them open to examination. Before the Wright brothers, the belief that 'man can never fly' was one of those kinds of principles. This belief was an *a priori*, or pre-existing, belief in the principle that human flight was impossible. The experimental phenomena available at the time reinforced that belief, so why would anyone question it? Those are examples of why you do not ever have to personally do any experimenting to a have belief in an experimental phenomenon. However, if we are going to reason like a pragmaticist, we must experiment. We must test our beliefs in experimental phenomena against the results which our beliefs produce, just like a pragmaticist does."

"Is this another example of beliefs interacting with experience?"

"Yes it is. Peirce addressed this issue earlier in this essay. This is what he means when he writes that 'all you have any dealings with are your doubts and beliefs, with the course of life that forces new beliefs upon you and forces you to doubt old beliefs'."

"I remember that."

"By the terms 'doubt' and 'belief,' Peirce does not mean specific doubts or specific beliefs. He means the processes of doubting and of believing. The issue is not 'whether' we operate upon belief in some experimental phenomena when we engage in purposeful action. The issue here is 'how do we habitually do this?' and 'how should we be doing this?' The non-verbal reasoning habits described in the Relational Thinking Styles model provide the answer to the 'how do we habitually do this?' part of the question. Peirce's pragmaticism shows us how we 'should' be doing this to reason rightly."

"What do you mean?"

"Let me sum this up in three points before we continue," I suggested. "First, whenever we automatically apply old habits and beliefs to select and achieve our purposes, we are not thinking. Secondly, when we are deliberate in the ways we go about making choices during each stage of a purposeful activity, we are acting as experimentalists. And thirdly, when we know what those certain ways are and can select and apply them appropriately, we are being pragmaticists."

"How can you be deliberate without knowing that you are being deliberate? That sounds illogical to me."

"When you walk over to the market, you probably think about where you are going or what you are going to be buying. I doubt that you think about how you are moving your feet. You know how to walk, so you do not need to think about how you walk, even though you are using your feet to deliberately move yourself from one place to another."

"I understand what you mean about walking. Are you saying that the same thing applies in thinking?"

"Sure, and that is what we show with the Relational Thinking Styles nonverbal reasoning model. We identify how people act in terms of their reasoning when they are not thinking about how they do this reasoning. Many people are like you. They are natural experimentalists, even if they are not scientifically inclined. For such individuals, reasoning like an experimentalist comes as easily as walking. Experimentalism is the automatic habit they use when they come across something new. Other people are not natural experimentalists. They have different automatic habits for dealing with the uncertainty of future outcomes. Their habits often keep them from even noticing that an outcome may be uncertain. Whatever way non-experimentalists use for dealing with uncertainty, that way is just as natural to them as your way is for you."

"I understand that. Is Peirce saying here that absolutely everything a person deliberately sets out to do is based upon a belief in some experimental phenomenon?"

I nodded.

"Not just scientific experiments?"

"Not just scientific experiments. Peirce means that, whenever we have a purpose or aim, we believe we can do something to achieve that aim. By acting on the belief that we will get what we intend, we take action based on a belief in an experimental phenomenon. That belief gives us a sense of control over the way something will turn out. That sense of control is what affects our future conduct, not whether we turn out to be correct. This sense of control applies to everything we do, whether we are doing scientific experiments, baking a pie, or minding a baby."

"Control of future conduct, then, refers to thinking ahead and making adjustments before the fact?"

"Yes, as well as looking ahead and not making adjustments. Having a 'sense of control' over the way something will turn out is not, however, the same as 'deliberately controlling future conduct'."

"What do you mean?"

"People who have the poorest abilities for deliberately controlling their future conduct often have the strongest 'sense of control' about the way something will come out."

"Is that another example of that bumper-sticker motto?"

"Which one?"

"The one that says 'often wrong, but never in doubt'."

"Exactly! Non-experimentalists often have the greatest confidence in future outcomes, because they do not consider changing conditions. They just act on prior beliefs."

"Would you say that their beliefs do not interact with experience then?"

"No, I would not say that. Their beliefs interact with experience, but they do not tend to notice the consequences of this interaction. They just keep doing what they have always done. That is their way of interacting with experience. Peirce sees the course of life experience as an uncontrolled experiment during which we apply our beliefs and settle doubts. We get a response whenever we apply beliefs. If we learn to recognize that response, that reaction to what we do, then we can learn to make effective interpretations. When we know how to recognize responses and correctly interpret them, then we can learn from experience by adjusting our future conduct accordingly."

"That must mean that people who do not know how to recognize and correctly interpret responses will not be able to adjust their future behaviors."

"You are right. They will not be able to self-correct, to deliberately adjust behavior on their own. Peirce's point here is that everything we do for a purpose is an example of belief and doubt interacting with experience. Whenever we act purposively, whenever we set out to accomplish something, we are either applying a habit or engaging in a formal or a common-sense experiment in order to settle doubt. Once we settle doubt, we are again able continue by applying our new belief."

"By 'common-sense experiments,' do you mean trial and error, like touching a hot iron a few times and figuring out it might be hot?"

"Trial and error is one way of performing common-sense experiments. More complex types occur as well. In any case, that is not Peirce's point here."

"What is his point then?"

"First, you need to remember that he is having an imaginary dialogue with a questioner. The sentence that we are discussing says, 'whenever a man acts purposively, he acts under a belief in some experimental phenomenon.' This is part of Peirce's concluding statement to the questioner on the topic of why pragmatism is not about single experimental phenomena."

Whenever a man acts purposively, he acts under the belief in some experimental phenomenon. Consequently, the sum of the experimental phenomena that a proposition implies makes up its entire bearing upon human conduct. Your question, then, of how a pragmaticist can attribute meaning to any assertion other than that of a single occurrence is substantially answered.

I paused here to see if this had all made sense and noticed that Hal was shaking his head thoughtfully.

"I thought I was understanding him until we came to this conclusion. I fail to see that he has answered any question."

"Maybe we should go back to the original question then."

"That might be a good idea."

"Here it is," I said, locating the hypothetical Questioner's query.

Questioner: Is it not obvious that [your doctrine] must wipe out every proposition of science and everything that bears on the conduct of life? For you say that the only meaning that, for you, any assertion bears is that a certain experiment has resulted in a certain way, nothing else but an experiment enters into the meaning. Tell me, then, how can an experiment, in itself, reveal anything more than that something once happened to an individual object and that subsequently some other individual event occurred?

"Oh, now I understand! The Questioner thinks that an experiment is a one-time thing. Peirce has put up an excellent argument against that."

"Would you summarize Peirce's argument for me?"

He glanced at the short space of text we had just explored so thoroughly.

"The meaning of everything we propose to do is located in the future. The reason for this is that you can only know what something means after you see its effects. Also, future conduct is the only conduct you can control. You cannot change what you have already done. You cannot change the present either, because the present is only a momentary instant and is gone before you know it. You can only change what you are going to do in the future. You change your future conduct by thinking out what you are going to do ahead of time, in advance of doing it."

"Good."

"Also," he continued, "experimental phenomena are what you get as a result of taking action on your purpose or proposal. They are not isolated events. They are connected to what has gone before and to what is going to be done later. If you can change what you do before doing it in order to change what you get as experimental phenomena, then you could do this again if you wanted to. That means that these phenomena are not isolated at all!"

"That was a great summary! Shall we continue?"

"Fine with me."

"Now, the Questioner asks a new question of the Pragmatist."

Questioner: I see that pragmaticism is a thorough-going phenomenalism. Only why should you limit yourself to the phenomena of experimental science rather than embrace all observational science? Experiment, after all, is an uncommunicative informant. It never expiates; it only answers "yes" or "no"; or rather it usually snaps out "No!," or at best only utters an inarticulate grunt for the negation of its "no." The typical experimentalist is not much of an observer. It is the student of natural history to whom nature opens the treasury of her confidence, while she treats the cross-examining experimentalist with the reserve he merits. Why should your phenomenalism sound the meagre jews-harp of experiment rather than the glorious organ of observation?

"This sounds like the Questioner is talking about positivism. He seems to be saying that description is the highest form of knowledge."

"Yes. Auguste Comte's version meant that."

"Is that what Peirce's Questioner is referring to when he talks about natural history and all observational science?"

"That would be it," I agreed. "Do you know what the Questioner was referring to when he used the word 'phenomenalism'?"

"I figured he meant having to do with experimental phenomena."

"That would be a logical assumption especially considering all we have just been through. Phenomenalism means something all on its own, though."

"And that is?"

"Phenomenalism is a theory of knowledge that says what we can know is limited to the totality of physical and mental objects that exist."

"That first part about physical objects sounds reasonable to me," Hal said, "but how would you know for sure what mental objects exist?"

"Phenomenalism comes in two different versions. The first is entirely sense-based. It is the 'what you see is what there is' version, based entirely on appearances. This version denies that any deeper reality lurks behind what you perceive or what you think about."

"And the other kind?"

"The other kind says that a deeper reality underlies surface appearances, but that you cannot possibly ever know what the deeper reality is."

"Why not?"

"Because, this version says that the real world is beyond our knowledge."

"Then, in the phenomenal world, either what you see is all there is, or else there is more, but you cannot ever know it," he said thoughtfully. "Either way you are out of luck if you want to dive below the surface. Right?"

"Yes."

"What does Peirce have to say about this?"

"We have to go back to the Questioner's last question, because Peirce answers this in his next sentence. The Questioner asked, 'Why should your phenomenalism sound the meager Jews-harp of experiment rather than the glorious organ of observation?' Here is what Peirce says in response."

Because pragmaticism is not definable as "thorough-going phenomenalism," although the latter doctrine may be a kind of pragmatism. The richness of phenomena lies in their sensuous quality. Pragmaticism does not intend to define the phenomenal equivalent of words and general ideas, but, on the contrary, eliminates their sential element, and endeavors to define the rational purport, and this it finds in the purposive bearing of the word or proposition in question.

"Now, this is where you and I part company with Peirce for a while."

"What do you mean?"

"Peirce says here that his pragmaticism does not intend to define the phenomenal equivalent of words and ideas, but instead eliminates their actual, or sense-based element, and sets out to find out what these mean linguistically. That is what Peirce means when he says that his pragmaticism finds rational purport in the purposive bearing of the word or proposition in question."

"Meaning in what someone is trying to say?"

"And the way it is interpreted by the listener or the reader."

"So, explain to me why we are parting company with Peirce here. Is it because we disagree with what he is going to say next?"

"No, not at all. We part company here because the Relational Thinking Styles model deals with the phenomenal equivalent of words and ideas and their rational purport. This model is the non-verbal version of Peirce's theory."

"What do you mean?"

"I am not going to go into it here. I would have to bring in the work of another pragmatist in order to explain what I mean. This is not a good place to do that. I just want you to make a note of it. Maybe we will discuss it later."

"That is fine with me. Does this mean that Dottie's non-verbal model is not a model of what a pragmaticist would do?"

"No. It only means that Peirce may have been mistaken when he eliminated phenomenally based purposiveness from the consideration of pragmatism. I believe that this omission caused Peirce problems down the line. By excluding the non-verbal equivalent of words and ideas, I think that Peirce excluded something he needed for proving his theory of abduction."

"Abduction," Hal repeated thoughtfully. "Which is the same thing as what we call multi-relational thinking, right?"

"Exactly. You cannot engage in abductive reasoning without making non-verbal relationships. All relationships, whether verbal or non-verbal, are made by comparing and contrasting qualities of things with one another for some purpose. Peirce believed that all relationship-making must involve a language of some sort if it is going to result in rational meaning. In all fairness, though, I should mention that Peirce defined the word 'language' broadly. However, he contended that the only way to get at the rational meaning of phenomena is to eliminate their sensory qualities and find meaning in the 'purposive bearing of the word or proposition' in question."

"Hmm," Hal nodded thoughtfully. "Peirce must have been one of those people who think that no rational meaning is possible without language."

"Yes," I agreed reluctantly, "at least, it appears that way. However, I suspect that, if Peirce could have seen a demonstration of our non-verbal expression of his theory, he might have come to a different conclusion. Anyway, what he did accomplish with this language-only bias was a remarkable model that is the basis for the study of signs. His thinking provided us with a new way of using language as a tool for reasoning. Besides, Peirce also made it possible for Dottie to construct her non-verbal expression of his theory."

"How so?"

"By making a system for using language scientifically, Peirce provided a tool for understanding the concept of methods. We now recognize methods as real things, which produce real consequences. Once it became possible to talk about scientific methods in the way Peirce conceived them, it also became possible to see method in general. Dottie constructed her theory from a visual-verbal model that someone else had constructed of Peirce's theory."

"Peirce made it possible to have a non-verbal version of his theory because he insisted that pragmatism was verbal? That is ironic."

"Yes, it is ironic. But it is perfectly understandable that Peirce would have insisted upon a language-only basis for conceptualizing. How else would you know for sure that you and someone else are talking about the same thing unless you can define your meaning in a way that both of you understand?"

"Good point."

"Language makes it possible to communicate complex ideas more efficiently because of its general, or generic, quality. General terms enable us to say 'our children,' instead of having to point to each one every time we want to refer to all of them at once. Many people have made the mistake of assuming that, since we talk about concepts by using language, concepts must necessarily require language for their formation. But that is just not so."

"What is not so?"

"Language is not necessary for the formation of concepts. Language allows us to put ideas out in a decodable form, so that, if you know what the words mean, you can understand what a person meant when those words were written or said. Peirce gave us a way of understanding language as signs whose meaning occurs within a context. He demonstrated that every context resides within a larger universe of discourse, a matrix. Value and purpose reside within this matrix and direct both the meaning of a context and the meaning of a sign within the context. Dottie constructed a non-verbal model of this same meaning-making process that Peirce developed. Her model of Relational Thinking Styles lets us decode the meaning-making process itself. That is how we know that concepts are formed non-verbally as well as verbally."

"I thought you said Dottie was mostly interested in the arts. How did she end up with something that was scientific?"

"She intended to identify creative processes. As she was doing this, she discovered that, at the non-verbal level, creative processes and reasoning processes might be the same. Once her model was complete, she developed the non-verbal assessment tool, so we could test her hypothesis. Now, after twenty-five years, you can see that she was correct."

"She sure was! I understand everything so far, if you want to go on."

"This is a good place to stop. Are you ready to call it a day?"

"This has all been a lot to think about. I guess I could use some time to think over what we have discussed before we continue."

We were both exhausted, but also satisfied with this day's discussion.

Eleven
GENERALITY

Essay lines 452-503

"We are finished with blackberry pies now," I announced as we began that morning. "We are going to be hearing more about generals today."

"Great!"

Glad as I was for his enthusiasm, I doubted that he would maintain it for long. This day's section was going to be challenging. Peirce had introduced some incredibly difficult concepts into just a few lines. In my opinion, this is the most difficult section in the whole essay, not only because it is so densely worded, but also because Peirce addresses an important concept of his semiotic here as if he is just playing with minute distinctions among words. I was not at all sure that I could explain what Peirce was saying here nor its significance. The concept of generality is central to Peirce's pragmaticism, however, so I knew I had to give it my best try. I returned to the text.

"Peirce has the Questioner ask the following:"

Questioner: Well, if you choose so to make Doing the Be-all and End-all of human life, why do you make meaning to consist simply in doing? Doing has to be done at a certain time upon a certain object. Individual objects and individual events cover all reality, as everybody knows, and as a practicalist ought to be the first to insist. Yet, your meaning, as you have described it, is general. Thus, it is of the nature of a mere word and not a reality. You say yourself that your meaning of a proposition is only the same proposition in another dress. But a practical man's meaning is the very thing he means. What do you make to be the meaning of "George Washington?"

"Where does the Questioner find that the pragmaticist is making 'Doing the Be-all and End-all'?"

"From what Peirce calls 'the purposive bearing of a word or proposition.' 'Purposive' means an intended action is involved, an action directed by a purpose. This is another way of suggesting that the meaning of something resides in its results. You have to deliberately, or purposively, do something to get results. The Questioner has wrongly interpreted this to mean that only 'Doing' matters."

"Oh, I see that now."

"Another big issue that the Questioner brings up here is the idea that people mean what they mean and that the listener is irrelevant. People used to believe that meaning was inherent in a word itself or in the intentions of the speaker. Here is what Peirce has to say about all of this:"

Pragmaticist: Forcibly put! A good half dozen of your points must certainly be admitted. It must be admitted, in the first place, that if pragmaticism really made Doing the Be-all and End-all of life, that would be its death. For to say that we live for the mere sake of action, as action, regardless of the thought it carries out, would be to say that there is no such thing as rational purport. Secondly, it must be admitted that every proposition professes to be true of a certain real individual object, often the environing universe. Thirdly, it must be admitted that pragmaticism fails to furnish any translation or meaning of a proper name, or other designation of an individual object. Fourthly, the pragmaticistic meaning is undoubtedly general; and it is equally indisputable that the general is of the nature of a word or sign. Fifthly, it must be admitted that individuals alone exist; and sixthly, it may be admitted that the very meaning of a word or significant object ought to be the very essence of reality of what it signifies.

"Uh," Hal interrupted here. "I understand the 'in the first place' part. I understand that we do not live for the sake of action alone. That makes perfect sense to me, since we would not ever be using reasonable judgment if we did. But I do not understand secondly, thirdly, and so on."

"The second part has the pragmaticist agreeing with the Questioner that a proposition describes a real, individual object. Remember," I reminded him, "Peirce's concept of general reals maintains that they stand for individual reals. By 'environing universe,' Peirce is referring to the context in which the individual real operates."

"What does that sentence mean then?"

"It means that, as often as not, the statement of a proposition is true of conditions in the context as well as the individual object itself."

"Oh, that makes sense," Hal said. "And thirdly?"

"The third point is that pragmaticism is not concerned with unrelated individual objects, meaning individual things in and of themselves. Peirce's pragmaticism does not concern itself with the translation, or meaning, of a proper name, or any other designation of an individual object."

"So a pragmaticist would not deal with the meaning of my name?"

"That is correct. Pragmaticists would not deal with the meaning of your name, though they might deal with the general class, or the categories, to which your name belongs, for example, its linguistic roots."

"And fourthly?"

"The fourth point is that 'pragmaticistic meaning is general' and that 'the general is in the nature of a word or a sign'."

"He says 'a word or a sign.' I thought that Peirce believed that meaning was only found in words, in language."

"Peirce assumes that conceptualizing requires a language, but not necessarily a language with words. Mathematics and music are both languages in the sense that Peirce means. We do not disagree that all meaning is general, but we do disagree that language is necessary for conceptualizing. Trying to explain our position from the non-verbal model would be much too complicated for me to go into here. Besides, we should not go off-track with the non-verbal part until we have thoroughly covered this verbal aspect."

"I remember what Peirce said about generals before, at least I think I do. It came under the section where he said general laws were also real things because they were true and whatever is true stands for something that is real. That makes it also real."

"Excellent! And fifthly, Peirce is saying that only individuals actually exist, even though pragmaticism only deals with generals. Does that make sense to you?"

He eyed me warily. "Duns Scotus?"

"Yes! Do you remember how Peirce defined the difference between the words 'real' and 'actual'?"

"I remember that it was tricky. I remember that something could be real, according to Peirce, but not actually exist."

"Yes. Peirce defined the term 'real' according to the medieval meaning used by philosophers like Duns Scotus. To be real means that a thing, an event, or a concept has properties, or aspects to it, whether it ever actually exists in time and space. Notice that Peirce did not say that only individuals are real, or true. He said that only individuals actually exist."

"What?"

"Individuals act upon one another, according to Peirce. In acting upon one another, they have an existence. They actually exist. Individuals, as he means the term, are unrelated, one-of-a-kind things that bump up against one another. When Peirce says that only individuals actually exist, he is referring to these unrelated individuals bumping into one another. Individuals in this unrelated state have no meaning."

"What are they, then?"

"They are just individuals. Individuals can only have meaning once they come into relationships with one another."

"Does that mean that they are not individuals anymore?"

"No. They still 'actually' exist, but they have to be connected up in some way to have any meaning. All meaning is general. Once you start connecting things, they become related to one another. Once individuals connect with one another, you have something that is general. This means that the individual object is also part of a pattern, or a category, or a system and that it has relationships among other patterns, categories, and systems."

"I do not understand the connection here. Why does connecting things make a difference in what they are?"

"Because of meaning and reality. This connecting part is Peirce's semiotic, his theory of meaning. We can only have meaning and reality when things connect up, when you have an inbetweeness operating."

He looked at me questioningly when I said this.

"You always engage an inbetweeness when you bring something into a relationship with something else. Inbetweeness is an invisible glue that connects things to one another. You can not touch or see inbetweeness. Inbetweeness words include connectives such as 'and,' 'also,' 'not,' 'but,' 'or,' and 'in addition to.' They presuppose general categories. However, we do not need words to express the inbetweeness of relationships. Most of the time inbetweeness is implied. For example, the relationship set up in the sentence 'This scarf is red' presupposes general qualities that the scarf shares with certain other individual objects, which we also call scarves, but not with dresses, shirts, or popcorn. This statement also presupposes a category exists which contains the quality of redness and which excludes everything that is not red. I suspect that hardly anybody thinks much about this inbetweeness glue. We all tend to notice things as complete packages, not as products that result from relationship-making. In another essay, Peirce called this inbetweeness factor 'the soul of a sign.' He said that 'a sign's soul gets its power from serving as an intermediary between its object and a mind.' This power of connecting things is the power that exists within everything in the universe to live and grow over time. In order to have meaning, or the potential for meaning, every isolated individual thing must carry within it the power of connectivity. This is what enables things to connect with one another, to form relationships between them. Even a sunflower's response to sunlight and rain is an act of semiosis, or sign making. The sunflower's response signifies that an inbetweeness is occurring between the plant and the sun and rain."

"I do not think I am tracking you here."

"Peirce called this inbetweeness factor 'mediation.' The plant reads and interprets those signs from outside itself as a means of its survival. Mediation is what enables communication between the plant and the elements it requires to live and grow. The 'soul of a sign,' the inbetweeness factor that connects one sign with another, is what allows a plant to interpret the signs of those elements which it requires to live."

"Are you saying that it does not take a human mind to connect signs?" he asked, puzzled. "I thought we were talking about words and what people think they mean."

"We are, but the power of relationship, of establishing inbetweeness, exists throughout the universe. By 'all things,' Peirce meant not only living consciousness such as that of human beings, plants, and other animals, but also what he called living constitutions."

"Like the United States Constitution?"

"That would be one example. By 'living constitutions,' Peirce meant those expressions of minds, those consequences of thought that have become ongoing systems, like newspapers and great fortunes. These living constitutions are signs mediated by inbetweenesses just as are the signs which connect in individual minds as ideas and propositions. In every sense, 'the soul of a sign' resides in its ability to bring individual things together in meaningful ways. Once you do this, you no longer have just unrelated individual stuff."

"What do you have?"

"You have general objects. You have forms, patterns, categories, things, systems, principles, concepts, thoughts, and relationships of all sorts. All of these are general objects to which individual objects belong. General objects do not actually exist. You cannot touch a category, for example. You can only touch individual things in that category. But, since general objects stand for things that are real, they are also real."

"I remember that! That was back when he said that the laws of nature are true and that means they are also real since they represent something real."

"Yes. The laws of nature represent relationships that things have among one another. Only isolated individual things actually exist. Yet, these general objects like categories, patterns, systems, and so forth, make up what we call reality."

"And Peirce defines real as what?"

"As having properties or qualities by which something can be identified, even if nobody ever identifies them."

"And actual?"

"As something that actually occurs in the past, present, or future."

"That is still hard for me to grasp."

"Just think of concepts like justice, or love, and other such general principles. Peirce would say that these concepts are real because they are general principles that have characteristics. Although only unrelated individual objects actually exist, all meaning is general. Nothing can possibly have meaning in and of itself alone. Meaning is the consequence of a relationship. To have meaning, you must have a thing, another thing, and a relationship between them. Relationship is the inbetweeness among things."

"Is that what Peirce means when he says that only individuals actually exist, but that pragmaticism deals with only generals?"

"Yes, but he is not only referring to principles like justice and love, when he says that pragmatism deals only with generals. He also means that categories of things, like tools, are real things. General categories are real things since they contain, or stand for, individual things."

"I can see that. And sixthly?"

"Sixthly, he is saying that 'the meaning of a word or significant object ought to be the very essence of reality of what it signifies.' By 'significant object' Peirce means an object that signifies something else. He is saying that the meaning of a word or significant object should be the essence of whatever piece of reality that it represents."

"And the word 'it' means the word or object?"

"Yes. The meaning of the word or the object that signifies something should be the essence of whatever it signifies."

"That sounds a lot like saying that 'the meaning of a proposition is a translation of the proposition'."

"Yes. Those two statements mean much the same thing. We can move quickly through this section now because what Peirce has to say here about language is related to what he had to say earlier about propositions and their meaning. We should review a little before continuing, though. I am going to paraphrase what Peirce has the Questioner ask him."

Why not have meaning be the same as doing? Everybody knows that individual objects and single events cover all of reality, and anyone who is practical should agree with that. Yet here is the pragmaticist saying that meaning is general—a mere word and not reality. But practical people mean whatever it is they mean.

"I think I understand all of that."

"Then Peirce grants the questioner all of the following points," I said, and wrote down a list for him of the six points we had just finished discussing.

1. Pragmaticism is doing-based, but doing is not the be-all of life.
2. Every proposition is true of a certain real, individual object.
3. Pragmaticism does not translate the meaning of a proper name or any other individual object.
4. In pragmaticism, meaning is general and in the nature of a sign.
5. Pragmaticism admits that only individuals exist.
6. The meaning of any sign is the essence of what it represents.

"I think I understand all of that," Hal said, after reading over the list.

"Next, after the pragmaticist allows in those six points without any reservations, Peirce says that the Questioner should be smart enough to infer that he has missed some major point. Then Peirce continues to put the pieces together for his hypothetical Questioner:"

Putting the admissions together, you will perceive that the pragmaticist grants that a proper name (although it is not customary to say that it has a meaning) has a certain denotative function peculiar, in each case, to that name and its equivalents; and that he grants that every assertion contains such a denotative or pointing-out function.

"You are back to incomprehensibility again."

"You may be right," I agreed, then explained. "When you put all six of these points together, you will notice that the pragmaticist does not translate the meaning of a proper name. He does, however, grant that proper names have 'a specific denotative function.' The words 'denote' and 'connote' are two terms that refer to the meaning of words." I explained. "Denote refers to a word that brings out a specific meaning of something, making it clear in the sense of unambiguous, and giving it a specific pointing-out function. 'Connote' suggests a fuzzier meaning, having more of a sense of implication."

"Such as?"

"'Poodle' is a denotative word in the sense that it refers to a specific breed of dog. It probably brings up the same image in the minds of everyone who knows what a poodle is. To someone who owns a poodle that word may also 'connote' feelings like warmth, companionship, and friendliness. To the victim of a poodle bite, however, the connotative meaning might be different."

"Then, can the same word be both denotative and connotative?"

"Yes. When Peirce refers to 'the denotative function of a proper name,' he means the word's specific pointing-out function, not its general meaning, nor what it implies. Notice, that Peirce adds that all assertions, not just proper names, have a denotative function."

"What does he mean by assertion?"

"An assertion is a claim or an allegation," I explained. "Every time we use a word for some purpose we are making an assertion."

"How so?"

"When we use a word, we are making a claim about its meaning. A proper noun, like Seattle, denotes one specific place and no other. You can easily see that a proper name is denotative, meaning that it points to a specific place. Peirce wants us to realize that all assertions, even general statements, are denotative in the sense that they point to one specific thing, even though they also point to others of the same sort as well."

"I do not understand what you mean."

"Think back to what Peirce said before about the translation of a proposition also being a proposition. Every proposition denotes, or points to, a specific translation of that proposition. Shannon's recipe, her general proposition for making blackberry pies, has a denotative function because it is directly related to whatever specific pie she makes with that recipe. Whenever we make a claim about something, the words we use are signs that denote whatever we are talking about, even if those same words have a general function as well."

"I remember you talking about specific things before. You talked about qualities and an apple that was here and not in the fruit bowl."

"We were talking about how each and every thing that exists is individual since it has qualities setting it apart from all other things."

"Is that what Peirce means here?"

"Yes, but he is referring mostly to words now. Peirce grants that proper names, and words equivalent to proper names, have a particular denotative, or pointing-out, function. He also grants that every assertion has a specific pointing out function. But pragmaticists do not think of this denotative function as having a rational meaning. A pragmaticist is not interested in one, specific, isolated pie. Pragmaticism only deals with the general meaning of things, recipes, laws, patterns, and principles."

"A word is not a recipe or a law."

"We will get to that in a minute," I assured him, then continued. "Peirce agrees that every proposition that is true is true of a single individual object. This is much the same thing as saying that only individuals actually exist."

"I see that."

"But, remember, the pragmaticist insists that all meaning is general. Peirce wants to establish that the pragmaticist does not deal with singular matters, only with the rational meaning of something. According to Peirce, rational meaning is always general," I added, then read the next passage:

> In its peculiar individuality, the pragmaticist excludes this [denotative function] from the rational purport of the assertion, although the like of it, being common to all assertions, and so, being general and not individual, may enter into the pragmaticistic purport. Whatever exists, ex-sists, that is, really acts upon other existents, so obtains a self-identity, and is definitely individual.

"I do not think I understand this."

"Peirce is saying that the pragmaticist excludes the specific one-of-a-kind instance from the rational meaning of an assertion. Remember our discussion about a proposition being plural and not singular?"

He nodded.

"Peirce's pragmaticism is not a theory of isolated anything. Nothing has meaning, according to Peirce, until it is generalized. In order to become generalized, a thing, or a word standing for a thing, must come into a relationship with something else. It must have a context from which it is to be understood. A context is a set of conditions which affects the meaning of a word or other sign. In the case of words, context is usually a sentence or a paragraph."

"How would a sentence make something general?"

"A sentence places a word into a relationship with other words."

"How would that make it general?"

"Because a sentence is a way of expressing relationships. Language is a system of relationships which we build by means of syntax."

"What is syntax?"

"Syntax is the way words are related together to make phrases and sentences. Every language puts words into phrases and sentences according to general rules of syntax for that language. Syntax is a form, or a type, of relationship that words have to one another in a phrase or sentence. Other non-word based language systems have syntactical relationships as well."

"Like what?"

"Like mathematics and logic, as well as the patterns of symbols that musicians and computer analysts use. Dottie's model of non-verbal reasoning patterns is built from syntactical relationships. Every system contains syntactical patterns that define the forms, or the types, of relationships that can occur within that system. These patterns are general objects, meaning that they are like propositions that apply to many different instances of something."

"Does a sentence make something plural because it is a form or a type?"

"Yes, even when that sentence has a denotative function, even when it points out something specific. Regardless of the words that you use, the rules of syntax remain constant. The rules of syntax are a general form, a type. Syntax is the reason why Lewis Carroll could put nonsense words together in ways that seemed as though they made sense. Do you remember 'Twas brillig and the slithey toves did gire and gimble in the wabes'?"

He nodded.

"That 'sentence' is an example of syntax giving the appearance of meaning. Peirce wants you to know that his pragmaticism is not interested in the particular meaning of a particular sentence for a particular situation. Pragmaticism is only interested in the rational meaning of a statement in terms of what is common in that statement to all assertions. Syntax is one thing that is common to all assertions. Now, I am going to repeat the last sentence. 'Whatever exists, ex-sists, that is, really acts upon other existents, so obtains a self-identity, and is definitely individual'."

"But," Hal said, "he is referring to a single, individual thing again."

"Yes. He is setting us up to realize that, in order to have meaning, a single thing that actually exists must enter into a relationship with other existents," I explained. "Meaning comes out of the relationship between a thing and whatever it acts upon."

"I still do not understand how a relationship makes meaning."

"Do you remember the Coke bottle that a pilot threw out of the airplane in the movie *The Gods Must Be Crazy*?"

"Sure."

"That Coke bottle was a single thing that fell out of the air and had no pre-existing meaning to the isolated tribe it fell upon."

"Yes it did. It meant that the gods had sent them something."

"The tribe did not know what it meant in a general sense," I countered. "They did not know why the gods had sent it. That Coke bottle as we know it was something outside of the context with which that tribe made meaning. In our society, it was just an empty Coke bottle. In their context, the bottle became something much larger. It eventually became a symbol of discord."

"From where I sit, that Coke bottle appears to be an example of an isolated singular thing having meaning all on its own."

"Not at all. It is an example of something 'not' having meaning until it is understood within a context. When that Coke bottle dropped into their midst, the tribe made assumptions about it based upon pre-existing beliefs."

"Do you mean their belief that it was sent from the gods?"

"Yes. That was a logical conclusion from their perspective."

"How was it logical?"

"It was logical in the sense that they made a typical inductive inference."

"What is an inductive inference?"

"It is a generalization. In this case the inductive inference would have had origins well before the Coke bottle incident," I said. Then I wrote out an inductive sequence for him, one that the tribe might have been using.

1. Rain falls from the heavens (which means it comes from the gods).
2. Rain is good.
3. All things that the gods send us from the heavens are good.

"The Coke bottle inference is just an extension of this one," I explained as I wrote down the second inductive sequence.

1. The Coke bottle fell from the heavens.
2. The Coke bottle (like rain) must be something that is good.
3. All things that the gods send us from the heavens are good.

"But they were wrong," he said after I finished writing down the lists. "The Coke bottle fell from an airplane, and it turned out to be a problem for them, not something good."

"Yes, you are right. Inductive inferences used all on their own can easily be wrong. Induction is the method of reasoning that should be used to verify and evaluate a conclusion, not to figure things out."

"What do you mean?"

"I mean that induction should be the last step in the reasoning process. First, abduction should be used to formulate a hypothesis, or possible explanation for a surprising fact. Then, deduction should be used to explicate the hypothesis and ready it for testing. Induction is the method we use for comparing what happens with our expectations. Some people confound abduction and induction. Peirce considered hunch-getting to be the same as abductive reasoning. He made a simple formula for hunch-getting. 'The surprising fact, C, is observed. If A were true, then C would be a matter of course. Hence, there is reason to suppose that A is true'."

"How is that different from what the people in that tribe did?"

"Well, Peirce's hunch-getting formula would say. The 'surprising fact, C,' is that a Coke bottle falls out of the sky. If 'A were true,' that the gods have gone crazy, then 'such things as C,' Coke bottles falling from the sky, would be an expected consequence. Hence, 'there is reason to suppose A,' that the gods have gone crazy, is true."

"It seems to me like that is the same thinking that the tribe members did."

"No, they did not 'suppose' anything. They drew a conclusion. The conclusion that 'all things that the gods send us from the heavens are good' was already a rule for them, one that they had previously applied countless times."

"But," he argued, "it seems to me that the only difference is that Peirce's formula uses the word 'suppose' and the other does not."

"If that were the only difference, which it is not, it would be a huge one. There is a big difference between a hypothesis and a conclusion. The word 'suppose' infers that you have some work ahead of you to figure out if you are correct or not. The words 'conclusion' and 'rule' infer that the matter is settled and that there is no need for analysis or testing to see if you are correct."

"Oh, I see that now."

"So, the inductive inference that the tribe made about that Coke bottle was that the gods had sent it and it must therefore be good. Based on this belief, they used deductive reasoning to try to figure out what the bottle was for. Then, when the bottle started causing discord within their previously harmonious tribe, they concluded that the gods had to have been crazy to send it to them. The tribe began with a belief that there are gods and that anything falling from the sky is good because it comes from the gods. The tribe did not make an abductive inference and form an explanatory hypothesis about the cause and effects of that bottle. Instead, they made an inductive inference based on prior assumptions, and then arrived at the conclusion that the gods must be crazy. Then, the tribe's leader acted upon this inductively derived belief by setting off to find the gods and return the bottle. Inductive inferences can start out with surprising facts, as abductive inferences do, but they end in conclusions. Abductive inferences, on the other hand, end in guesses, or hypotheses, which require further analysis and testing."

"So, the tribe reached a conclusion instead of making a hypothesis?"

"Yes, that remote tribe reached a reasonable conclusion as far as their experience was concerned. They knew nothing about Coke bottles or airplanes. They figured that the bottle had to have come from the gods and, therefore, had to have been a good thing. Then, they tried to figure out what its purpose was. They tried to generalize that bottle by using it as a tool for different chores. Eventually, the bottle became a symbol for the discord it caused among tribal members, who began competing for turns at using it. To make sense out of this isolated event, the tribe had to imbue the bottle with meaning. As Peirce would have said, that specific Coke bottle 'ex-sisted and had effects upon other existents.' That made it truly singular. However, that bottle could not mean anything to the tribe members in-and-of-itself. It was the relationship of that bottle to the other existents that eventually imbued it with meaning."

"They could have just worshiped the Coke bottle," Hal suggested. "Then it would have been a single thing with meaning."

"It would still have had a pre-existing, relationship to their 'gods' category. And that relationship would rest upon the assumption of an inexplicable ultimate, violating Peirce's doctrine of continuity which says that inexplicable ultimates are *verboten*. So, even if they had worshiped the bottle, they would have been relating it to something else, a pre-existing 'gods' category. Many people still classify surprising facts into the category of 'the divine' when they do not know what else to do with them."

"Good point," Hal said, smiling at that last remark. "Still, there is something wrong in the way that they made their hypothesis."

"Yes, there is. Do you know what is wrong with it?"

"It has to do with the 'god' part, about something you said earlier."

"About inexplicable ultimates, perhaps?"

"Yes!" he said then, remembering. "You said that Peirce had a doctrine about that."

"That would be his doctrine of continuity, which he covers later in this essay. Next, Peirce writes that 'whatever exists, ex-sists, that is, really acts upon other existents, so obtains a self-identity and is definitely an individual.' He excludes this singular, individual existence from having meaning in the sense of rational significance. However, he includes what he calls 'the like of it,' or general qualities that the singularity shares with others. The tribe was seeking 'the like of it' as they tried to figure out what that Coke bottle meant."

"Such as when they used the Coke bottle like a rolling-pin?"

"Yes. Peirce begins to explain next what he means about generals and individuals when it comes to language. This explanation may be one of the most confusing sections in the entire essay," I warned. "You can comfort yourself as we go through this next paragraph by knowing that the information we are going to be covering here is embedded in Engaged Intelligence training in the form of simple exercises. I just hope you do not become discouraged as we go through this passage because it is very dense. I think that one reason it is so confusing may be because Peirce uses George Washington as an example."

"Why would that make it confusing?"

"Because Peirce wants to explain two different kinds of generality. Most people think of Washington as 'General' George Washington, which mentally adds in a third meaning of the word 'general.' Different meanings for the word 'general' tend to get snarled up here, so I am going to substitute the name 'Benjamin Franklin' for 'George Washington.' Doing this might help to make the explanation easier to follow."

"That is fine with me."

"Now, I am going to read this paragraph with the name substitution 'Benjamin Franklin' for 'George Washington'."

As to the general, it will be a help to thought to notice that there are two ways of being general. A statue of a soldier on some village monument, in his overcoat and with his musket, is for each of a hundred families the image of its uncle, its sacrifice to the Union. That statue, then, though it is itself single, represents any one man of whom a certain predicate may be true. It is objectively general. The word "soldier," whether spoken or written, is general in the same way, while the name ["Benjamin Franklin"] is not so. But each of these two terms remains one and the same noun, whether it be spoken or written, and whenever and wherever it be spoken or written. This noun is not an existent thing, it is a type or form, to which objects, both those that are externally existent and those which are imagined, may conform, but which none of them can exactly be. This is subjective generality. The pragmaticistic purport is general in both ways.

"What is he trying to get across here when he says that 'each of these are one and the same noun'? Does he mean the statue and Benjamin Franklin are the same noun?"

"No. At first, he is referring to the specific statue that represents any soldier who served in the Civil War. That statue of a soldier is objectively general because it represents any person who performed certain actions under certain conditions. The word 'soldier' is also objectively general in the same way because that word stands for all civil war soldiers in general, in a generic way. However, this is not true of the name 'Benjamin Franklin.' The name 'Benjamin Franklin' is not objectively general because it stands for only one particular person. However, these two words, 'soldier' and 'Benjamin Franklin,' remain the same words whenever and wherever they are spoken. This means that these words have a kind of generality that is common to both of them."

"I do not think I am getting this."

"What Peirce is trying to say here is in the same vein as what he said earlier about experiments and propositions. Remember, for the pragmaticist, the phenomenon you get from an experiment is not singular. Every time an experiment is conducted in a particular way under particular conditions you get the same phenomena."

"I remember that, but what does that have to do with words?"

"A proposition is a statement about what phenomena will occur if such and such is done under certain conditions."

"I remember that as well, but I still do not see the connection."

"Nouns, which are words standing for persons, places, or things, are like the phenomena that a proposition predicts. These predicted phenomena are not the actual events. The events are the actual part, not the prediction. The same thing holds true with nouns. Peirce tells us that a noun is not an existent thing. It is 'a type, or form, to which objects may conform...but which none of them can exactly be.' He calls generality of type or form 'subjective generality'."

"Does he mean that subjective generality is like syntax?"

"Yes. Syntax is a type or form of relationships among words. Here, Peirce refers to a single word, a noun. A single word is also a type or form because it stands in place of something else."

"I am not sure that I am getting this. First, he says that 'Benjamin Franklin' is not a general term, and then he says that he is."

"Neither a proposition nor a noun is an actual thing," I explained. "They are both concepts used to signify a thing. That physical statue of a soldier is an actual individual thing that is objectively general because it represents a category of persons who were soldiers. The actual Benjamin Franklin was an actual individual thing. However, the word 'soldier' and the word 'Benjamin Franklin' are both symbols that represent something else. That makes the words, 'soldier' and 'Benjamin Franklin,' general things. In the case of the word, 'soldier,' the meaning is objectively general because it stands for many different people who perform certain tasks under certain conditions. The word 'soldier' does not point to one particular person but covers a whole category of people. The name 'Benjamin Franklin,' is subjectively general because it is a proper noun standing for one particular person. However, neither the common noun, 'soldier,' nor the proper noun, 'Benjamin Franklin,' are existing things. A noun is a type, or form, by which we can identify actual or imagined objects. None of these forms can actually be the thing they represent. The word 'soldier' and the word 'Benjamin Franklin' remain the same whenever and wherever they are spoken or written. This generality of type or form is subjective generality."

Hal still had a confused look on his face.

"Think of it this way," I suggested, "you cannot ever be a word. You can only be the physical, mental, emotional being that is you. Benjamin Franklin could not be the word, 'Benjamin Franklin'."

"I can see that."

"So, even a proper noun is general in the sense that it is a noun. This type of generality comes from a noun being a type or form that stands in place of something else. The term 'Benjamin Franklin' is a symbol that stands for the person. A word continues to stand for something else whenever and wherever it is spoken or written. A word is always general, even if the thing it stands for is a one-of-a-kind specimen, like Benjamin Franklin. Peirce calls generality of type or form, as with nouns and syntax, subjective generality, even when the thing it refers to is not general."

"And you are saying that the word 'Benjamin Franklin' is subjectively general even though Benjamin Franklin himself is a one-of-a-kind thing?"

"Yes. The word 'soldier' is also subjectively general in the sense that it is a type or form and not an existent thing. Since the word 'soldier' also refers to a category of people, it is objectively general as well. Pragmaticism deals with both objective and subjective generalities."

"Let me see if I understand. Pragmaticism deals with things that are objectively and subjectively general, but not with single, one-of-a-kind things?"

"Yes," I answered, adding, "and this is a good place to end for today."

"Are we ever going to go into why this matters? I think I understand about generals and individuals, but I do not see why they make a difference."

"Then we should talk about that tomorrow."

At that, we agreed to stop for the day.

Twelve
REGULARITY

Essay lines 504-560

Since, as usual, Hal and I had not been paying too much attention to such mundane things as the days of the week, we had failed to notice that the day of our last conversation was a Friday. Our oldest son Dave and his wife, the Shannon of blackberry pie fame, had arranged to drive up here for that weekend. They had recently added Ethiopian food to their broad gastronomic repertoire and proposed to create a memorable feast for us. We invited several friends to join us. It had been a terrific weekend and entirely non-intellectual. It took us a while on this morning to figure out where we had left off.

"Let me see. On Friday, we discussed Peirce's assertion that all meaning is general. Do you remember anything we talked about?"

"I remember *The Gods Must Be Crazy*. I remember we talked about that Coke bottle that fell from the sky and that it had to fit into some general category before it had meaning to the tribe."

"Good. Anything else?"

"I just do not understand what the point of it all was."

"Oh, right," I said, remembering only then that I had promised to explain the point of generality. "We were supposed to start off with a discussion of why the issue of generals and individuals matter. Do you have any ideas of your own on this matter?"

"No. I think I understand what you have been saying about generals and individuals, but I do not understand why it matters."

"Do you remember when I said that back in Peirce's day, and before that as well, people believed that words themselves had meaning?"

"I remember that."

"And do you remember how Peirce wanted to clean up philosophy to get the gibberish out? He wanted to bring the methods for studying philosophy up to the standards of science."

"I remember that too."

"To do this, Peirce had to establish the reality of general objects such as categories, propositions, and patterns. He needed to establish the reality of generals because he wanted to establish the importance of purpose as the director of action. Purposes, like ideas and beliefs, are general objects. They stand in place of any number of future instances of something. Up until Peirce, nobody had paid all that much attention to the way in which purposes are formed. Philosophers treated the formation of purposes in the same way that most people treated the meaning of words. Things just were what they were and meant what they meant, period. The concepts of generals and individuals are important for formulating purposes and identifying the effects of these in advance of pursuing them."

"What about the 'sign's soul' and what you said about plants and newspapers?"

"Signs are general objects because they are types, or forms. The 'soul of the sign' is its faculty for serving as an intermediary. In order to have meaning, we must have one sign, plus another sign, plus the power of inbetweeness to connect these to one another. All meaning arises because of signs. Signs are the general mechanism by which the universe operates. Everything alive operates by means of signs, and these signs operate by means of the action, reaction, and interpretation loop that Peirce described earlier."

"That is what an experimentalist does!"

"That is also what everything alive does," I added. "Everything acts, receives reactions back from its environment, and interprets the reaction in some way. This could be at a primitive level. For example, a single celled organism uses this loop when it is taking in food, putting out waste, and going in search of more food. How long and how well that cell and its progeny survive depends upon how their environments react to their actions. Their survival also depends upon the interpretations which the cell and its progeny make of these reactions."

"What does this have to do with words?"

"People get much of their meaning by way of signs that are purely mental constructions, like remembered or imagined events, images, sensations, and words. These internal images, sensations, and words are types, or forms, by which we think of things. These are not actual things or events. We always think by means of signs, which are general objects. In addition, general objects, in the form of purposes and beliefs, guide our choice-making process when we decide to do things. For Peirce, the power of general objects to guide behavior extended beyond the behavior of living things. He held that general systems—forms, laws, types, and other such generalities—guide everything that occurs in the cosmos. That is why he can say that generality is a property of everything that has form and meaning."

"Would Peirce have thought the universe is intelligent?"

"I think he did believe that. He would have said that our job is to discover the general principles of this intelligence so that we shape our conduct to be more in line with those principles. Peirce based his concept of generality upon his definition of reality. We discussed this before, but he brings this up in his next passage, so we should go over it again."

As to reality, one finds it defined in various ways; but if that principle of terminological ethics that was proposed be accepted, the equivocal language will soon disappear. For *realis* and *realitas* are not ancient words. They were invented to be terms of philosophy in the thirteenth century, and the meaning they were intended to express is perfectly clear. That is real which has such and such characters, whether anybody thinks it to have those characters or not. At any rate, that is the sense in which the pragmaticist uses the word.

I stopped at this point and looked at Hal questioningly, expecting a comment or response.

"Peirce is just saying what we talked about before. He is saying that whatever is real is real, whether anyone thinks it is real or not."

"Yes. Do you know what he was referring to when he said, 'if that principle of terminological ethics that was proposed be accepted, the equivocal language will soon disappear'?"

"He is referring to not tinkering with other people's terminology."

"Yes. Peirce offers the definition issue surrounding the word 'real' as an example of something that would be cleared up if his principle of terminological ethics were to be accepted. Peirce's meaning of 'real' ties with this next statement:"

Now, just as conduct controlled by ethical reason tends toward fixing certain habits of conduct, the nature of which (as to illustrate the meaning, peaceable habits and not quarrelsome habits) does not depend upon any accidental circumstances, and in that sense, may be said to be destined; so, thought, controlled by a rational experimental logic, tends to the fixation of certain opinions, equally destined, the nature of which will be the same in the end, however the perversity of thought of whole generations may cause the postponement of the ultimate fixation.

I stopped again to see if Hal was following.

"I think I understand this."

"How about paraphrasing it just to be sure."

He looked over his copy of the text and then summarized the section.

"Peirce is saying that when we deliberately behave in an ethical way, then behaving ethically becomes a habit. That is why we should not be surprised when we continue to behave ethically in the future. Since it is not accidental, we could say that this ethical behavior is destined to be. Along the same lines, Peirce says that thinking 'controlled by rational experimental logic' causes certain opinions to become fixed. Once these opinions are set, they appear to have been destined from the start."

Hal paused at this point.

"This next part of the sentence is a little complicated to follow," he said, reading from his copy of the essay, "'...however the perversity of thought of whole generations may cause the postponement of the ultimate fixation'."

"Peirce is pointing out the difficulty of getting new ideas to take hold, even if they are proven to be scientifically valid. Now I am going to finish up that paragraph:"

If this be so, as every man of us virtually assumes that it is, in regard to each matter the truth of which he seriously discusses, then, according to the adopted definition of "real," the state of things which will be believed in that ultimate opinion is real.

"If what be so?"

"If certain habits of conduct become fixed because they are used so much and if the result of that conduct appears to be destined because it is so closely tied into prior behaviors."

"Is he saying that the same thing is true of experiments?"

"Yes. Remember, Peirce considered logic to be a species of conduct. He means that conducting scientific reasoning in certain rational, experimental ways produces results that are destined to be rationally true, just like the habit of behaving in a peaceful manner is destined to produce more peaceful behavior in the future."

"The opposite would also be true, then."

"What do you mean?"

"I mean that, if certain habits of good behaviors produce predictable, or destined, good results, then certain habits of bad behaviors would produce predictable bad results."

I knew what Hal was getting at here and figured that one more foray into the non-verbal realm probably would not take us too far off track.

"It might seem so, but we are fallible and cannot predict every future context. But, if we happen to know the context, certain actions taken under certain conditions can produce predictable results, good, bad, or otherwise."

"And that is what the non-verbal reasoning patterns show!"

"Yes."

"Then, the non-verbal thinking patterns must be generals," he concluded. "I mean they are types or forms, and stand for different ways of doing things."

"Good reasoning!" I was surprised that he had already made this connection. "I want to go back over Peirce's last statement again:"

If this be so, as every man of us virtually assumes that it is, in regard to each matter the truth of which he seriously discusses, then, according to the adopted definition of 'real,' the state of things which will be believed in that ultimate opinion is real.

"Is he saying, then," Hal interrupted incredulously, "that what is real is what someone believes is real?"

"Not exactly. Do you recall the definition of 'real' that he gave earlier?"

"He said that real is what is true whether anybody ever thinks so or not."

"Yes. You may remember that earlier Peirce described the word 'real' in more specific terms. He said 'real' is 'that which has such and such characters, whether anyone thinks it to have those characters or not'."

"What are 'such and such' characters?"

"They are whatever particular properties a thing has that makes it real, regardless of whether anyone thinks it has those properties or not. Peirce is saying here that what is real under this definition are the things that will be believed in that ultimate opinion."

"What ultimate opinion?"

"The ultimate opinion that results from 'thought, controlled by a rational experimental logic' even if several generations of blockheads are too thick-skulled to recognize such truth." I added this part with my own emphasis.

"Is he saying that truth is a matter of opinion? What happened to something being real no matter what?"

"Peirce means that what is real is the destined consequence of thought controlled by rational experimental logic. The truth discovered in this way by means of signs and other general objects is not just made up, according to Peirce. It is something that we uncover or discover. We can know the meaning of these general objects when we identify the consequences that come from following them out. According to Peirce, reality, in the form of knowledge, results from the formation of certain opinions by means of this rational experimental logic. Rational experimental logic is a continuous process of different minds testing out one another's findings and building upon these. Over time, opinions as to what is true become fixed into beliefs, which Peirce says should be called a state of 'belief unassailable by doubt,' instead of truth."

"Which is nearly the same as being true?"

"Just barely. For Peirce, the ultimate opinion based on these destined opinions is what is real."

Hal shook his head thoughtfully at this.

"I just cannot get used to the idea of reality being a matter of opinion."

"Peirce believed it should be a matter of 'considered opinion.' Besides, you need to keep in mind that Peirce contends that what is real has certain characteristics whether anybody thinks it has those characteristics."

"Is there a 'real' reality as well as 'a considered opinion of' reality?"

"Peirce said he was not sure if these would be different or not. However, he did contend that there were two kinds of ordinary truth, which he called 'holding for true.' He said one type is 'the practical holding for true,' which is alone entitled to the name 'belief.' The other is a 'provisional holding' for true, such as you would have when exploring a proposition."

"What about truth with a capital T? Did Peirce believe in such a thing?"

"Sure. Remember, he held that whatever was real was still real whether anybody ever figured it out."

"Oh, sure. I remember that."

"Here is what he says next:"

But, for the most part, such opinions will be general. Consequently, some general objects are real. (Of course, nobody ever thought that all generals were real; but the Scholastics used to assume that generals were real when they had hardly any, or quite no, experiential evidence to support their assumption; and their fault lay just there, and not in holding that generals could be real.)

"Question! What is he saying here?"

"Just what he has already set us up for. Remember when Peirce said that generals could be reals if they were true because whatever is true represents a real, and, if something stands for a real, it is itself a real?"

"I remember that."

"Then Peirce wrote, 'Now the laws of nature are true'."

"And, therefore real. I remember that, too."

"Peirce is just saying that, for the most part, the considered opinions about what is true will be in the form of generals, such as laws of nature, not a specific instance of these. Thus, he says, 'some general objects are real'."

"Some but not all?"

"Yes. And although nobody ever thought that all generals were real, the Scholastics had a problem with this because they made assumptions about generals being real without any experimental data to back them up. Peirce wants us to know that the problem lay in making these unsubstantiated general assumptions, not in the assertion that generals could be real."

"I can see that."

I read the next section:

One is struck with the inexactitude of thought even of analysts of power, when they touch upon modes of being. One will meet, for example, the virtual assumption that what is relative to thought cannot be real. But why not, exactly? Red is relative to sight, but the fact that this or that is in that relation to vision that we call being red is not itself relative to sight; it is a real fact.

I stopped reading at this point, without even being asked. I knew I would need to explain this statement.

"Do you know what Peirce means by the phrase 'modes of being'?"

"I assumed I did, but now that you are asking, I am not so sure."

"'Modes of being' is one of those incredibly general phrases we can all hear and assume we understand. However, even different philosophers have different shades of meanings for this term."

"Then, what are 'modes of being'?"

"We are going to define them here as modes of consciousness. You already know what these modes are. We deal with them in Engaged Intelligence training."

"Just refresh my memory then."

"Modes of being refer to the internal states by which we have our being and through which we filter information in and out."

"Like temperaments?"

"Yes. Temperament is a psychological offshoot of this concept. Peirce may have had a particular way he wanted us to think about these modes of being. He applied three categories to consciousness: 'being,' 'existence,' and 'reality.' He applies these categories to everything else as well, but that is another story. These modes also correspond to the three categories in the qualification portion of Engaged Intelligence training. 'Being,' Peirce's term for the first category, corresponds to what we call the affective mode of consciousness. This mode has to do with attitudes or feeling states. 'Existence' corresponds to the sensory mode, because we can only experience the actuality of existence by means of our senses. 'Reality' corresponds to what we call the logical, or rational, mode because it deals with making relational judgments. Rational judgments come from noticing and comparing qualities of existence and usually have to do with things such as size, number, capacity, form, and other aspects of that sort."

"You were right. I do know these from Engaged Intelligence training."

"Good. Now, I am going to re-read the last section:"

One is struck with the inexactitude of thought even of analysts of power, when they touch upon modes of being. One will meet, for example, the virtual assumption that what is relative to thought cannot be real. But why not, exactly? Red is relative to sight, but the fact that this or that is in that relation to vision that we call being red is not itself relative to sight; it is a real fact.

When I finished re-reading the passage, I said, "Peirce was making a big distinction here. This passage is preparing you to accept that qualities having to do with reasoning or, as he says, with thought, are just as real as qualities having to do with the senses."

"Does 'relative to' mean 'having to do with'?"

"Yes. Qualities allow us to make relationships among things. We relate or differentiate one thing to or from another, based upon qualitative similarities and differences. Peirce believes that logical qualities, which are relative to thought, should have the same claim to reality as qualities relative to vision. Peirce asks, why not agree that qualities used in the performance of reasoning functions are just as real as the qualities related to seeing something?"

"What is a 'something' that would be relative to thought?"

"Logical qualities are those having anything to do with figuring something out inside your head, as opposed to just experiencing a feeling or perceiving by means of your physical senses. Suppose you have a cold and I want to make chicken soup to help you feel better. 'Wanting' you to feel better is a quality of feeling which causes me to make the soup. As I prepare the soup, I notice qualities of sensation, such as smell, taste, color, temperature, texture, and so on. However, I must use the qualities of reason to make judgments as I set about to prepare the soup, as well as during the actual cooking. These judgements of reason will have to do with such things as quantity, degree, time, space, and transformation. Peirce is contending here that the qualities of reason, by which we figure things out, are just as much a legitimate fact of being as are the qualities of sensation, by which we experience such things as redness."

"That makes perfect sense to me."

"Now, remember, we are still talking about how some generals are real. Peirce has already explained his meaning of 'real' to us. He has also explained that conduct controlled by ethical reason leads to the fixing of certain habits of conduct that appear destined and that the same thing happens when thought is controlled by rational experimental logic."

He nodded to let me know he was following this summary.

"Peirce shows us how ultimate opinions about what is real are going to appear to have been destined, just like peaceable conduct, if these ultimate opinions are determined by good reasoning. Then he says that these ultimate opinions are going to be mostly general. He finishes up the paragraph by arguing that what is relative to thought is just as real as what is relative to sight. Just as red is a real fact, so, too, are qualities having to do with thinking."

"I understand all of that now."

"Next, he explains some practical ways that generals are reals."

Not only may generals be real, but they may also be physically efficient, not in every metaphysical sense, but in the common-sense acception in which human purposes are physically efficient. Aside from metaphysical nonsense, no sane man doubts that if I feel the air in my study to be stuffy, that thought may cause the window to be opened. My thought, be it granted, was an individual event. But what determined it to take the particular determination it did, was in part the general fact that stuffy air is unwholesome....

"By 'physically efficient,' does Peirce mean 'causing you to do things'?"

"In a sense. He means that general principles, rules, and laws are physically efficient because you do not have to deal with every issue as an isolated event. If the room is stuffy, do I open the window or not? Of course you do, because a general belief exists that stuffy rooms are bad for your health. Peirce is saying that a thought motivates you to open the window. This thought is a general one because it is based upon a general principle about the unhealthy effects of stale air. In this way, general ideas are physically efficient because general ideas can cause you to do something, like open the window."

"That makes sense."

"Next Peirce refers to Dr. Carus who had written an article for *The Monist* called 'The Foundations of Geometry':"

> My thought, be it granted, was an individual event. But what determined it to take the particular determination it did, was in part the general fact that stuffy air is unwholesome and in part other Forms, concerning which Dr. Carus has caused so many men to reflect to advantage....

"We do not need to go into these other forms or talk about Carus here. Now, listen carefully to this next sentence. It is a famous statement by Peirce."

> For truths, on the average, have a greater tendency to get believed than falsities have.

"Why is it famous? I am not even sure I agree with it."

I knew Hal was thinking about some of the strange religious belief systems floating around these days.

"First, note that Peirce said 'on the average.' Secondly, Peirce was thinking of truths in terms of those that are amenable to scientific inquiry. Here is the rest of that statement:"

> For truths, on the average, have a greater tendency to get believed than falsities have. Were it otherwise, considering that there are myriads of false hypotheses to account for any given phenomenon, against one sole true one (or if you will have it so, against every true one), the first step toward genuine knowledge must have been next door to a miracle.

"Do you understand what Peirce means?"

"He just means that truth tends to be believed more often than falsities because, otherwise, nothing would ever have been discovered or invented."

"Yes. This next statement will finish up the section:"

> So, then, when my window was opened, because of the truth that stuffy air is *malsain*, a physical effort was brought into existence by the efficiency of a general and non-existent truth. This has a droll sound because it is unfamiliar; but exact analysis is with it and not against it.

"Then Peirce says some more things along the same lines of explaining the value and validity of generals."

And it has besides, the immense advantage of not blinding us to great facts—such as that the ideas "justice" and "truth" are, notwithstanding the iniquity of the world, the mightiest of the forces that move it. Generality is, indeed, an indispensable ingredient of reality; for mere individual existence or actuality without any regularity whatever is a nullity. Chaos is pure nothing.

"I take it that an explanation is on its way."

"Justice and truth are generalities. Peirce is saying that, in spite of all the wickedness in the world, justice and truth are the mightiest of the forces that move human behavior."

"Maybe they used to be, but justice and truth are not having much influence these days."

"Then we can say they 'should be' the mightiest forces. Something general is driving the world, the human part of it at least. That 'something' is a generality, even if it is something bad, like greed."

"I will agree to that."

"Peirce wants you to understand that generality is an indispensable ingredient of reality."

"By generality, does he mean general principles?"

"And laws of nature, man, justice, and beauty, as well. Generality provides us with the means to motivate behaviors, organize ideas, communicate, create proposals, and imagine. We follow and we discover general principles. They are what allow us to construct ideas, as well as analogies to ideas. Generalities allow us to form the hypotheses that we need to discover or create something new."

"This is starting to make sense now."

"Good, because to understand Peirce's pragmaticism, you need to realize that generality is an indispensable ingredient of reality. Peirce wants you to know that you have to have generality in order to make reality, and that reality is something we know exists because of its regularity."

"What is it that makes something regular? Is it the same thing that makes something real?"

"Good question. The qualities, or properties, that distinguish one thing from another are what makes that thing real. The qualities that one thing shares with another contribute to its regularity."

"So, differences make things real and similarities make them regular?"

"Yes, but similarities and differences are a pair. They must both be considered at the same time in order to have regularity. I can use a piece of Dottie's theory of non-verbal reasoning to explain this."

"That might help."

"Dottie's theory claims that, at any given moment in time, you can do one of two things. Either you can 'vary,' which means that you can do something different than you did before. Or else, you can 'repeat' something that has been done before. Varying corresponds to Peirce's state of irregularity, and repeating corresponds to his state of regularity."

"I can see that. It also sounds a lot like what you said earlier about doubt and belief and the binary code."

"Good insight! The two methods of varying are 'random' and 'deliberate.' Both varying methods are 'means directed.' That is to say, means and materials direct the selection of a goal, instead of the other way around. Because they are means-directed instead of goal-directed, the outcomes of both of these processes are unpredictable. Other than their unpredictability, however, these two methods are nearly opposites. Random varying is capricious and produces only transient goals. It involves jumping from one thing to another without making meaningful connections between them. This type of varying feeds chaos. Deliberate varying, however, involves the careful selection and rejection of options based on contrasting, combined with occasional forays into random varying as a method for encountering new means, such as new possibilities, methods, and materials. Abductive reasoning uses a means-directed action pattern of deliberate varying. Because the abductive process is means-directed, however, the process offers no predictability as to what a pattern of deliberate varying will produce, if it produces anything at all."

"The random varying would cause transient thinking, and the deliberate varying would be the same as multi-relational thinking, which you also call abductive reasoning. I know you would not have much in the way of regularity from either of these. That must leave the regularity job to repetition, then."

"You are right. We get regularity from pattern or repetition. The non-verbal model also includes two sorts of repeating, 'simple' and 'complex.' Both types of repetition are goal-directed. Thus, the selection and rejection of materials and methods is based upon a desired outcome. Simple repetition is the direct replay of a pattern or process that is connected to producing a specific outcome. This would be like following a chocolate chip cookie recipe to produce chocolate chip cookies. Complex repetition involves the construction of a process or a general method in order to produce a new version of something. This would be like using the general method of cookie-making to develop a new recipe."

"And that is what I do. I like to make new versions of things."

"You certainly do. Now, I said earlier that both sorts of repetition are goal-directed, but the goal for complex replication is much more general than the kind used for simple repetition. Method, in this sense of complex replication, is a lot like Peirce's concept of having a hypothesis. Complex replication is not a sure thing. When you begin to make a new version of something, you have to think your way from the desired end backwards through potential materials and processes that you can adapt to achieve that end. In the course of doing this, you construct a pattern or plan for producing your outcome. Earlier, Peirce talked about needing to have a verifiable hypothesis. A hypothesis is a proposition similar to the general kind of goal you would have when you select and reject for complex repetition. Both simple and complex repetition make the biggest contributions to what Peirce refers to as regularity."

"Can you relate this to what Peirce means by regularity?"

"Imagine that you were composing a piece of music. What if random variation was the only basis you ever used for making choices? What if you completely avoided the actions of repetition and contrasting? What if you selected your next note only because it was different from whatever note you last used? What do you think would happen?"

"Not much. The piece of music would certainly not have a melody."

"Yes. It is possible that someone else might interpret such a haphazard collection of notes as an awful sounding piece of music. But we will pretend that there is no form of regularity in your choice-making process, only variety. All that you can produce with variety alone are different unconnected notes and not the thing, or pattern, that we call music. Now, imagine that we are talking about the way the whole universe works. Imagine what it would mean if every individual thing that exists, down to the smallest thing imaginable, were to operate independently of every other thing."

"Ah ha! That would be chaos."

"Right. If all that existed were differences among things, without any similarities, you could not possibly have what we know as reality. You could have an infinite number of differentiated individuals, but not reality. You have to have patterns to have reality. Patterns are forms, and form gives us regularity. Regularity is habit."

"So, patterns are ways of having regularity," Hal summarized, "and existence without regularity, which is habit, is nothing."

"Such existence is chaos. Chaos is the absence of any sort of regularity, pattern, or organizing system. For Peirce, chaos is every isolated, individual potentiality moving around randomly in an unrelated state. In other words, chaos is every isolated, unrelated possibility and nothing more. Therefore, just as unrelated notes are not music, chaos is no 'thing,' because you must have regularity to have either music or things. Since pure chaos contains no relationships, it has no regularity and is, therefore, nothing." By then I had started to wind down and said abruptly, "I guess that is it."

"Are we finished with this topic or with what we are going to do today?"

"We are finished with both for now. You appear to have a good grasp of this generals issue."

"I understand it now. Who knows if I can retain it until tomorrow."

"I bet you will!" I said, hoping to sound encouraging.

"Until tomorrow then," he said, kissing me on the cheek. "Thanks for doing this, honey. I am greatly enjoying it."

I was relieved that we had managed to survive this difficult section with his interest still intact.

Thirteen
EVOLUTION
AND THOUGHT

Essay lines 561-585

The following morning was wetter than usual, but still typical of the Pacific Northwest. Both of us were glad to nestle into the cottage, our steaming mugs of coffee in hand.

"Today, I am not going to bother with a review. We are just going to take up where we left off yesterday. Peirce had just finished off a paragraph by saying that 'generality is an indispensable ingredient of reality.' He begins the next paragraph by saying something you already know:"

That which any true proposition asserts is real, in the sense of being as it is regardless of what you or I may think about it. Let this proposition be a general conditional proposition as to the future, and it is a real general such as is calculated really to influence human conduct; and such the pragmaticist holds to be the rational purport of every concept.

"It sure does not sound like something I already know."

"What about the part that says that which any true proposition asserts is real, regardless of what you or I may think about it?"

"I understand that part. The second part stumps me."

"Peirce is just referring to what he said earlier, that the proposition is conditional because contained in the proposition are the conditions under which the phenomena predicted by that proposition will occur."

"And 'conditional to the future' means that it will happen in the future because it is a proposal?"

"Yes, and this proposal is a general also, because whenever the conditions are met, the proposal will be true."

"I understand that."

"Then I am going to read this excerpt again."

Let this proposition be a general conditional proposition as to the future, and it is a real general such as is calculated really to influence human conduct; and such the pragmaticist holds to be the rational purport of every concept.

"The reason why the pragmaticist's proposals influence human conduct," Hal offered, "is because you can change what you are going to do in advance of doing something, if you decide you want to, that is."

"Excellent! Here is the next part:"

Accordingly, the pragmaticist does not make the *summum bonum* to consist in action, but makes it to consist in that process of evolution whereby the existent comes more and more to embody those generals which were just now said to be destined, which is what we strive to express in calling them reasonable. In its higher stages, evolution takes place more and more largely through self-control, and this gives the pragmaticist a sort of justification for making the rational purport to be generals.

"*Summum bonum?*"

"It is Latin for the greatest good. Peirce is still responding to the fictitious Questioner here. He is addressing what the questioner said about pragmaticism making 'Doing the Be-all and End-all of human life'."

"Then, does Peirce mean that the pragmaticist makes generals the 'Be-all' instead of doing?"

"No. The pragmaticist makes the process of the evolution of generals the 'Be-all,' but only because they have come into being by means of thought controlled by rational, experimental logic."

"Yet he calls this 'evolution.' Does he mean evolution in the same sense as Darwin?"

"In part. The word 'evolution' meant unfolding well before Darwin used it. In another essay, 'Evolutionary Love,' Peirce says that there are three different modes of evolution. The first mode of evolution, fortuitous variation, is brought about by chance mutations that pop up within a species. The second kind occurs because of mechanical necessity, having to do with such things as changes in geological and climatic conditions."

"Like an asteroid hitting the earth?"

"Yes, and you could include global warming, or an ice age, or volcanic eruptions as well. Peirce said that the first two sorts of evolution involve conflict, survival of the fittest in a win-lose sense."

"What other kind could there be?"

"The third category according to Peirce eliminates the need for conflict. It is the type of evolutionary process proposed by Jean Baptiste Lamarck."

"Who is he?"

"Lamarck was a French naturalist who lived between 1744 and 1829."

"Is that the same time as Darwin?"

"They overlapped, but only slightly. Darwin was born in 1809. His *Origin of Species* was not published until 1859. He would probably have known about Lamarck's thesis that living things could inherit characteristics acquired by habit, use, or disuse. However most evolutionary biologists, right up to present times, have ridiculed Lamarck's theory of the inheritance of acquired characteristics."

"But Peirce liked Lamarck?"

"Yes. Lamarckian evolution appealed to him as an evolutionary concept built on a higher order of things, on a principle of universal harmony."

"Is there a problem with that?"

"That depends on who you are. As I said, most traditional evolutionary biologists think that evolution of acquired characteristics is an absurd idea. Peirce did not. In the essay, 'Evolutionary Love,' he wrote that Lamarckian evolution 'takes place in the domain of consciousness.' Peirce defines consciousness broadly, by the way. He also says we cannot deliberately make this type of evolution happen. We cannot 'will it' into being. This conscious evolution is done by means of a particular process, which we will discuss later."

"What is that process called?"

"Abduction. I do not want to go into that right here. What you need to realize for now is that Peirce's concept of evolution included a type of evolutionary process that practically every biologist on the face of the earth would exclude. Peirce considered evolution as the means for unfolding entities, including ideas and systems, into ever higher and more evolved forms already implicit in the system, that is, into waiting ideal forms."

"That is not what Darwin meant?"

"No. Darwin's concept of natural selection means that organisms that survive are the ones most able to adapt to their environments. That is not the same as saying that evolution is unfolding something waiting to be unfolded, or that it has any higher, or lower, stages. Nor does it mean that, at a higher level, evolution will take place by means of self-control."

"I think I see what you mean. Was Peirce wrong about evolution, then?"

"I am not so sure he was wrong. As far as I am concerned, the jury is still out on this. We need to know much more about consciousness and cosmology, before we can make such a judgment. Now, listen again to what Peirce says. 'In its higher stages, evolution takes place more and more largely through self-control, and this gives the pragmaticist a sort of justification for making the rational purport to be general'."

"By 'higher stages,' does Peirce just mean more deliberate?"

"In a sense. Remember, Peirce believed a reality exists out there and that good scientific method leads us closer and closer to discovering that reality. He compared discovery to the process of evolution. In his understanding, evolution can lead to the unfolding of organisms toward their ideal form, which is general. That is why he called abduction 'a logic of discovery,' instead of a logic of discovery and creativity, as you and I would call it."

"Hmm," Hal nodded thoughtfully at this. "I am starting to see the implications of this."

"Of what?"

"Of thinking that evolution takes place more and more through self-control," he said ominously. "That sounds like genetic engineering."

"Peirce could not possibly have meant that back then, though he could have been referring to the sorts of deliberate choices which farmers used for breeding certain qualities into plants and livestock. I am almost positive, though, that he is referring to Lamarckian evolution by means of abduction when he says that, 'in its higher stages evolution takes place more and more largely through self-control.' Even if he is also referring to the practice of controlled breeding as causing higher stages of evolution, he also means ideas. He also means higher stages of knowledge."

"Meaning that ideas evolve deliberately?"

"Yes. Peirce uses evolution to explain how he believes that thought evolves into higher stages along a continuum. His basic premise throughout this essay is that generals, as they are used for thinking, promote or retard the production of those consequences that he calls 'experimental phenomena'."

"I do not see the connection here."

"Evolution is a process by which certain characteristics are favored and others are not. In the first two kinds of evolution, chance variation and mechanical necessity, no apparent force controls the outcome. Something comes along and abruptly forces things inside the system to change or die out. In the third kind of evolution, a guiding force, or intelligence, controls the evolution of characteristics. In this third type of evolution, deliberate promoting and retarding of general characteristics occur under the direction of an intelligent force which, in the case of thinking we could also call a general proposition."

"What do you mean by 'promoting and retarding'?"

"'Promote' means to enable something to come into being, and 'retard' means to hold it back from coming into being. Both words connote the aspect of having deliberate control of future behavior. Peirce believed that a force exists in the universe, which he called evolutionary love. Evolutionary love is a fundamental force that guides the evolution of everything into harmonious balance. This force splits into patterns, habits, forms, and all other sorts of regular manifestations. When we discover a law of nature, we are discovering a general expression of one of these forms. This general expression provides us with general principles that we can use to effectively shape our future behaviors."

"Why do we shape our behaviors?"

"To bring ourselves into harmony with that law. We know if a law of nature is true or not by the outcomes we get when acting according to the principles of that law. Peirce proposes that the principles of right reasoning are a law of nature by which true ideas evolve. The principles of right reasoning are real things by which we can deliberately control our future behaviors to promote and retard the consequences we produce. By becoming more able to apply the general principles of right reasoning, we become more able to use our thinking process to deliberately promote the occurrence of some future consequences and retard the occurrence of others. According to Peirce, the ability to do this would mean that we are tapping into some fundamental law of nature.

This deliberate promoting and retarding of characteristics, mental or physical, is the fundamental process of all experimental research."

"Is one kind of proposition used to promote and another to retard?"

"No. Promote and retard work together. When I seek to promote one consequence, it means that I am also putting the brakes on something else. Sometimes, I may be more focused on getting something to not happen than I am on getting it to happen, or the other way around. Regardless of my focus, promoting and retarding are an inseparable pair. They are an inseparable pair that we use deliberately when we seek to control future conduct."

"How does that work?"

"Think back to Shannon and her blackberry pie recipe. Her recipe is a method for promoting certain characteristics in her pie and for retarding others. For example, oven temperature and baking time are a basis for promoting the outcome of certain qualities and retarding the production of others. Time and temperature are the means for producing a thoroughly baked pie with a golden brown crust. At the same time, they are also a means for retarding the production of those qualities that would result if it were underdone or overdone. If you are not aware that a double-edged nature exists when promoting or retarding certain characteristics, you can end up with unintended consequences. Sometimes these consequences can be disastrous, like the ones I see ahead from global warming and genetic engineering."

"I see that too."

"Just as all forms of scientific methods do, Peirce's pragmaticism deals with this process of deliberately promoting and retarding certain traits. However, Peirce also addresses the promotion and retarding of the consequences due to over-riding values, purposes, and hypotheses as well as those resulting from testing a particular proposition."

"Can you give another example of promoting and retarding?"

"Sure. Growers, for instance, can deliberately promote the qualities that give ripe tomatoes a longer shelf-life by retarding those characteristics that cause them to rot quickly."

"True, but as a result, you have tomatoes that taste like cardboard."

"I agree. Perhaps the qualities of taste and texture were not high priorities for whoever developed the tomato proposition. However, the general proposition of creating a longer shelf-life for ripe tomatoes carried within it the aim of promoting certain characteristics and retarding others. The results of promoting and retarding are experimental phenomena. Sometimes, as with the cardboard tomatoes, you also promote or retard some unintended characteristics as well. Cardboard tomatoes are just a trivial example why the formulation of a hypothesis matters so much for an inquiry. If you just grab goals out of thin air, the way science and technology does these days, you can end up creating bigger problems than the ones you are trying to solve. Cardboard tomatoes can stand for all kinds of environmental and social degradation brought about by poorly formulated hypotheses. If people knew how to construct propositions in the way that Peirce proposed, we would not have so much junk science and spooky technology going on as we do today."

"I know what you mean. I bet no one was minding the consequences of the industrial age back in Peirce's day, just as no one is minding the consequences of things like genetic engineering today."

"These are reasons why ordinary people need to learn how to engage intelligence on a day-to-day, moment-to-moment basis. Carl G. Jung wrote, back in 1947, that our minds are at such a low state of development compared to our technological advances that we are like 'primitives left in charge of dangerous playthings.' The situation is even worse today. All sorts of consequences are being promoted and retarded by both deliberate and non-deliberate conduct, and few people are even aware that potential problems might be ahead. I remember hearing someone comment a while back that the biggest problem that we have in the world today is population of several billion 'rusting brains.' The gears cannot engage when brains are rusted, and that is why our work matters so much."

"Because of rusting brains?"

"Yes. Regardless of intelligence, culture, or educational levels, people need to learn to be reasonable, how to be 'reason' 'able.' We know from raising Tonya and Andrea that a person does not have to be either intelligent or highly educated to be reason-able. We also know countless examples of people who are both highly intelligent and well-educated who cannot reason well. This world needs a population made up of rational minds if we are to promote good consequences for our planet and effectively retard negative ones. We can only effect change by changing our conduct. We can only effectively change our conduct by understanding what needs changing and how to change it."

"Figuring that out is a tough order. I wonder which is harder, knowing what to change or knowing how?"

"Peirce thoroughly covered both of those issues in his theory of right reasoning. He believed that an ideal reality is available to us by which we can check out our choice-making. By means of abductive reasoning, we can come ever closer to discovering what that ideal reality is."

"How do we know if we are discovering the ideal reality of something?"

"Because, if we are wrong about something, our proposition will not play out properly. It will not produce the effects that we say it will if it is not unfolding in accordance with general laws that govern the way things really are."

"Are these general laws the same things as the laws of nature?"

"Yes. Peirce conceives these laws as general forms just waiting to be unfolded into, in the same sense that he thinks that living organisms evolve into ever higher forms. When we discover and validate a general law, we have formulated a proposition that has correctly predicted the occurrence of certain experimental phenomena. In this sense, these phenomena, or consequences, come under the governance of general principles. These general principles are destined because they are available for discovery by means of rational thought. This is what pragmaticists mean when they call something reasonable."

"I do not think I understand what you mean by that."

"By what?"

"I do not understand what pragmaticists mean by 'reasonable'."

"Reasonable means able to be determined by means of reason."

"Or able to reason?"

"Yes. Reasonable also means 'able to reason.' Although that is not exactly what Peirce means here, you must be able to reason if you are to discover and develop something capable of being reasoned about."

"I wager that most people think they are being reasonable even when they are not."

"You are probably right about that. As I have said before, 'it is not what people don't know that causes problems.'"

"'It is what they don't know that they don't know,' right?"

"Right. Other than having never encountered something, whenever we are ignorant and 'don't know that we don't know,' either we are not noticing reactions to what we do, or else we are incorrectly interpreting the meanings of these reactions."

"That reminds me of an article I saved for you from the *New York Times*," Hal said. "I brought it out here for you to read, so it must be somewhere in that pile of stuff on your desk." He began searching through a stack of papers on my desk. "The article is about the research of David Dunning, who is a psychology professor at Cornell. His research shows that most incompetent people have no idea that they are incompetent. Here it is:"

One reason that the ignorant also tend to be so blissfully self-assured, the researchers believe, is that the skills required for competence often are the same skills necessary for recognizing competence.[7]

"That is exactly what I am getting at!" I said enthusiastically. "As a teacher, my most difficult problem was getting students to want to develop the skills for noticing consequences and for interpreting these correctly. I often found that I needed to put on a theatrical performance, just to wake some students up long enough to get them to recognize that they did not already know everything. I have heard from some teachers that this problem is even worse today. I wonder if it is a consequence of too much television-watching."

"We have had the same problems working with corporations," Hal reminded me. "Just think how difficult a time we have had trying to get anything across to managers and workers who 'do not know what it is they don't know.' That blissful self-assurance of the ignorant is a big problem in corporate America as well."

"In education," I added, "students are not the only ones who can display the blissful self-assurance of ignorance. I hate to think how many teachers are operating from that state as well. Getting students to pay attention is only one part of the process. Once you wake them up, what do you do then? Do you teach them facts and data? Do you help them learn how to engage their minds in the learning process? Can you do both? Teachers and students become co-learners when they develop the skills for recognizing competence. To develop these skills, both teachers and students need to have the ability to engage their intelligences. They both become participants in learning instead of one being the performer and the rest spectators."

"I imagine that could be threatening to some people," Hal said, "especially those who like to perform."

"I imagine so, though I am one of those who likes to perform. However, teaching reasoning skills is much more difficult than performing is. It is much easier to hand out facts and data, especially if the students like you. Yet, even when students like their teachers, they may become upset when required to learn how to reason more effectively. Learning how to reason well is hard work for both the teacher and the learner. Outside pressures also work against teaching children how to reason. Not only are many parents unaware of the need for their children to develop reasoning skills, but some highly vocal parents even oppose their children learning anything but facts and information. Just try getting people to engage their minds in learning when they absolutely believe that learning is the same thing as gathering facts and information. Reasoning ability of the sort Peirce proposes is not a pencil-and-paper skill. It is an engaged process."

"Then, maybe Peirce was adding a fourth 'R'."

"What do you mean?"

"I mean," Hal said, "maybe Peirce was adding 'reasoning' to the old-fashioned three 'R's of 'reading, writing, and 'rithmetic'."

"Yes. He would have agreed that we should add reasoning to the basic curriculum. Reasoning should be one of the basic skills that all students should be expected to master. It is something you need to be able to do in order to make use of knowledge. Unfortunately, this fourth 'R' is still practically invisible to most people."

"Contributing to the bliss of ignorance?"

"Probably so," I agreed. "In any case, reasoning is a process of formulating relationships among qualities and the things they qualify. This process is invisible, and that is the main difficulty in bringing reasoning into focus as an educational basic. Most people think that they reason perfectly well and do not see why they need to learn how to reason more effectively. Listen to this. It is from one of Peirce's early essays."

> Few persons care to study logic, because everybody conceives himself to be proficient enough in the art of reasoning already. But I observe that this satisfaction is limited to one's own [reasoning process] and does not extend to that of other men.[8]

"Interesting. So people think that other people need to improve their reasoning abilities, but not themselves?"

"Yes, and this is a big problem, an especially big problem when teaching well-educated people to reason more effectively. Most well-educated people figure that they must be doing it just fine, or they would not have their degrees. Teachers are among the toughest nuts to crack when it comes to recognizing the need for upgrading their reasoning skills."

"Why do you think that is?"

"Peirce had something to say on this matter. I keep this quote from one of his 1887 Cambridge lectures taped right here to the side of my computer."

In order that a man's whole heart may be in teaching he must be thoroughly imbued with the vital importance and absolute truth of what he has to teach; while in order that he may have any measure of success in learning he must be penetrated with a sense of unsatisfactoriness of his present condition of knowledge. The two attitudes are almost irreconcilable.... Just as it is not the self-righteous man who brings multitudes to a sense of sin, but the man who is most deeply conscious that he is himself a sinner...; so it is not the man who thinks he knows it all, that can bring other men to feel their need of learning, and it is only a deep sense that one is miserably ignorant that can spur one on in the toilsome path of learning. That is why, to my humble apprehension, it cannot but seem that those admirable pedagogical methods for which the American teacher is distinguished are of little more consequence than the cut of his coat, that they surely are as nothing compared with that fever for learning that must consume the soul of the man who is to infect others with that same apparent malady.[9]

"Wow!" Hal said. "Peirce sure did have some opinions about this!"

"He sure did. Peirce would have argued that it is much more vital that teachers learn how to help students ask and explore the right questions than to smugly hand over information. People who believe they have already asked the right questions, or that they already have the answers, can be exceedingly dangerous. They are unaware of so much that they can be lethal."

"Is that because they 'don't know what they don't know'?"

"Yes. Peirce contended that, to be a good educator, you must be a good pragmaticist," I explained. "Educators should be experimentalists and never lock up their minds. Pragmaticist educators are learners as much as teachers."

"But teachers have to teach something. Children have to learn basic skills like reading and math."

"Sure they do," I agreed. "And I would add that learning to think like an experimentalist is one of those skills. But Peirce was mainly referring here to the fact-mongers, to people so full of facts and information that they do not know anything about learning."

"I recall that Peirce used a word for teachers like this."

"Was the word 'pedant'?"

"Yes."

"Pedantry means stressing the trivial details of learning," I reminded him. "I am not as radical as Peirce was, however. I do not think that such a dichotomy between teaching and learning is necessary, or even wise. All students need to know certain fundamental facts, skills, and bodies of knowledge. All teachers should be required to help students learn these. I consider it a crime that there is no standardized curriculum for grade levels."

"What do you mean?"

"I mean that, at many schools these days teachers are free to cover whatever they want to cover. Some students never read a Shakespearean play during high school, while some read the same play twice. Many never read *The Odyssey*, or encounter an historical time-line. We have practically a whole generation of young adults among us who do not even know what *Aesop's Fables* are, nor even what the word 'fable' means."

"Do you think that everyone should be taught the same things?"

"I agree with those who think that there should be a basic core curriculum at each grade level," I answered. "Everyone who makes it through that grade level should have experienced the same subject matter and should have developed the same core competencies for that grade level. I am not totally opposed to rote work and repetition, either. In some cases, the only way to get skills and information across is by throwing it at children as facts and information and requiring them to engage in rote work and repetition to reach a level of mastery. Besides, that is the only way that some people learn."

"By rote work and repetition?"

"Yes. As you know, direct reasoners learn best this way. Regardless of reasoning habits, however, certain skills can only be mastered by means of repetition. This is especially so in the elementary grades. Besides, not every child comes to a classroom imbued with natural curiosity. Some children are probably never going to become curious, no matter what you do. The best you will ever be able to do for those children is require them to master skills through repetition and try to put lots of information inside their brains."

"We sure know that is true!"

Hal and I understand that some people have a temperamental preference for gathering up archaic facts and data. Their quest for more data is not the same thing as "the will to learn" in Peirce's sense. Just as many dedicated teachers are not pre-disposed to become learners, so too, many students (even some with straight A grade averages) are not learners as well. At least, they are not learners in the way Peirce meant.

"Keep in mind that teachers are in the trenches and that Peirce never was," I added. "He never even attended elementary school. He was tutored at home by his father, who was a mathematics professor. Peirce never raised any children either. Based upon his own narrow experience of life, Peirce made untested assumptions about what everybody who is intelligent should or should not be innately capable of doing. We know he was wrong about many of these assumptions because of the testing we have done with Dottie's non-verbal assessment. Peirce's theory provides us with the ideal, with what we should all be aiming for, but he does not provide much of a roadmap for getting there. That is why Dottie's non-verbal model and Engaged Intelligence training matter so much."

"What do you do about people who only want to gather or teach data? We know lots of them are bouncing around out there. What would you do about that?"

"Just what we do in Engaged Intelligence training. I said before that facts and information are important. They are like the raw materials for thinking. I consider teachers who are subject matter experts to be valuable commodities in the educational system."

"Even if they just want to teach facts and information?"

"Sure. Just because people want to do one thing does not mean that they cannot do something else as well. Everyone can learn how to do this type of thinking that Peirce proposes, and anyone can apply it to helping students learn to reason better in any subject. Subject matter experts are vital for improving the educational system. They should begin sharing their stores of knowledge with other teachers who may be less experienced or less knowledgeable in subject matter than they are. One of the things I liked least about teaching was working with teachers whose petty jealousies kept them from learning from other teachers. I also disliked the stinginess of some teachers, who were not interested in sharing materials they had developed. Educators should think of themselves as part of the same team, regardless of what they teach and where they are teaching. There should be no petty fiefdoms, professional jealousies, or stinginess among educators. Educators should cooperate among one another to raise the quality of learning in everyone's classroom. In education, as in science, nobody wins unless everyone does."

"I wonder how you would convince educators to do that."

"Do what?"

"How would you convince educators to work as a team? From what I saw when the kids were in school, most teachers act if they are free agents."

"It would take a paradigm shift, that is for sure, but this shift must happen if we are to reform the educational system. My guess is that the schools having the most success helping children learn have faculties made up of educators who operate like 'a loosely compacted individual.' According to Peirce, this is the only way for knowledge to evolve, by engaging critical thinking skills and by sharing knowledge with each other."

"That sounds like a good goal."

"I think so, too. But we would have to get past the solid brick wall made up of those people who do not think they need to infect students with the 'will to learn.' An even bigger wall is the one made up of those who think they already know everything they need to know."

"Do you mean the ones who are 'so ignorant that they cannot even recognize the skills needed for competency'?"

"That would be them. Ignorant people tend to block the route of inquiry. Peirce contends that human minds are far too fallible to have enough certainty to justify closing off any direction as a route for inquiry. All people who think they already know everything about something, regardless of education or intelligence, are not only likely to be dead wrong, but they are also sure to be dead weights. They are sure to be holding back the advance of knowledge."

"That same thing is true in business as well," Hal added.

"Yes, it is. Peirce wants to demonstrate that a particular logical method exists for discovering new relationships, for unfolding the relationships that are waiting to be discovered. He contends that his new logical method is the mechanism by which higher levels of knowledge evolve. This is the logical method by which new discoveries are made."

"Is the unfolding of discoveries the main point of his theory?"

"He feels that this method for unfolding discoveries is the main point," I answered. "But Peirce's theory is an interconnected whole. It includes three kinds of logic. The first is the logic of asking the right questions, which he called 'abduction.' The second is the logic of figuring out how to answer those questions, which is 'deduction.' And the third is the logical method for generalizing and fixing beliefs, which is 'induction.' Peirce's theory of a logic of discovery is vital, but not the main part. Peirce's pragmaticism contains no main part because it is all one piece. Peirce explains this in his doctrine of continuity. However, that has not prevented people from extracting pieces and parts of his theory for different purposes, without bothering to figure out how it connects together as a whole."

"I can see why people would chop it up into pieces," Hal said. "This theory is hard to get your arms around."

"I know what you mean. However, we need to have a complete and coherent system of reasoning. Just think of what it would be like if each logical method were separate unto itself. What if all that humankind did was to use abductive reasoning, relating things to one another in interesting ways? What if no one bothered to set up plans or construct methods for testing out relationships? We might create and discover many interesting things, but we would never arrive at the necessary general principles for figuring out how to make them applicable to future situations. Or, what if humankind only used general principles already in existence? Peirce called these *a priori* principles. What if humankind spent all of its energies on the development of things based on these *a priori* principles, without ever re-examining them to see if they remain valid? We might manage some innovations, but would never discover or develop anything truly new. However, if all that humankind did was replicate versions of things already in existence, we would have neither new discoveries nor improvements, just more of the same. And, if all that humankind did was respond randomly to whatever popped up in a given moment, we would not have much of anything at all."

"Those sound like the non-verbal reasoning processes."

"Yes, I am describing the four primary reasoning habits, which are multi-relational, analytical, direct, and spontaneous. Using Peirce's terms, we could call these abductive, deductive, and inductive."

"I can only count three there."

"You count only three, because there is no formal reasoning method for the spontaneous habit. People who employ this habit jump capriciously from thing to thing and idea to idea. Unlike the others, spontaneous thinkers make inferences randomly, as someone might during a brainstorming session. They usually come up quickly with an option of some sort, though their ideas are poorly thought out. As you know, spontaneous thinkers are the most flexible of all the types, and the most ineffective as well."

"We have sure seen enough of that before," Hal said, ruefully. He once hired a salesman who operated this way, and we lost several customers due to that fellow's unpredictability and lack of follow-through.

"We sure have!" I agreed, then continued. "Just as for Peirce's *logica docens*, the *logica utens* habits of Dottie's non-verbal model need one another to produce good effects. No single process on its own is going to get us out of the big messes we have created for ourselves. We need each of these methods operating appropriately on what each is best suited to do. This is one reason why Peirce was so emphatic about his version of scientific method. He was the victim of a science for which *a priori* truths were the norm and of a society for which authority, habit, and tradition were the only valid sources of social reasoning. Peirce argued for his theory of the logic of discovery as a way to overcome what he felt were the negative aspects of science and society as a whole. He was a great believer in the power of the human mind to reason rightly. To lay out what this meant, he had to address this issue of generals and specifics."

"Is that because generals guide what we think about?"

"Yes! Peirce believed that if we used his version of the method of science to discover general laws, then the consequences of what we discovered would also be beautiful, moral, and true. That was a main purpose of his pragmatism," I added, "to lay out the way that general laws should be discovered, developed, and put into practice."

"I can see that."

"Good." I then continued reading from Peirce's text.

There is much more in elucidation of pragmaticism that might be said to advantage, were it not for the dread of fatiguing the reader. It might, for example, have been well to show clearly that the pragmaticist does not attribute any different essential mode of being to an event in the future from that which he would attribute to a similar event in the past, but only that the practical attitude of the thinker toward the two is different. It would also have been well to show that the pragmaticist does not make Forms to be the only realities in the world, any more than he makes the reasonable purport of a word to be the only kind of meaning there is. These things are, however, implicitly involved in what has been said.

"All Peirce is saying here is that he is not claiming that someone's mode of being was any different when he experienced an event in the past as it might be in the future for a similar event."

"I thought he did say that!"

"Peirce is talking about 'mode of being' here, not about propositions and changing future conduct. 'Mode of being' is a person's way of being conscious. Your mode of being, your 'isness' or 'essence,' does not need to change in Peirce's pragmaticism. All that needs to change is the practical attitude from which you approach the future."

"So, my practical attitude changes as to what I am going to choose to do in the future, but my basic mode of being does not change," Hal repeated. "This whole theory of Peirce's sounds a lot like *Groundhog Day!*"

If you have never heard of *Groundhog Day*, you will need to know that Hal was referring to a movie that came out during the 1990s. The plot details the problems of a ne'er do-well television weatherman sent out to cover *Groundhog Day* ceremonies in Paduca, Pennsylvania. As a bizarre cosmic retribution for his perpetually obnoxious behavior, this weatherman has to endure the exact same day repeatedly. Day after day, everything that occurs, down to the smallest detail, is exactly the same. All that he can possibly change are his own future behaviors and his 'practical attitude' toward the future.

"*Groundhog Day* is an excellent example of how the 'control of future conduct' issue works. This is a good place for us to stop."

"Fine with me. Besides, I could use another cup of coffee."

"That sounds good to me."

At that, we gathered up our umbrellas and headed down the block to the Wild Coho. There we were sure to meet up with at least one or two of our neighbors also seeking escape from the dreariness of that morning's insistent drizzle.

Fourteen
CONSTRUCTING
A CONDITIONAL PURPOSE

This day, I had to make a decision about whether I should leave something out of this discussion. Peirce's original essay included a long paragraph about a distinction between his logic and Aristotle's logic. I could see that adding in this passage would do little more than take us on a long diversion. I would have to discuss Aristotelian logic in order to demonstrate Peirce's distinction, one that did not matter all that much for my purposes anyway. I decided to ignore the passage altogether.

"We are starting to wind down," I said as we began that morning. "I am going to begin here with the end of the paragraph we discussed yesterday. Here is what Peirce adds to what he omitted in this essay:"

It would also have been well to show that the pragmaticist does not make Forms to be the only realities in the world, any more than he makes the reasonable purport of a word to be the only kind of meaning there is. These things are, however, implicitly involved in what has been said.

"What does he mean by forms? He did not say anything about forms."

"Sure, he did! Peirce talked about forms and patterns when he discussed generality and regularity. He explained that nouns are forms, as well. We also talked about rules of syntax as the form of sentences?"

"Oh, yes. I remember that now."

"Peirce concedes that forms are not the only realities in the world. Nor is the 'reasonable meaning of a word' the only kind of meaning there is. But, the reality of form and the reasonable purport, or meaning, of words are implicitly involved in what he has been discussing here."

"Meaning?"

"Meaning that, even though form and rational meaning are not the only kinds of meanings that exist, they are to be understood as belonging to what Peirce calls pragmaticism."

"Like nouns and general categories?"

"Right! Now, in true Peircean form, just as he is about to end his essay, he introduces a new concept."

"What is it?"

"Abduction."

"But we have talked about that before."

"That we have, but I did not explain how it works. Peirce leads us into the topic with his usual wordiness."

Suffer me to add one word more on this point—for, if one cares at all to know what the pragmaticist theory consists in, one must understand that there is no other part of it to which the pragmaticist attaches quite as much importance as he does to the recognition in his doctrine of the utter inadequacy of action or volition or even of resolve or actual purpose, as materials out of which to construct a conditional purpose or the concept of conditional purpose.

I stopped here to explain.

"This does not mean that it is impossible to 'construct' a conditional purpose. It means that 'when constructing' conditional purposes, 'action, volition, resolve, or actual purpose' are not enough. They can even get in the way."

"Then, does that mean that you do not do anything at all?"

"No. Do you know what he means by 'a conditional purpose'?"

"Is that the same as a provisional truth?"

"Conditional...provisional," I repeated, "I can see how you would mix these up. But no, they are not the same. A provisional truth is more like a belief. It is something you act on as if it were true. Provisional truths can even become 'beliefs unassailable by doubt.' Conditional purposes are propositions, or hypotheses."

"Then a provisional truth is like a belief, and a conditional purpose is like a proposition or hypothesis?"

"Yes." I decided that this was a sufficient definition of terms for now. "Now, think about these terms when Peirce says that the most important part of his pragmaticist theory is the 'inadequacy of action, volition, resolve, or actual purpose' as materials out of which to construct a conditional purpose."

"What does he mean by materials? How can 'action' or 'purpose' be materials?"

"A purpose is like a goal. Peirce means you cannot construct conditional purposes or even the concept of conditional purposes by taking action or by rearranging what you already know to be true into a goal."

"Why not?"

"Because a goal, or a 'conditional purpose' as Peirce calls it, presupposes an end-point or outcome," I told him. "Remember, once you begin to take action, or decide to take action, or actually have a goal, you are acting on a belief in an experimental phenomenon. This belief functions just like any goal. Whenever you have a goal, or belief in an outcome, that goal directs what you select and reject. You cannot, according to Peirce, construct a conditional purpose when you already have a purpose directing what you choose to do. "

"What do you do with a conditional purpose?"

"You can do pretty much the same thing with a conditional purpose as you do with an actual purpose, once you have it, that is. However, Peirce is addressing the 'construction of a conditional purpose' and 'the construction of a concept of a conditional purpose'."

"Then what makes it conditional if you do the same thing with it?"

"The conditional aspect of a conditional purpose is that it is a hypothesis has not been thoroughly tested yet. Thus, it is open to change, revision, or even complete abandonment should circumstances warrant. Even actual purposes are conditional in the sense that they are subject to future conditions. But Peirce is addressing the 'construction of' a conditional purpose here, not what you do with it."

"Let me see if I understand this. Are you are telling me that Peirce makes a distinction between 'figuring out how to accomplish' a purpose and 'constructing a purpose' in the first place?"

Hal's question took me by surprise. How could we have come this far without my having made a clear distinction between "having" and "constructing" a purpose? All along, I thought Hal realized what Peirce meant by abduction and hypothesizing, because he knows what our non-verbal theory means by multi-relational thinking. I decided to ask a few questions to see how far apart we were in his understanding of this.

"Is that unusual to you?" I asked casually.

"Not unusual, just picky. Constructing a purpose is a straightforward activity as far as I can tell. You decide what you want and then figure out how to get it. I fail to see the big deal about it, or why Peirce should say that this part of his theory has the greatest importance."

I sighed at this. We were going to have to spend some serious time together discussing abduction, multi-relational thinking, and continuity. If Hal did not understand the connection, given all he knows about non-verbal reasoning, maybe an analogy would help.

"I want you to suppose that we know three couples who are going to have a home built," I proposed. "Building a home is the intention. We will say that each couple uses a different method for developing a conditional purpose, or goal, for building a house."

"What are the methods?"

"Choosing, planning, and designing. I will call couple number one, Mr. and Mrs. Blue. I will call couple number two, Mr. and Mrs. Orange. Couple three, will be Mr. and Mrs. Red. Now, suppose that Mr. and Mrs. Blue decide that they want to have their home built in a particular subdivision. The developer of this subdivision has three different models of home styles available. Once the Blues decide which home they want built, they are allowed to choose the lot they want and to select the colors of tile, paint, carpeting, and so on."

"That sounds to me like the way Tonya and Merrill built their house."

"It is," I agreed. "So, which method would you say that Mr. and Mrs. Blue used to build their home?"

"Choosing."

"Yes. Mr. and Mrs. Blue are operating on what Peirce would call an actual purpose."

"I see that."

"Mr. and Mrs. Orange, on the other hand, love the Cape Cod colonial style of houses and have decided that they want to have a home of this sort built for them. They find a lot in a neighborhood they like. Then they contact an architect to help them describe all of the special amenities they want to include in their home. Together, the Oranges and the architect develop and refine the plans for the new home. Which method would you say this couple used?"

"What are my choices?"

"Choosing, planning, or designing."

"Uh, planning probably, but there was designing going on too. There had to be, since they were building a custom home."

"But they already knew what style of home they wanted," I countered. "In their case, they already had a general idea of what they wanted in the end. Planning was the highest level of reasoning that the Oranges used."

"Oh, I see that."

"This planning is like figuring out how to prove a general proposition. The Oranges began with a conditional purpose. They already had a general proposal of what they wanted. Then they set out to develop plans for putting their general proposal into action."

"I understand that."

"The Reds are an entirely different story. Well before ever deciding to build a home, Jim Red found an interesting piece of castaway aluminum sheeting that had an accidental design element to it. He thought that the sheeting might look interesting in relation to some chain-link fencing. He imagined a balcony overlooking a living area that used the chain-link fencing as balcony railing. Then the aluminum sheeting could be used above the fireplace, giving an interesting visual element to the balcony. Throughout the whole process of deciding on a home, the Reds are never completely sure how their new home will end up looking."

"You are describing Jim and Rachel Cliftons' home!" He interrupted, referring to a family we know whose house is a favorite of design magazines.

"Yes, it is. And there was even more of this relating going on before they ever bought their land, decided how to lay out the flow of the house, or chose a builder."

"That would be the designing sort, or multi-relational thinking, for sure."

"Yes, multi-relational thinking is correct. The Cliftons' method of house design reflects the 'construction of a conditional purpose.' Multi-relational thinking, what Peirce called 'abductive' reasoning, always deals in constructing conditional purposes. The Cliftons eventually had plans and even used them to communicate with their builder, but these plans came at the end of a long process of formulating the qualities that they wanted for their home. The formation of the conditional purpose, the overall design of that house, took up most of their mental time and energy. Even after they defined the conditional purpose in the form of blueprints, plans still evolved in a sense. Even during construction, the design still continued to change and evolve as new possibilities came along."

"That sure is true. Do you remember when they bought up those stainless steel cabinets and the shelving from the old Cabrini Hospital?"

"Yes, I remember, and I remember the giant food mixer as well. Those cabinets and other kitchen tools entirely changed the plans for the kitchen. This is a physical example of 'means directing the development of a goal,' instead of 'a goal directing the means selected.' In both the subdivision and the custom homes, the goal was an existing plan which dictated what could and could not be used as materials. Neither of those pre-planned homes could accommodate the style and dimensions of those hospital kitchen cabinets and cooking tools."

"Is that what Peirce means by a 'conditional purpose?' Does he mean that the materials change the goal?"

"That is what he means by 'constructing a conditional purpose.' Once a conditional purpose is constructed, you set about to prove it, or in this case, to build it."

"How does that apply to the Cliftons' house? The Cliftons acted conditionally all the way through."

"No, they did not act conditionally all the way through. They did get their home built, so they had to move into production at some point. They had blueprints and building permits that let them do this. The Cliftons employed a reciprocal process for designing and building that house. The word 'reciprocal' signifies that first the means, which include materials, ideas, tools, and other resources, direct the formation of a goal. Then that goal directs the selection of means for a while. Then, when something new comes along, the new option directs the formation of the goal again. That ongoing reciprocity is characteristic of multi-relational reasoning tempered by analytical reasoning."

"And of abductive reasoning?"

"Abduction tempered by deduction and induction," I corrected. "The Cliftons home-building experience is an example of how to 'construct a conditional purpose.' A conditional purpose is only one part of the equation. In the case of Peirce's *logica docens*, his formal logic, you would be in another mode once you made blueprints and started construction. The Cliftons house is an original, one-of-a-kind outcome, like an original piece of art. But Peirce was not after one-of-a-kind outcomes. His concept of 'constructing a conditional purpose' implies that abduction is going to be used in conjunction with deduction and simple induction to construct, develop, and validate a hypothesis."

"Is that because pragmaticism does not deal with single phenomena?"

"Yes. Pragmaticism concerns itself with general laws and principles. The process of abductive reasoning is general in the sense that it is a form. It is a pattern of mental and physical actions that are generative, rather than deductive or inductive."

"Just what is abduction then?"

"Abduction is a pattern of actions which, when applied to creative endeavors, produces unique and original ideas. These may then be manifested as artistic expressions or...."

"Where is the general part in this?"

"The general part is in the method used to make the discoveries or create the unique and original ideas. Abduction is the pattern of actions for making unique and unusual relationships among things and ideas. The 'pattern of actions' is the general here."

"If you get one-of-a-kind ideas as a result of using abduction for doing art, then what do you get when it is applied to science?"

"You get the same thing. Only in science the ideas are formed as hunches that are eventually expressed as hypotheses."

"Yet, you said using abduction for art produces original, one-of-a-kind things," he argued. "That would make each one a single phenomenon."

"The methods of art and the methods of science are the same methods, but applied with different emphasis, for different purposes. Artists want to produce a single phenomenon. The qualitative singularity of an artistic creation adds to its value. Once someone makes a plan to reproduce a unique piece of art, we could say that this plan is a 'conditional purpose.' When artists make multiple copies of the same thing, they reduce the value of the original piece. Replication is bad news in art, because it results in cliché, or knock-offs, as they are called in some circles."

"And science?"

"Science is just the opposite. In science, the whole point is to be able to replicate something. In science, you want to be able to establish conditions and predict the phenomena that will occur under those conditions by repeatedly testing these. The point of science is to make a good hypothesis and to replicate the conditions and actions of the proposal until you prove or disprove its validity. Nevertheless, good science starts at the same place where good art begins. Unique, or single, phenomena are the property of all creative reasoning, even in science. This is where I think Peirce became stuck."

"On single phenomena?"

"No, on abductive reasoning, his logic of discovery. As Peirce struggled to define his theory of discovery, he used two terms, 'abduction' and 'retroduction.' In most of his writings, it appears that he is using these terms interchangeably, even though he also appears at times to be describing several different types of abduction." I reached over and found a recent article by Jaakko

Hintikka in the summer 1998 *Transactions of the Charles S. Peirce Society.*
"Here, listen to this."

> It is sometimes said that the highest philosophical gift is to invent important new philosophical problems. If so, Peirce is a major star in the firmament of philosophy. By thrusting the notion of abduction to the forefront of philosophers' consciousness he created a problem which, I will argue, is the central one in contemporary epistemology.[10]

"What is epistemology?"

"Epistemology is the branch of philosophy that has to do with theories of knowledge," I told him, "with investigating the origins, forms, methods and validity of knowledge."

"Does Peirce's theory belong in the branch of epistemology?"

"Many issues he brings up belong there. Dottie's non-verbal reasoning model is epistemological. This means that Relational Thinking Styles is a theory about how we come to know things."

"Oh."

"The author I just quoted is making the claim that Peirce's notion of abduction is 'the central problem in contemporary epistemology'."

"I see that."

"Another philosopher, Tomis Kapitan, divided Peirce's different descriptions of abduction into four separate theses," I said, then read directly from Kapitan's list, which Hintikka had cited in his article.

1. Inferential thesis. Abduction is, or includes, an inferential process or processes.
2. Thesis of purpose. The purpose of 'scientific' abduction is both to (1) generate new hypotheses and (2) to select hypotheses for further examination, hence, a central aim of scientific abduction is to 'recommend a course of action.'
3. Comprehension Thesis. Scientific abduction includes all the operations whereby theories are engendered.
4. Autonomy Thesis. Abduction is, or embodies, reasoning that is distinct from, and irreducible to, either deduction or induction.[11]

"Which one of them are we using?"

"We are using all of them. Peirce described abduction in all four of those ways. We loosely group together numbers one, two, and four, the 'inferential,' 'purpose,' and 'autonomy' theses to cover our meaning of the term 'abduction.' We use number three, 'comprehension' thesis, for the reciprocal process that we refer to as 'retroduction.' Dottie's theory defines retroduction as abduction deliberately tempered by deduction and induction."

"Are you saying Peirce did not mean retroduction the way Dottie did?"

"No, he did not."

"You said Peirce had a problem with his theory of abduction. What if he had just divided things up the way you have here?"

"It would probably not have helped," I answered. Then I decided I should explain why. "Peirce did not believe a logic of creativity could exist in an aesthetic sense. He believed that aesthetics could only be a firstness state. Firstness includes impulse, feeling, intensity, and beingness. I suspect that he was trapped by this belief that aesthetics is only a firstness state and that this kept him from noticing that aesthetics requires forms of reasoning comparable to logic. The logic of discovery and the logic of creativity use the same methods. I suspect that separating abduction from retroduction would only have helped if he could have brought himself to think about aesthetics differently."

"Why do you think he became stuck there?"

"One reason was because he could not leave language out of the equation. Dottie's non-verbal model demonstrates where he was mistaken. Peirce's pragmaticism is concerned with the construction of conditional purposes, with identifying, forming and eventually, researching good hypotheses. To construct conditional purposes for philosophy, science, or anything else, you must approach matters in the same way as the Cliftons did when they built their home. This approach requires that you apply the same aesthetic processes that Dottie addresses. The Cliftons engaged in an act of first creating something new and unique, instead of developing an existing hypothesis and then setting out to prove it. Unique art unfolds multi-relationally, or abductively, by the interaction of materials, methods, and ideas. These interact within the context of certain principles, but without ever getting into the construction and development of actual goals."

"Was Peirce interested in goals?"

"He was interested in discovery instead of creation. This leads to a bias for the formation and proof, or disproof, of hypotheses, which are sorts of goals. Peirce believed that both natural science and philosophy should be a process of unfolding truth. They should be aimed at developing greater understanding of natural laws and principles."

"I can see a big difference between discovery and creation. I guess I am on Peirce's side, though. I fail to see how you could use the same process to both discover and create."

"The difference is in what you use abductive reasoning to do. If you are noticing qualitative similarities and differences and your mind is focused just on the act of making qualitative relationships among things, you are going to undergo an experience aesthetically, regardless of your topic. Even though Peirce identifies aesthetic as an impulse instead of a method, you cannot perform abductive reasoning without applying aesthetic methods, regardless of subject matter."

"Would this be true even if the subject is say, cleaning out a sewer?"

"Sure. We use John Dewey's definition of aesthetic as a way of doing something, rather than as an appreciation of art. Dewey defined the opposite of aesthetic as anesthetic."

"What is anesthetic?"

"Not being conscious of what you are doing. You can do things anesthetically by mindlessly applying habit or capriciously moving from one thing to another. Anesthetic activity uses habit or whim, both are types of 'disengaged' intelligence. Aesthetically undergone activities require 'engaged' intelligence. Aesthetic and anesthetic methods can be applied to any activity, from scrubbing floors to painting a cathedral ceiling. So, for us, aesthetic means the way something is done, regardless of the subject matter of the activity. Science and art both deal with unpleasant materials at times."

"Is abduction a particular way of dealing with materials?"

"Yes, and also with ideas. We count ideas as materials, too."

"At what point is there a difference between discovery and creation?"

"The difference comes at the point of having a goal, or a hypothesis. Once you have a hypothesis, you are no longer discovering something new or creating something original."

"What are you doing then?"

"You are producing, or figuring out how to produce, an outcome. Or else, you are proving, or figuring out how to prove, a hypothesis. Once you are doing any of these things, then you have moved out of abduction."

"Where do you move to?"

"You move into what most people would call analysis or planning," I answered. "Analysis and planning require deductive reasoning, in the most flexible sense of that word. You move out of the construction of conditional purposes into the analysis and testing of conditional purposes. Science is set up for the purpose of analyzing and testing conditional purposes. Peirce wants science to apply this same degree of attention to the discovery and formulation of hypotheses as it does to analyzing and testing them."

"What about philosophy?"

"Peirce feels that philosophy has not done a good job of either formulating or testing conditional purposes. He would like philosophy to take a lesson from science concerning the analysis and testing of hypotheses, and he would like for both fields to take a lesson from him regarding the construction of hypotheses."

"Oh, I see that. So, back to the one-of-a-kind thing. Are you saying that the other pragmatists were one-of-a-kind people and not scientific?"

"Not at all. I only meant that they were coming at things from a different perspective than Peirce. The three best-known of the early pragmatists, Peirce, John Dewey, and William James, all came at pragmatism from a different point of view. Each of their views provided something of use to the others, but none of them entirely understood one another. Peirce felt misunderstood by everyone, except for the philosopher Josiah Royce, whom he considered his only real student."

"Then what is the difference between the Cliftons' one-of-a-kind home and Peirce's single phenomenon?"

"At one level, the difference is that the Cliftons' home exists and continues to exist in physical reality. At another level, their ideas coalesced into a conditional purpose, which were the blueprints for that house. Once you have a goal or hypothesis, then you can set out to test and re-test the proposition."

"I thought that the Cliftons never had a goal or hypothesis."

"Sure they had a goal, but it changed and evolved as they proceeded. Their goal evolved because it developed, and changed according to what they discovered along the way. They did not retain their goal in the same form as when they started."

"But the Oranges changed things too."

"Yes, but their changes did not change the shape of their goal, which Peirce might have called the 'form of their proposition.' Their changes were adjustments made to achieve the goal more effectively, not to change or alter the goal itself. The Oranges made adjustments as necessary along the way, but they did not come across something interesting and then change major design or functional elements of the project. Mr. and Mrs. Orange might have adjusted a color scheme here or added a porch on there during the process of building their house. The Cliftons, however, changed entire portions of the house plans *in media res* to incorporate interesting new materials as these became available to them. When a conditional purpose is being constructed by means of abductive reasoning, the entire process, including goals, methods, and materials, is open-ended and evolving. The Cliftons' house became what it is today through a process different from the process that resulted in either the Oranges' custom home, or the subdivision home of the Blue family. A conditional purpose is formed out of an interplay among all the elements in a process, including goals, materials, plans, and anomalies, as well as adaptations made possible or necessary by some unforeseen event."

"Are you saying that the Cliftons only used a conditional purpose?"

"I am saying that they 'constructed,' in an almost literal sense, a conditional purpose, while the Oranges 'used' a conditional purpose. Someone could review the Cliftons' building plans and the myriad of changes to the plans, as well as those details that never made it onto a plan and put the whole process into a full set of plans. If this were done, then that set of plans could be used to build another version of that home, even to make a direct copy of it."

"Then their house would not be one-of-a-kind anymore."

"You are right. That hypothetical set of plans that someone put together by going back and identifying the probable processes for constructing the Cliftons' home would be a 'conditional purpose.' After these plans are used to build one or more houses, then we can say the plans reflect an actual purpose."

"Why then?"

"Because, at first, those plans become a general proposition, a hypothesis, which proposes that 'if you do all of these things then you will have a home just like the Cliftons.' Once you have fully experimented with these plans, in the sense of eliminating problems as you build a few homes based on them, those plans become an actual purpose. They become like a well-tested recipe."

"Would that work?"

"Would what work?"

"Would someone be able to construct a home just like the Cliftons' with a set of plans? I cannot see how you would incorporate all of those subtle details into a set of construction plans."

"Those plans would be like any other conditional purpose, hypothesis, or general proposal. Whether they are true or, in this case, whether they 'would work,' depends upon how well the proposal is stated."

Hal interrupted me excitedly at this point.

"I understand it now! When you construct the conditional purpose you use abductive reasoning. When you are setting up to achieve the conditional purpose, you use analytical reasoning. Right?"

"Yes. Peirce would have called this 'deductive reasoning.' When you are analyzing in advance what probably will and will not work and analyzing what did or did not work before, you are using deductive reasoning. Following plans requires you to make simple inductive inferences by checking your plans as you test. Induction is conclusive: 'this means this, that means that'."

"Yes," he agreed impatiently, "and the reason that you cannot use any of those...things...that Peirce said...." Hal struggled for a brief moment to remember the phrasing.

"Do you mean the 'inadequacy of action, force of will, determination, or actual purpose'?"

"Yes," he said, gratefully. "I can see now that the reason you cannot use any of those to construct a conditional purpose is because of what Peirce said about propositions."

Although I was stunned when he said this, I did not let any reaction show outwardly. I tried not to interrupt his train of thought. Had he made a connection here? Would he be able to state it if he had?

"And?"

"All other ways that Peirce says will not work for constructing a conditional purpose will not work because, to do them, you must already have your proposition."

"How so?" I asked, feigning only casual interest.

He looked as though he was settling in for an act of deep verbal reasoning. "If you are taking action on something, or trying to make something happen by force of will or determination, that means you have already settled on your goal. Trying to make something happen is the same as having an actual or conditional purpose, which means you already have your proposition."

"But what if your purpose is to construct a conditional purpose?" I asked, deciding to play devil's advocate. "What if you just set your mind to constructing a conditional purpose or the concept of a conditional purpose?"

"It would not work."

"Why not?"

I had stumped him. However, that was no surprise. This statement of Peirce's has stumped scholars for nearly a hundred years.

I decided to bail him out. "You are right that action, volition, resolve and actual purpose all presuppose a goal. But the reason that these are inadequate as materials for constructing a conditional purpose is that qualitative anomalies are the raw materials from which conditional purposes can be constructed."

"Meaning?"

"Meaning that conditional purposes arise from exploring things that we do not already know or understand. The ongoing process of exploration brings new information by means of making relationships that we have not yet made, or discovered, as Peirce would say. Therefore, what we can discover cannot be known to us in advance of our making the relationships that bring new relationships into our awareness. These new relationships become present to us only after we have made a series of prior relationships among things. The new relationships are possible because of the synthesis of prior relationships. They are possibilities that could not have existed for us until we made the necessary prior relationships to have discerned them."

"Which is what I meant! I meant that action and volition are inadequate because you cannot plan out what unknown thing you will discover or how you will explain it before you know what it is."

"Good! That is exactly right. Once you set out to discover something, you are setting out to prove something. You are acting on a hypothesis. You already have a hunch that something is true and you are checking it out. Abduction gets you the hunch in the first place."

"I understand that. But what do you start out with if not to discover?"

"You start out with exactly what you have, in exactly the present moment, with whatever is there and whatever you bring with you. These taken together become your raw materials. As you relate them to one another, new relationships form which lead you to synthesize out whatever qualities you decide are the best, or most interesting, or most useful. In doing this, you uncover further possibilities along the way that you could not have considered before because you had not yet made the necessary prior relationships. That is why we say that abduction is a generative process."

"I see that now."

"Are you ready to call it a day?"

"I guess so, if you think this is a good place to stop."

"It is a good place to stop. We can begin tomorrow with a review."

"Till tomorrow, then," he said, blowing a kiss in my direction.

Fifteen
CONTINUING INTO CONTINUITY

"Yesterday we spent the whole time talking about what Peirce means by 'constructing a conditional purpose.' Do you think you can give me a summary of what he means by this?"

"I think I can do that. A conditional purpose can be like a hypothesis or a goal. If the conditional purpose is a hypothesis, it still needs to be analyzed and tested. If it is a goal, then it still needs to be planned out and achieved."

"Good, but Peirce is not talking about 'having' conditional purposes."

"Oh, right," Hal said, self-correcting the course of his thought. "He is talking about the 'construction of conditional purposes.' He says that no amount of will or actual purpose is going to enable you to construct a conditional purpose."

"Or the concept of a conditional purpose," I added. "And why is that?"

"Because if you have put your mind to do something, you already have a purpose. When you have a purpose, you will do your picking and choosing based on that purpose, like the Blues or the Oranges."

"Yes. Do you remember the distinction I made between abductive and retroductive reasoning?"

"Sure. You said that abductive reasoning is what you do to construct conditional purposes. Abductive reasoning is the same as multi-relational reasoning, and you use it to create or discover new ideas. Retroductive reasoning, in the way we use it for Dottie's model, means using abductive, deductive, and inductive reasoning for different stages of doing something."

"Good! Next, Peirce brings up his doctrine of continuity:"

Had a purposed article concerning the principle of continuity and synthesizing the ideas of the other articles of a series in the early volumes of *The Monist* ever been written, it would have appeared how, with thorough consistency, that theory involved the recognition that continuity is an indispensable element of reality, and that continuity is simply what generality becomes in the logic of relatives, and thus, like generality, and more than generality, is an affair of thought, and is the essence of thought.

"Peirce begins this section with some whining. He had received little recognition in his life and things were rough for him. Peirce never wrote the article that he refers to here because he was never contracted to write it. Most of what the world knew of pragmatism came through William James and John

Dewey. James, especially, was deeply influenced by Peirce. That is a major reason why Peirce wrote this particular article."

"What is?"

"When Peirce wrote this article, James had just recently given him credit for coming up with the name for the philosophy of pragmatism. This was gratifying to Peirce, who had lived in relative obscurity most of his life. He was fond of James, who even arranged to help him out with money over the years, but Peirce felt that James was too psychologistic."

"What did he mean by that?"

"'Psychologistic' is a term that philosophers use when philosophical topics are approached as subjective psychological issues. This term is used as a reproach by those philosophers who feel that objective and logical factors should take precedence in philosophy."

"And was Peirce one of those who thought that objective and logical factors should win out?"

"Yes. However, we should just ignore Peirce's *Angst* here and focus upon what he has to say about continuity:"

[Pragmaticism involves] the recognition that continuity is an indispensable element of reality, and thus, that continuity is what generality becomes in the logic of relatives, and like generality, and more than generality, is a matter of thought and is the essence of thought.

"I do not follow what he means by 'continuity being like generality'."

"We have already discussed that the essence of Peirce's doctrine of continuity is that you cannot use something that is inexplicable as the basis for explaining something else. You must always begin with an observed fact and combine your observation with what is known and with the understanding that all knowledge is fallible. Peirce believed that continuity rests upon fallibility. Fallibility, or openness to doubt, enables us to open our eyes to the significance of a fact."

"How is that like generality?"

"Generality, remember, is what gives us reality. Generality enables regularity, habit, representation, and whatever else Peirce includes as 'thirdness.' Continuity gives us this same regularity in the mental realm. Because of continuity, we can generalize from one experience to another. However, because of fallibilism, we are able to revise our knowledge. If we know we are fallible then we know we cannot ever be absolutely sure that our generalizations are correct."

"What do you mean?"

"As I just said, continuity rests upon observed facts and has to do with thought. I see an apple and remember from before that it is an apple. Fallibilism, the fact that our knowledge is never absolute, makes it possible for me to reorganize observed facts and look at them in a different way. Sometimes an apple is not an apple. Sometimes it is a piece of plastic made to look like an apple. Continuity provides us with mental regularity in the same way that generality provides form and regularity to what would otherwise be unrelated individuals. In partnership with fallibilism, continuity allows us to reformulate ideas in new ways. Thus, because of continuity informed by fallibilism, I can adapt to the fact that, sometimes, what appears to be an apple is really a piece of plastic made to look like an apple."

"I think I understand that."

"Good. The word 'continuum' implies a series, an order proceeding from one direction to another. Peirce would say the direction was from past to future, since you cannot change the past. Peirce also says that all things 'swim in the continua' at the same time, meaning all things and possibilities are present, even if we do not know they are there."

"Then, would all of those things and possibilities be real?"

"Yes, they would be real because they have qualities, whether or not we know what those qualities are. Possibilities are like propositions in the sense that their meaning resides in the future. Peirce's doctrine of continuity rests upon observed facts, so the possibilities from which we form our hypotheses must be related to observed facts."

"Is that because you cannot base a hypothesis on inexplicable ultimates?"

"Yes, good memory! Now, regardless of how we acquire them, we use our beliefs to build our expectations about what will happen when we do something in the future. When we come across something that causes us to notice that a belief may be in error, the power of doubt takes over for a while. We must settle that doubt in some way before we can continue. Doubt causes a break in our mental habits. It provides us with a discontinuity."

"An example?"

"The Coke bottle example is a good one. The people of that tribe repeatedly attempted to figure out why the gods had sent that bottle to them. Those people had a belief about their gods that was 'unassailable by doubt'."

"What belief was that?"

"They believed that the gods only sent things that were useful and harmonious. The continuity of this belief was interrupted when the Coke bottle fell out of the sky. The only explanation that ultimately made sense to them was that the gods must be crazy. They would not have imagined that their conclusion might be based upon an inexplicable ultimate, that there were no gods tossing Coke bottles down to them. Therefore, when the bottle became a problem for the tribe, the only option was to return the Coke bottle to the gods. They had to settle the discontinuity in order to continue on with their lives."

"But, there were no gods. How could they straighten things out?"

"That was the whole point of the movie. You and I knew that there were no gods involved in this, but they did not. Even in this modern world, every one of us has some beliefs founded on inexplicable ultimates. We all have beliefs that seem so true that we cannot possibly believe otherwise. When experience, or greater knowledge, comes along and challenges one of these fixed beliefs, different people will react differently to the challenge. *The Gods Must Be Crazy* is just another example of belief interacting with experience."

"That was a movie. How about something more like real life?"

"Here is an everyday example of what continuity is 'not.' A train derails killing everyone aboard. Suppose we say that the reason that the train derailed, killing everyone, was because it was God's will and that the ways of God are inexplicable. Now, according to Peirce, you cannot ascribe the cause of something to something else that is inexplicable and still have continuity."

"I understand what continuity is not. I just do not understand what continuity is."

"Continuity is the opposite of that example I just gave. For a thought or a proposal to have continuity, whatever it is based upon must be explicable. It has to continue from something that can be explained. We can address the problem of that same train derailment according to the doctrine of continuity. We already know from experience that certain factors having to do with mechanics, weather, rails, human error, or deliberate sabotage can cause a train to derail. A train derails killing everyone aboard. The reason the train derailed and everyone was killed is probably due to one of the above-mentioned factors. However, we are fallible people and do not know everything, so we know that there may be some other factor involved that we have not even thought of. Now, the point of continuity is that you have prior knowledge that explains certain facts. You can rely upon this information because it is based on prior research and testing. You can use this information to check if something went wrong with the rails or train mechanics, or if sabotage was involved."

"Can you prove things one way or the other with continuity?"

"Not necessarily, but you can quickly eliminate the less likely reasons and consider only explanations that have high probabilities of being correct. The doctrine of continuity covers all purposes for reasoning, including the formation of explanatory hypotheses. You form such hypotheses by using abductive reasoning, which we talked about earlier. Using this doctrine of continuity, you select the most likely possibilities for analysis and testing."

"I see that you could not scientifically prove anything based on God's will, but attributing the cause to God's will could make the whole tragedy easier to handle for those who lost family and friends."

"Possibly, and who is to say that, on a higher level, everything that happens is not God's will? Elsewhere, Peirce puts up a good argument for the reality of God. However, Peirce would have said that you cannot just ascribe the cause of a phenomenon to God's will or any other inexplicable cause because that would mean the cause is not connected to something that can be known. If we cannot know something, then we cannot adjust our behavior to deliberately alter what we do based on that particular thing and expect predictable results."

"Ah ha!" Hal said, his mental light bulb flicking on. "I see! This has to do with deliberate self-control of future events!"

"Yes it does. Peirce's doctrine of continuity allows us to figure out what went wrong and find ways to change things and improve future conditions. If you just ascribed the whole derailment tragedy to God's will, you would not have a way of knowing if something could be done, in practical terms, to prevent future derailments. Peirce's doctrine of continuity insists that we must build upon what has already been explained when we seek to discover the reason for something else. We make back-and-forth relationships between what we know to be so and what might be so."

"I can see that."

"You can also think of continuity as a web of connections between established knowledge and what may be possible. If you are trying to solve a particular problem, like finding the reason for a train derailment, the doctrine of continuity gives you a way of analyzing data and eliminating some explanations. Perhaps the weather was perfect, and there was no sign of damage to the tracks. Those two preliminary explanations can be eliminated by checking out the facts. Then, we can eliminate other possibilities through research and experiment. After narrowing possibilities down to the most probable causes of the accident, we have potential answers that can be thoroughly checked out. If one of those answers turns out to be true, action can be taken to find ways of correcting the problem so that it does not happen again."

"Does God's will come in if the detectives fail to find a reason?"

"No. Maybe the investigators never come up with a reason for that particular accident to have occurred, but that investigation provides vital information in-and-of itself. Someday, a similar event might occur, and the second investigative team can examine the findings of the first group. Perhaps, because they are able to eliminate some explanatory possibilities more quickly, this team might have the mental energy to come up with an entirely new explanatory hypothesis. Maybe, by building on the earlier process, the second team will come up with a possibility that had not even been considered before. This possibility might be the one that correctly explains what happened, opening the door to preventing future accidents of this sort."

"That just sounds like typical reverse engineering to me, figuring something out by working backwards."

"The working backwards part is reverse engineering. You use standard deductive reasoning to do that. Abduction is used for selecting which explanatory hypothesis to single out for deduction. It is the inference method for deciding which, out of a myriad of possible explanations, has the highest probability of proving to be true."

"You must have to know a lot about trains and tracks to do that."

"Sure. Having knowledge about a subject is a given. However, using that knowledge abductively to make a guess about an unknown is a particular way of using knowledge. In this same sense, deduction and simple induction are also particular ways of using knowledge."

"What about continuity?"

"All three ways of gaining and using knowledge are necessary in Peirce's doctrine of continuity."

"Can you relate this train example to the Cliftons' house?"

"Let me see," I said, caught off guard by his query. "The way that the Cliftons built their house is a physical manifestation of what someone would do mentally when constructing an explanatory hypothesis."

"How so?"

"They started off with an unusual fact or anomaly, in this case an interesting piece of aluminum. They then related the qualities of that anomaly to other qualities of other things, gradually evolving an idea, which eventually became a conditional purpose. In other words, the Cliftons started out in a state of not being settled on one thing or another."

"I see that."

"From that state of not being completely settled on one thing or another, they began exploring possibilities."

"Are you saying that the Cliftons' house was a solution?"

"Sure, at least it was in the sense that the house they built and the process they went through to design and build it expressed their way of settling doubt."

"What about the Blues and the Oranges? They found solutions as well."

"Ah ha! You just asked the million-dollar question!"

"Which is?"

"Which is the one that lets me explain this whole theory in a nutshell."

"Including continuity?"

"Yes. Just now we were talking about continuity and the construction of conditional purposes and how the Cliftons started off with a problem to solve."

"And I asked 'what about the Oranges and the Blues'?" Hal added. "That is when you said I had asked the million-dollar question."

"I have said before that Peirce's pragmaticism addresses how problems 'should be' identified and how solutions 'should be' sought during particular stages of an inquiry. Our non-verbal model addresses how people 'habitually' identify and solve problems, regardless of what they 'should' be doing in a particular context. Both *logica docens* and *logica utens* are methods by which the identifying and solving of problems can be done. *Logica docens* is deliberate and *logica utens*, non-deliberate. Yet, we must use one or the other for identifying and solving problems, for settling doubt. Mr. and Mrs. Blue found the solution to their problem by selecting from what was made available to them by someone else. Mr. and Mrs. Orange solved their problem by finding someone who could help them to develop a new version of an existing idea."

"And the Cliftons?"

"The Cliftons began by playing around with an interesting piece of aluminum. Their home design process was not driven by a specific problem, or goal, as were designs of the Blues and the Oranges. They played with possible relationships among materials, rather setting out to solve a specific problem.

Since they explored possible relationships, rather than deciding in advance to build a particular type of house, or even to build a house at all, the deciding part of their process took a long time."

"It sure did!"

"The design for that house evolved from relationships that interacted with one another. Jim and Rachel played around with ideas, took out what they wanted from them, and juxtaposed these ideas with other things. They kept extracting and synthesizing as they went along. When something new and interesting appeared, they explored that new thing as an option. If an option irretrievably intrigued them, they found a way to adjust their design to use it. They incorporated interesting materials as those materials came along. They even entirely changed whole chunks of the plan to accommodate new relationships as these evolved during the process. At the end of the whole process, the Cliftons created a home that is a design phenomenon. Someone else, someone who did not possess their innate multi-relational abilities, might have ended up with an expensive junk pile."

"I sure would not have been able to end up with a place like that! And the irony is that Jim's a cardiologist, not an architect."

"That is not ironic. Jim probably does not practice subdivision cardiology either. He probably practices cardiology the same way a good train derailment detective would work."

"What do you mean?"

"A good train derailment detective and a good cardiologist would work in much the same way. They would enter a given situation with all of the necessary basics of medical knowledge or derailment detecting. Both a good detective and a good cardiologist would habitually go where the information leads them, not where they think it should lead."

"I am missing the distinction here."

"Going where you 'think' something will lead, instead of where it does lead is like deciding to build a Cape Cod colonial-style home and then selecting materials that fit that type of home. You will not be paying attention to anomalies like stainless steel cabinets or unusual pieces of aluminum or metal cyclone fencing. Those things just will not come into your awareness as having any point to them, because you are building a Cape Cod colonial-style home. Things outside of your goal will appear irrelevant because they do not match up with your image of the Cape Cod colonial-style home."

"What does that have to do with train derailments and cardiology?"

"This is where continuity and conditional purposes come in. Think of what Peirce said earlier about specifics and generals."

"Do you mean when he said that they were both reals?"

"I was thinking more of when he was explaining about isolated phenomena and general laws or principles."

"Do you mean how pragmaticism does not deal in isolated phenomena?"

"Yes. This house-building situation is a good example of continuity and of generals. All three sorts of house-building methods are examples of a particular relationship of generals to specifics."

"What do you mean?"

"In the first case, the builder's plans for Mr. and Mrs. Blues' subdivision home, which are the generals in this case, are already concrete and specific. They have already been proven by the building of a model home, which represents, in most details, the home the Blues will actually have. Several homes will be built in that subdivision using those same plans."

"Are these plans still general propositions? Does their meaning still reside in the future even if they are used to build many homes?"

"Yes. Each set of plans will always be a proposition, just like Shannon's pie recipe, because its meaning is located in the future whenever it is used to build a particular home. After several homes have been built using a particular set of plans, you might compare these building plans to what Peirce called 'beliefs unassailable by doubt.'"

"Do you mean," he asked, "that you can be almost certain that those houses will come out in a particular way?"

"Yes. The most significant part of the Blues' home-building experience will be the building part. All of the pre-planning has been done so that, for them at least, no need exists to use abduction or deduction to make decisions about their home. The concept of continuity is easy to see here because it is based upon 'direct replication' of something that already exists. Mr. and Mrs. Orange are similar to the Blues, but they reflect a more complex approach."

"Because they are getting a custom home?"

"Yes. The Oranges are operating from the goal of creating a 'new version' of an existing type or form of a house, instead of using a set of available plans for making a particular house. They are going to end up with specific plans, but they are not starting out with these. They have a general idea of the type of home design they want to have. Their biggest chore is the planning part, the part of developing the general plans that will become blueprints for building the style of home that they already know that they want."

"But the Oranges' outcome would be less certain than the Blues'."

"Yes. The Oranges' outcome is going to be more like the outcome of a conditional purpose that Peirce discussed. Their home will probably turn out in a particular way. You can be almost sure that it is going to look like a Cape Cod colonial, because those features are well-established. We could even say that they are operating from an *a priori*, or preexisting, concept. Their home will have an obvious connection with other houses of the same sort. However, since they are building a custom home, lots of pre-planning will be required of the Oranges and their architect. Changes and adjustments may also occur along the way as certain problems arise."

"What kinds of changes?"

"Oh, like switching from oak cabinets to birch because the builder found a good price for birch. They could even decide, after the foundation was poured, to divide up the downstairs family room into two smaller rooms and gain a downstairs bedroom for Mrs. Orange's recently widowed mother."

"Are you just saying that the Oranges are more involved in the planning than the Blues are?"

"Yes, and they are more involved in making ongoing adjustments as well. The Oranges are operating from a conditional proposition. Because of this, they may need to adapt some of the specifics as they go. These adaptations will be reflected in the expression of the proposition, which is their house. Once that house is built, others can replicate it again and again."

"I understand about the Blues and the Oranges, but what about the Cliftons' house? That house is so unusual, and it evolved instead of following a planned outcome."

"That is exactly what happened. The Cliftons' house did evolve, at least in Peirce's sense of unfolding. This is where continuity comes in."

"How so?"

"It should be easy for you to see how continuity worked for the Blues and the Oranges."

"Yes, I see how continuity worked for them," Hal said, "and generality, as well. Their houses were similar to other houses. They were of a type or a sort. They were based on styles of houses that had gone before."

"Right. Now, the Cliftons' house-building project started with a piece of aluminum, not with an idea of building a home as the others did. When the idea of building a house emerged, the Cliftons dealt with this idea differently than the other two families did."

"How so?"

"The Cliftons started by exploring materials and possibilities. They did not start by choosing which floor-plan they would use, or with a preconceived idea of what their home would look like when it was finished. They began their home-building project by confronting an anomaly. They embraced doubt, instead of relying upon pre-conceived certainty for formulating their purpose. They went swimming among the options within the 'continuum of uncertainty and indeterminacy' that Peirce described. The Cliftons' home-building process reflected Peirce's idea of continuity as 'fallibilism objectified.' They spent most of their thinking time exploring possible relationships and synthesizing various elements that evolved into a conditional purpose. This evolutionary process eventually culminated in the conditional purpose, which were the blueprints for their home. But just 'action, volition, resolve, or actual purpose' would not have been enough to end up with their unique and original ideas."

"How is that continuity?"

"The Cliftons did not construct this conditional purpose out of nowhere. They began with the qualities of one thing, which connected with others in meaningful ways."

"Unlike Harry the phone man?" he offered playfully.

"Ah yes! Harry the phone man." He had taken us on a wild ride after we hired him to add extra telephone lines in our home. "Harry's home design and building practices reflect discontinuity."

We came to know Harry when we first moved to town. He advertised in the local paper as an expert in wiring telephone lines. Yet, he was so clearly inept as a phone man that Hal had to show him how to wire the extra lines we needed. During this brief acquaintance, we also learned of his personal home-building methods. These were the polar opposites of those the Cliftons used. Harry never synthesized the best from anything. He just used whatever he found as-is and then added it on nowhere in particular. He did not fool with such nitty-gritty things as building plans, foundations, or insulation. Harry's helter-skelter addition of rooms and hallways onto an ancient travel-trailer, ended up looking more like a poorly constructed rabbit-warren than a home."

"What kind of purpose would you say that Harry had?"

"Immediate or temporary."

"Would temporary be like conditional?"

"Not in the sense Peirce meant. Harry moved abruptly from one inexplicable option to another. He tacked things on to one another, without making contiguous relationships. He did not connect things together purposively."

"Are you saying that the Cliftons' home-building method had continuity because things connected together in a purposeful manner?"

"Yes, we could say the Cliftons enabled things to evolve, or unfold, in a purposeful manner. Almost the entire home-building project operated for the Cliftons as the 'construction of a conditional purpose.' A retroductive element also occurred there as well."

"What do you mean?"

"Since building plans and specific directions were involved, Jim Clifton had to use pre-planning as well as designing skills. If this project had been something like a painting or sculpture, he could have created it entirely on his own without blueprints and permits. He could have used an entirely multi-relational, or abductive, process."

"I can see that."

"Because of the way in which the Cliftons went about building their home, they were able to create a unique and original dwelling. This dwelling has all the best qualities of a well-built home, but it was designed by making unique and unusual relationships among materials."

"Where does the continuity come in?"

"In the evolution part. From Peirce's perspective, in the higher stages of evolution, a process starts from some particular real point and then unfolds into a higher form without losing the connection to that original point. That starting point can be established principles. It can also be a series of prior relationships that eventually synthesize, or meld, into an outcome. The outcome can then become a new beginning. The Cliftons began with an interesting piece of corrugated metal which they juxtaposed with other materials to form the possibility of a home in which that metal might work. They allowed themselves to play with possibilities throughout the conception and construction of their home. Because of this, the Cliftons kept themselves open to exploring, altering, adapting, synthesizing, and changing things in significant ways, or even altogether, if they had so desired. When confronting new materials, unforeseen problems, or unusual opportunities, they could take advantage of these in ways that the other types of home builders could not. Yet, they never lost connection with underlying principles of good design and home-building."

"And Harry the phone man tacked things on until he ran out of room."

"Yes."

"What does this have to do with train derailments and cardiology?"

"Would you want Harry as your cardiologist?"

"Absolutely not!"

"Peirce did not include Harry's spontaneous method in his theory of pragmaticism, unless you count it as the first step in abductive reasoning. However, taken all on its own, Harry's helter-skelter method is nearly the opposite of abduction. It is more like an example of Peirce's doctrine of chance."

"Doctrine of chance?"

"Chance is tied into Peirce's theory of probability about the predictability of something, or lack of predictability. Harry might qualify as a loose cannon on the deck in Peirce's doctrine of chance, a random event that comes and goes nowhere in particular. Harry is 'predictably unpredictable,' meaning that his basic premise for selecting among options is simple variation. Given a choice of repeating what he just did or doing something different, Harry will opt for different. He is a good example of discontinuity."

"Then, is discontinuity the opposite of continuity?"

"Not quite. In Peirce's theory, discontinuity is an integral part of continuity, since it provides anomalies that instigate abductive thought. However, for people like Harry, discontinuity is a habit of mind all on its own. It helps to know how Harry's mind works when you are trying to understand abduction."

"Why?"

"Because most people find both Harry and Jim Clifton incomprehensible. People who are like the Blues understand how to apply existing goals and patterns. Those like the Oranges know how to use goals to construct new versions of things. Both sorts of thinkers have a difficult time when they try to understand non-goal directed reasoning. When people who habitually operate like the Blues and the Oranges first see people like Jim Clifton and Harry they may mistakenly assume that they are both operating in the same way."

"I remember that I used to think those processes were the same."

"You sure did. People have a hard time grasping abduction unless they can see it play out over time and space. They often mistake the shallow and capricious reasoning of a spontaneous thinker, like Harry, for the ongoing confrontation of qualitative anomalies of an abductive thinker. Many people misunderstand abductive reasoning without the contrast of its random opposite."

"Because?"

"Because neither abductive thinkers nor spontaneous thinkers use sequence to guide the order in which they do things. Abductive thinkers are guided by the making of qualitative relationships and spontaneous thinkers by whatever happens along. To an observer, abductive reasoning sometimes appears random while it is happening. Both abductive reasoning and spontaneous thinking are means-directed, which is to say that the means direct the formation of a goal for both of these types of thinkers. Both the Blues and the Oranges operate in an opposite way from the Cliftons and Harry. The Blues and Oranges use goals to direct the selection of materials and methods. For any goal-directed thinker, the products of an abductively directed process might end up looking as if they were produced in an inexplicably mysterious way."

"Are you saying that what Jim Clifton does is inexplicable?"

"No, just that it seems that way to people who are goal directed. Goal directed people can sometimes infer that multi-relational, or abductive, thinking has occurred when they see an original or creative outcome, but they cannot be sure unless they have observed how those results came to be. Dottie has always said that whenever something is separated from at least a minimal understanding of the system that produces it, the results always look like magic."

"Good point. That is like the metaphysical street lights."

"Oh yes!" I said laughing at the reference. "That is an excellent example of an invisible producing system!"

Hal and I had recently learned of one of the latest proofs of the New Age power of mind to change physical reality. If you are spiritual enough, this proof can be demonstrated by parking a spiritually energized car under a city street lamp on a dark night. After a few moments of deeply spiritual concentration by the car's inhabitants, the street light will almost invariably flicker or shut off, giving proof of the power of mind to effect physical changes. What is really happening, however, is that some of the older streetlights turn off and on via antiquated photosensitive mechanisms. These turn the lights on at dusk and off as daylight arrives. When a light-colored or highly polished car is parked under one of these street lights, its reflection temporarily confuses the photosensitive cell, causing it to flicker and, sometimes, even to briefly shut off altogether.

"Metaphysical streetlights are an example of people worshiping phenomena instead of trying to figure something out. Some people tend to worship phenomena when they do not understand a producing system. Some people choose to deny that an anomaly has even occurred. Neither type of person is using pragmatic reasoning."

"Magical thinking is a good place to leave off for today."

"That is just fine with me," he agreed.

Sixteen
COSMOLOGY

Essay lines 628-647

"Yesterday we discussed Peirce's concept of continuity," I began as we settled in that next morning. "We went off onto several divergent paths, so I am wondering if you remember what we discussed."

"I remember that Harry the phone man is the opposite of continuity."

"That is a good start. Do you remember anything else?"

"I remember that the kind of continuity that the Blues and Oranges used was different than the kind Jim Clifton used."

"How is it different?"

"The Blues and Oranges started off with goals that connected up to things that are just like, or similar to, what has been done before. Jim Clifton started out with a piece of metal."

"How did the Cliftons' home-building method show continuity?"

"Their continuity came from starting out with an odd piece of metal sheeting and designing the home from that point, but never letting go of established principles of good home-building. That is why even though their house is unique and one-of-a-kind, it is still well built and structurally sound."

As a civil engineer, Hal knows that to be true, while I greatly admire the clever ways that the Cliftons managed to adapt dramatic design elements into their home, yet still create cozy spaces.

"The continuity in Jim Clifton's process also came from the process of relating qualities and making relationships among things based on these qualities. These relationships led him to synthesize whatever he decided was the best from these prior relationships and to uncover further possibilities along the way that he could not have considered before he had made the prior relationships. Abduction is a generative process. Generation always has a history behind it, a starting point to which all that follows is connected. You cannot generate from nothing. However, you also cannot know in advance what the connections will be when reasoning abductively, because future connections will depend upon relationships that have not yet been made."

"Oh. I can see that, then."

"Can you sum up continuity?"

He sighed deeply. "You have caught me too early in the morning for a summary. Can I just say that continuity is the opposite of the way Harry the phone man operates and leave it at that?"

"I suppose, if you can remember what continuity is not, you probably do have a good idea of what it is. Besides, we will be getting to habit next, and then we will find out for sure if you know what continuity means."

"Fire away!"

"Yesterday, Peirce told us that the articles he did not get to write would have shown how his doctrine of continuity is an indispensable element of reality. He said that 'continuity is what generality becomes in the logic of relatives. So, continuity is generality, only more so.' Do you have any idea what Peirce meant by that?"

"No, I have no idea of what that means."

"Peirce wanted to use geometry to explain his doctrine of continuity," I explained, "but plain old geometry was not enough to handle his doctrine. He proposed an optical geometry that had to do with rays. He contended that Euclid and even earlier Greeks had known about this geometrical optic, and he tied this into what was then a new branch of geometry called 'topology'."

"I know about topology from engineering school, but I cannot imagine what that would have to do with continuity."

"Topology in Peirce's sense, which he called 'Topic' to rhyme with metric and optic, deals with the connections among the parts of continua."[12]

"Oh. That makes sense then."

"It does?"

"Sure. Topology is the geometry of hypothetical space, multiple dimensions of hypothetical space. These dimensions all connect up in one way or another."

"I am no mathematician," I began, understating the obvious, "but when I put together what Peirce has to say about continuity and abduction and topology, I cannot help but think about fractal geometry."

"Ah ha! That would be chaos theory."

"Just take a look at that fractal," I suggested, pointing to the computer-generated design Hal gave me several years ago for my birthday. "This fractal design is an excellent metaphor for continuity, if nothing else. Look at how the pattern, which Peirce would have referred to as habit, plays itself out for a while. Then it becomes irregular, corresponding to the end of a process, or to the action of some surprise or chance that disrupts the pattern."

"Or doubt?"

"Or doubt," I agreed. "The system adjusts itself to deal with the irregularity, to settle the doubt. Then it settles into a pattern again. In the case of fractals such as this one, the same pattern of order and chaos will continue indefinitely. The formula that drives the pattern is set up to iterate, to repeat itself over and over again. In the case of the mental or physical universes, however, chance events occur to interrupt patterns. These chance events cause the system to adapt itself to the change, so the resulting new habit will not exactly match the old."

"Do you think that the universe might be a great big fractal?"

"I have no idea if it is. I suspect that Peirce might have thought so, though. Peirce believed that an absolute ideal reality exists in terms of forms and patterns, and that the process of evolution unfolds toward this ideal. Fractal geometry would have provided a metaphor for him of how that might play out. Here is Peirce's next statement:"

> Yet even in its truncated condition, an extra-intelligent reader might discern that the theory of those cosmological articles made reality to consist in something more than feeling and action could supply, inasmuch as the primeval chaos, where those two elements were present, was explicitly shown to be pure nothing.

"What does 'truncated condition' mean?"

"Peirce is telling us that the incomplete early series of articles he wrote left his theory in an unfinished, or abbreviated, condition."

"And cosmological articles?"

"Do you remember that early in our discussion of this essay, Peirce talked about how he extracted the 'precious essence of metaphysics to give light and life to cosmology and physics'?"

"I think so. Cosmology is about the origin of the universe. Is that right?"

"The origin, structure, and processes of the universe," I amended. "The early articles that Peirce refers to here were philosophical treatments of cosmology from his particular pragmatic point of view. Peirce contends that, even in his theory's incomplete condition, a smart person might have been able to recognize that reality consists in something 'more than feeling and action could supply.' He says the reason a smart person might recognize that there is more to reality than feeling and action can supply is because, in the primeval chaos, there was pure nothing."

"What does the primeval chaos have to do with feeling and action?"

"Only feeling and action were present in that state, which is another way of saying that no pattern or regularity existed, or as Peirce wrote, 'only impulse and action' but nothing of the habits we need for producing regularity."

"How could he say that feeling was present in the earliest chaos? How could you have feeling without having beings to feel?"

"Remember we are talking cosmologically now. Peirce is referring to his articles on cosmology."

"That makes it even more confusing. Why would he use the word 'feeling' to refer to cosmology?"

"Feeling is one name for the category that Peirce also called firstness. He described this category of firstness in many different ways. He used such terms as 'quality,' 'being,' 'feeling,' and 'impulse.' In the firstness state, everything exists as a potentiality, as a possibility. There is no action or relationship in this state, only quality or beingness. According to Peirce, the secondness state is where action takes place. You have to have action before you can start the process of making connections among things based on their qualities. In this passage, Peirce is referring to qualitative nature of firstness as feeling."

"What about the kinds of qualities we use for Engaged Intelligence?"

"Do you mean affective, sensory, and logical?"

"Yes, you used the word 'feeling' for affective. How do these fit in?"

"'Affective,' 'sensory,' and 'logical' are general categories for sorting different kinds of qualities according to different modes of being so that we can talk about them. What we call 'affective' qualities have to do with feelings, attitudes, and emotions. However, anything having to do with qualities of value, including objective value such as 'redness' or 'hardness,' belongs in the category of firstness as long as these remain unrelated to anything else. Peirce would have said that any of these are qualities of beingness, or firstness. Firstness is pure potentiality and has no separate parts."

"Then is firstness just potential without any action to go along with it?"

"Yes."

"And Peirce is now calling this 'feeling'?"

"Yes. I can see that this is confusing."

"How about an example?"

"Suppose you wanted to make a bird house," I suggested. "In this case, the 'wanting' part would be firstness, as feeling or impulse."

"Wanting is the same as feeling?"

"Yes, at least, it is a kind of feeling. Wanting, desire, fearing, and hoping are feelings having to do with future outcomes. Desire is the underlying component of purpose. How you formulate and achieve purposes boils down to the mental relationships you make among feeling, action, and outcome."

"What do you mean?"

"I mean just what Dottie's theory shows. Multi-relational thinkers use feeling, or what she calls intensity, to drive them as they formulate a purpose. Feeling in this sense is a state of highly focused attention for selecting and rejecting among the qualities of options. This intensity, or feeling, governs how a multi-relational thinker uses time, space, and materials. Intensity is a non-issue for those who are random thinkers. They do not confront options so much as they randomly accept what comes by. That is why their actions and outcomes rarely hook together well."

"What about the others?"

"Analytical thinkers use a high degree of intensity to figure out how to achieve a purpose, once they have one. They do not like to spend much time constructing purposes, like multi-relational thinkers do. Analytical thinkers like to strategize. They like figuring out how to achieve a goal, how to work the glitches out, and how to solve problems. For analytical thinkers, the projected outcome, the goal, becomes the driver of both feeling and action."

"What about direct thinkers?"

"For direct thinkers, the goal directs the action, and the action directs the feeling. This means that the outcome, the actions for getting them, and the desire to have them are all hooked together in a straight line. Direct thinkers desire what they have already had, or done, or seen before. They want more of the same. For them, desire is subjugated to the action, to the getting part. At the same time, action is subjugated to outcome. We could go back to the birdhouse for an example."

"Great!"

"Regardless of how you ultimately apply the components of feeling, action, and outcome, desire is the force that initializes action. If you think like a multi-relational thinker, you might not end up building a bird house, even if you started out to do so."

"Is that because multi-relational thinkers generate new ideas?"

"Yes. Multi-relational thinkers may start out at the same place as everyone else. They may begin with a particular goal or idea. However, intensity which is the confrontation of different qualities among materials, guides each of the relationships they make as they work. Multi-relational thinkers decide what to do next based upon the outcome of these prior relationships in juxtaposition with whatever subsequent options and materials arise. Every idea and every material possesses many possible qualities and potential qualitative relationships. Since the materials are being considered without a specific outcome in mind, the possible relationships among the qualities of differing materials is enormous. In addition, a variety of outcomes are possible for each act of relating the qualities in one thing to the qualities of another. That is why the manner in which these qualities are perceived and then related to one another may produce any kind of outcome or nothing at all. But it rarely produces what was originally intended. Outcome is a starting place for multi-relational thinkers, not an end-in-view."

"What about random thinkers?"

"They might hammer some pieces of wood together, but they would ignore directions. If they came across any problems, or something that needed figuring out, they would use the 'bubble-gum and Band Aid' approach, taking the easiest option available even if the whole project falls apart as a result. They might also quickly become bored and abruptly drop the whole project. Their immediate being of feeling is usually shallow and transitory."

"And a direct thinker would like to follow plans. Right?"

"Right," I agreed. "Direct thinkers like to follow plans, and analytical thinkers like to construct plans."

"But analytical thinkers rarely follow the plans they construct," Hal said, speaking from experience.

"Not all that rarely," I countered. "Analytical thinkers follow plans when first learning how to do something. And they follow plans at other times, especially when using the plans as a template to be adapted or altered in some way. Analytical thinkers like to innovate and develop new applications."

"I can see that."

"Now, we should go back to Peirce's point here. His point is that 'wanting,' which he called firstness and feeling, is what starts action. When you put the wanting together with action, or secondness, then you have 'action propelled by the immediate being of feeling'."

"By 'action,' do you mean I would have started to build the birdhouse?"

"Not necessarily. This was Peirce's point. Desire, or feeling, may start you and keep you going, but feeling and action as a pair are incomplete. They do not lead anywhere. There must be a pattern to the action, or else all you have is chaos. Thirdness, what Peirce also calls habit, representation, relationship, and so on, provides pattern to the actions propelled by feeling. This is what makes feeling and action play out into a form of some sort. If you want to build a birdhouse, the pattern of actions propelled by feeling result in a birdhouse, unless you are a random or multi-relational thinker. In the first instance, you are likely to end up with a poorly constructed mish-mash. In the case of multi-relational thinking, the outcome may be something else entirely."

"Is Peirce saying that this works the same for the universe?"

"Yes. If you are building a universe, the pattern of actions propelled by feeling, impulse, or whatever you want to call that energy, results in planets, solar systems, and the patterns of planetary motion that keep them in operation. In the earliest chaos, only feeling and action existed, no sequence, or habit. Because of this, Peirce says there was pure nothing. That is why an extra-intelligent person should have been able to figure out that something more must be going on. He gives more information about this next."

Now, the motive for alluding to that theory just here is, that in this way one can put in a strong light a position which the pragmaticist holds and must hold, whether that cosmological theory be ultimately sustained or exploded, namely, that the third category—the category of thought, representation, triadic relation, mediation, genuine thirdness, thirdness as such—is an essential ingredient of reality, yet does not by itself constitute reality, since this category (which in that cosmology appears as the element of habit) can have no concrete being without action, as a separate object on which to work its government, just as action cannot exist without the immediate being of feeling on which to act.

"What?" Hal asked, confused. "That sounds like one of those sentences we had early on."

"Let me see what I can do with it. Peirce mentions his cosmological theory to illuminate what the pragmaticist holds and must hold as a premise."

"And that is?"

"That the third category which we talked about earlier...."

"Do you mean representation?"

"Yes, and we also called it habit and sequence. By the phrase 'third category,' Peirce is referring to the category of thought that he calls representation, triadic relation, mediation, and, sometimes, relationship. 'Genuine thirdness,' he calls it. That category of thirdness looks real, because it is the part you can see, hear, touch, talk, and argue about."

"What else could be real? He included thought in his category of thirdness. What else do you need for reality?"

"Make a guess."

"I think Peirce is just playing with words here. Being able to touch something or talk about it would make it real as far as I'm concerned. I bet most people would agree with me."

"But not Peirce. Thirdness is an essential ingredient of reality, but is not by itself reality. Thirdness includes such things as habit, pattern, sequence, representation, and relationship."

"Do the parts you cannot touch or talk about make up reality?"

"No. All three categories are essential to reality. You could not have something that means anything if action did not exist, because actual existence requires that something must actually move around in time and space. This thing we call action, put into motion by feeling, or intensity, or energy, is what provides us with the dynamic part of the system from which we get reality."

"Are you saying that action makes reality?"

"I am saying that reality, in order to be real, must involve action, even if that action is in the form of duration or movement in time, as it is in Dottie's non-verbal theory."

"Are you saying that action is like duration? Action seems more like energy to me."

"Not in Peirce's categories. Energy enables action, but it is not action. In this same sense, action enables the expression of patterns, things, and events but action is not the substance of these. Think of it like this. You and I and everything else that exists are dynamic systems and parts of dynamic systems, meaning that motion is a fundamental aspect of existence."

"I am not sure I understand what you mean."

"For the planets to move, for our blood to flow, and for our minds to think, we must have movement, or action. We must also have some force to get the movement started and keep it going. This force must necessarily be of an energetic nature. It must be an impulse, a burst, or any source of energy that can get things moving, like the Big Bang did for the universe. However, the word 'system' implies something more than action and energy."

"It implies a pattern."

"Yes. A dynamic system must have energy to fuel it. It must have action to make it dynamic. It must have a pattern to make it a system."

"And energy is what Peirce is calling feeling? Why not call it energy?"

"Because feeling is the term Peirce uses to refer to unrelated qualities of value, regardless of whether they are affective, sensory, or logical qualities. Also, I suspect that Peirce used the term 'feeling' for the firstness state in his cosmology because he believed that a conscious force guides the universe. He hinted at this when he discussed Lamarckian evolution in his essay, 'Evolutionary Love.' He also hints at this in what he has to say about God."

"Maybe the 'dark matter' that the astronomers talk about contains the consciousness of the universe."

"Maybe so. Peirce sometimes described firstness as an aesthetic impulse. He contended that the 'immediate being of feeling' drives all thought. In the case of people, we can probably be safe in assuming that, by the word 'feeling,' Peirce was including intuitions, flashes of insight, enthusiasm, appreciation, and senses of incongruity. He would also mean instincts and whatever else brings about movement or desire and the awareness of logical or intellectual discontinuities. He would have included the discomforts of doubt and the comforts of habit as well. But, in the case of the universe, he would mean energy, impulse, and potentiality."

"Does this mean feeling is everything that is not action or a system?"

"Yes," I answered, then continued. "Peirce has established continuity as the essence of thought because continuity is the capability of a mind to generalize from one event to another. Based on generalizations, we develop propositions about what might occur in the future. Then, we act based on our propositions. Here is what Peirce says next:"

> The truth is that pragmaticism is closely allied to the Hegelian absolute idealism, from which, however, it is sundered by its vigorous denial that the third category (which Hegel degrades to a mere stage of thinking) suffices to make the world, or is even so much as self-sufficient.

"Uh," Hal interrupted, "Hegel? I am not familiar with that name."

"Thesis, antithesis, and synthesis," I offered. "Does that ring a bell?"

"Only vaguely, from college days, I think."

I know I must have sighed at this. I thought we would be able to finish quickly. Having to deal with Hegel put speedy completion at risk. Perhaps I could find a way to say just enough to get Peirce's point across, yet still complete the essay discussion in a timely manner.

"And that is enough for today!" I said in my best school-marm manner. "We will start off with Hegel tomorrow. Maybe we can finish soon."

"I thought you said that Peirce was winding down."

"I guess he does not wind down in this essay so much as he brings up a major issue into the last paragraph and then stops abruptly."

"I guess that is to be expected," Hal said fatalistically, "considering what we have already gone through."

"We will deal with Hegel tomorrow."

"That is fine with me!"

Seventeen
HEGEL

Essay lines 643-655

I began slowly and a bit formally that next morning, wondering how little I could get away with in this explanation.

"Hegel was a German philosopher who lived from 1770 to 1831. He wanted to determine the methods by which ideas become true. He asserted the necessity of a thing carrying its own opposite, or contrast, you might call it. Truth was the third thing that emerges, or is synthesized, from settling the conflict between the first two."

"Then, Hegel was saying that truth came out of reconciling the opposites? That sure sounds like Zen to me."

"Hegel's triad was most definitely not a Buddhist-like concept! It takes a balancing act to reconcile the opposites of *yin* and *yang*. Hegel's synthesis presupposes conflict and an improvement of some sort, instead of balancing. Like nearly all Westerners, Hegel operated out of the typically Western perspective of salvation time."

"What is salvation time?"

"Salvation time drives the Judeo-Christian perspective which probably came down to us via the Egyptians. Salvation time has us thinking that we are headed somewhere that will be an improvement upon where we are now. Some people call it linear or goal-directed time, as opposed to the circular time perspective you find in Eastern and some other non-Western philosophical systems."

"Such as?"

"Such as Native American traditions, for one. Our Judeo-Christian notion of time is heavily influenced by geometry and spatial metaphors such as, 'that is too far into the future to see' and 'we should put that behind us, in the past.' For us, time is a place that you can be in or out of."

"I have heard of the term 'linear time' before, and circular time is familiar to me from studying Buddhism. It is just strange to think of a perspective on time as influencing someone's ideas. But I can see that it would, now that you mention it."

"Our Western time perspective has us operating under the assumption that we are progressing in a spatial sense, in the sense of moving closer toward something. This idea of progressing, of striving to improve oneself or one's lot over time is embedded in our Western concepts about time, space, and energy. That is probably where we get our discovery bias."

"Discovery bias?"

"The bias we have in Western culture toward discovering things. The Eastern perspective is not progressive in that way. Or at least it was not until the East started to Westernize."

"I bet that is because the traditional Eastern perspective assumes cycles like birth-death-rebirth."

"Yes, as in 'To everything there is a season'."

"But that is from the Bible," Hal protested. "Ecclesiastes."

"And it is also from the *Tao Te Ching*. From my perspective, that phrase is much more compatible with the rest of the *Tao* than it is with the rest of the Bible. But that is not the point. The point is that Hegel, and everybody else in Western philosophy, considered thought as a progression, as coming from some point toward another. Hegel conceived of thought in terms of improving over time, as heading toward an ideal."

"Peirce thought that too," Hal argued. "That is what his unfolding thing was about."

"Do you mean evolution?"

He nodded.

"Yes, and Hegel considered thought as a progression too, but a progression resulting from a synthesis out of conflict instead of from evolutionary unfolding, as Peirce did. Still, as I said before, both Peirce and Hegel thought of ideas in terms of advancing over time, as heading toward an ideal reality."

"Then what was the difference between Peirce and Hegel?"

"Some people would say that Peirce was an Hegelian, meaning that his work fit Hegel's philosophy in a general way. Maybe we should first take a look at some of the key things on which they agreed."

"That is probably a good idea."

"Peirce and Hegel were both idealists as opposed to objectivists," I explained, "meaning that both Peirce and Hegel held that there was a perfect truth out there toward which we are, or should be, aiming."

"What about objectivists?"

"Some objectivists believe that what you see is what you get, that material reality is reality. Others believe that you cannot trust sense experience. That is, you cannot trust what you see, hear, smell, taste, or touch, to give you the truth about things."

"Then how do you find the truth?"

"By means of primary qualities. Primary qualities are objective things like shape and relations. Secondary qualities are what you know through the five senses. These sorts of objectivists believe that secondary qualities give us subjective and deceptive appearances. They would say that what is real are atoms and molecules moving according to the laws of nature. What we experience is an illusion."

"Ah," he said, "*maya*."

"What?"

His comment had thrown me off track.

"Maya. It means illusion. Remember? It is the Hindu term for illusion. What you just described as the second version of objectivism sounds just like the Hindu version of reality to me. The moving molecules would be Shiva dancing."

"However, unlike Shiva's dance, modern objectivists trust only formal logic and mathematics to yield truths about reality, not metaphors, sense observations, or experiences."

"I like Shiva better."

"Me, too. But our point here is that Peirce and Hegel were both idealists as opposed to objectivists."

"I can remember that."

"They were not idealists in the regular sense of the word," I cautioned. "Idealism is a broad category, covering lots of different kinds of idealism. Hegel and Peirce's kind of idealism was linked to perfect forms of real things. That is to say, they proposed an idealism hooked to the reality of forms and to the importance of method for bringing us closer to an understanding of these forms. I guess you could call them realistic idealists."

"Realistic idealists?" Hal queried. "Now what would that mean?"

"For one thing, they both believed method and doctrine are inseparable."

"What does that mean?"

"For Hegel, it meant that method is grounded in the idea of the synthesis, or resolution, of a conflict between two opposing doctrines. For Peirce, the issue was to figure out how synthesis occurs, especially in the context of the discovery and development of new ideas. For Peirce, method is a series of reasoning processes that produce right reasoning."

"Which we would call retroduction."

"Yes, that is what we refer to as retroduction in Dottie's theory. But Peirce's concept of retroduction concerns the deliberate application of an appropriate method for performing reasoning during certain stages in the construction of a hypothesis. Sometimes deduction and induction are required during the creation of a hypothesis in addition to abduction, before the whole theory is ready for explication and testing. For right reasoning to occur during the construction and testing of a hypothesis, logical method must be directed by ethics, and ethics, in turn, by aesthetics."

"I remember you mentioned this earlier. It sounds complicated to me."

"Way back at the beginning of our dialogue we discussed how Peirce was using the term 'ethics'," I said. "Do you remember?"

"I think he said that ethics has to do with human conduct."

"Good memory! Do you remember why Peirce thought that logic was a species of conduct?"

"Because you could think it out ahead of time."

"Meaning?" I prodded encouragingly.

"Meaning you can work out what to do and how to do it ahead of time."

"Right! That means that logic can be deliberately self-controlled. Since it is subject to self-control, reasoning is, therefore, also subject to praise or blame, as is all deliberate conduct."

"Does Hegel's method have an ethical component to it as Peirce's did?"

"It is not the same, but he does have an ethical component. Hegel believed that you could not analyze rational powers. You could just use them to explore concepts. He believed that this exploration gave insights into the mind of God and that history was the unfolding of a divine plan."

"That is an odd thing to believe. It is strange to think of history as the unfolding of a divine plan."

"Why is it strange?"

"Because," Hal said, "that would mean that whatever happens in the future is not subject to self-control."

"You are right, unless self-control means following a divine plan."

"How would you figure out what this divine plan was?"

"According to Hegel, history tells you what the plan is, plus whatever the situation is in the present, meaning the *status quo.*"

"Are you saying that Hegel believed that whatever happened in the past and whatever is happening in the present is because of a divine plan?"

"Yes, but he meant the word 'divine' as Peirce meant the term 'system,' as laws of nature or of an over-riding system."

"If Hegel believed that whatever happens in the future is a divine plan, did he believe that things inside the system do not affect other things?"

"No. Hegel just believed that the over-riding system controls deliberate changes in conduct as well as the outcomes of these changes. It is a hard theory to refute. You cannot prove it one way or another."

"Why in the world would Peirce go along with Hegel? Surely Peirce at least believed that you could affect the outcome of something in the future."

"Peirce believed that you could deliberately change your conduct to get more in line with what is ultimately right or real. That is not the same thing as affecting the ultimate outcome of something. Peirce liked Hegel because Hegel proposed a system, a method, by which God's plan played itself out. Hegel said that for every proposition, or thesis, there was an opposite proposition, an antithesis."

"Now I am beginning to remember this from college!" Hal interrupted excitedly. "Thesis, antithesis, synthesis. Is that right?"

"Yes it is. Peirce was interested in Hegel's idea of system, or method, connected to doctrine. He was not interested in Hegel's particular doctrine. Like Hegel, Peirce believed that method reveals the truth about ideal reality."

"What does that mean?"

"For Peirce, it meant just what he wrote about in this essay, that 'the sum of the effects that you might conceive a thing to have is the whole of your conception of that thing.' Or, in other words, the method, the way in which you conceive of something, determines what you can know about it and what you can do about it as well."

"But that would be the opposite of Hegel. If the past, present, and future are just the unfolding of God's will, how can you do anything about anything? I mean, what is the point?"

"For Hegel, the doing part came through conflict. Thesis and antithesis come into conflict and eventually produce a synthesis of the best of the two concepts."

"How did Hegel know what was the best? After all, sometimes the bad guys win."

"For Hegel, whoever wins is supposed to be the winner. He believed that history is a progression from lesser to greater synthesis and that every system that has been defeated held within it the seeds of its own destruction. So, getting from the conflict between thesis and antithesis to the synthesis part is seen as a necessary consequence of whatever system contains the conflict."

"That progression part sounds a lot like Peirce's evolution. What does all that mean?"

"It means that whatever synthesis results as the resolution of a conflict between a thesis and its antithesis is the correct result for the context within which it was formed. Whatever is, is supposed to be."

"How would that play out in the real world?"

"Take slavery. This is an example that Jayne Tristan likes to use in her classes." I found Jayne's example in my email files and read it to Hal:

In slavery, the master desires to be recognized and honored. The slave is dishonored to bring honor to the master. However, in dishonoring the slave, the master dishonors himself and so does not deserve honor. The slave does not have honorable standing, so he cannot honor the master. The value of a worthless slave's honor is worthless, yet the master needs this honor and recognition. The master-slave dilemma harbors the seeds of its own destruction.[13]

"Now, here is the contradiction that brings about a synthesis in the master-slave dilemma:"

Everyone desires recognition, honor, and respect. Therefore, the new truth that can be synthesized out of the conflict is that all people deserve equal recognition.[14]

"I can see how that worked," Hal said, then amended, "how it does work. But you said that Hegel believed that something was right just because it was so. That would be like saying that slavery was right when it was going on because it was going on. That is not idealistic."

"The idealism, for Hegel, comes from his premise that each of those syntheses brings us closer to a higher and better truth, or goodness, or whatever might be higher and better. Since history is the unfolding of a divine plan, everything that happened in history had to be correct because it was the unfolding of this plan."

"I still cannot understand how he could believe that what ever is, equals whatever is supposed to be!"

"That is a problem with Hegel. You might say that he envisioned progress as a spiral moving upward toward the ultimate truth or good. Some people even use the idea of a spiral shape to explain how the thesis-antithesis-synthesis thing works," I added, drawing a spiral on a piece of scrap paper. "Now, just imagine that this spiral has been going on since the beginning of human time. At the first point we have a thesis. Opposite that, we have its antithesis," I filled in these words as I spoke. "Then you have the conflict that is resolved by synthesis, and that synthesis rests higher on the spiral and becomes the new thesis. Then you start the whole thing all over again until you reached perfect truth."

"Did Peirce agree with Hegel on this? Did he agree that whatever is, is what should be?"

"Not at all! Yet, Peirce did hold with the methods-consequences perspective. He believed that method was the means by which we can discover more about an ideal reality. Peirce also has a three-part system, like Hegel, but he was disdainful of Hegel's dismissal of the first two categories. He did not like the way Hegel proposed his third category 'synthesis' as sufficient for describing the world. Here is what Peirce says about that:"

The truth is that pragmaticism is closely allied with Hegelian absolute idealism, from which, however it is sundered by its vigorous denial that the third category, (which Hegel degrades to a mere stage of thinking) suffices to make the world, or is even so much as self-sufficient.

"What does that mean?"

"Remember when I said that Hegel's system is like a spiral?"

Hal nodded.

"That spiral was headed upward, toward ever better conceptions."

"Like salvation time?"

"Yes, just like salvation time."

"Still," he argued, "Peirce's unfolding was heading toward ever better conceptions also."

"Yes. Peirce was caught up in salvation time, just like the rest of Western civilization. Nonetheless, Peirce felt that the parts of the unfolding that you could not see, the feelings of firstness and the actions of secondness, were as necessary to reality as the third category, which Peirce called thirdness, and which Hegel referred to as synthesis."

"Did Peirce see his unfolding in a spiral, as Hegel did?"

"No. For Peirce, the development of knowledge did not progress in a spiral or in any of our ordinary geometric ways."

"How did he see such development then?"

"Based on how he described abduction and what I have seen of his graphs, I would say Peirce saw knowledge as emerging out of a reticulated pattern, that is, as a multi-dimensional web."

"Reticulated?"

"Yes. Reticulated means web-like. Peirce's unfolding came from his concept of a network among relationships. Most of us think of relationships as familiar connections. We mentally sort things into categories based on the qualities that identify kinds of, parts of, stages and phases of, things and operations. Peirce's theory of abductive reasoning, at least in the way we have developed it from Dottie's model, shows how we can dismantle our familiar mental categories. When we do this, we can rearrange things and their qualities in completely unique and unusual ways."

"Would these happen to be the kinds of relationships," Hal asked wryly, "that the Cliftons used for building their house?"

"Yes. Hegel held that the system was the entire context which caused something to be true or not. Peirce, on the other hand, had the system as a context from which you could exit by means of abductive reasoning into the region that, for the sake of simplicity, I call "matrix." This matrix includes all options including those of value and purpose. This concept of a matrix is connected to Peirce's doctrines of continuity and fallibilism."

"And what is fallibilism, again?"

"Fallibilism has to do with our being imperfect creatures," I reminded him. "It means that we can never be absolutely certain that we are correct about something. Peirce did not use the term 'matrix,' however. My particular use of the word 'matrix' comes from John Dewey, who used it as a term for defining this hypothetical realm. Albert Upton took Dewey's meaning and wrote that 'a matrix contains everything else and every other possibility in the universe, other than what you are trying to explain'."

"That sounds like a violation of terminological ethics to me."

"What does?"

"Using a word from John Dewey to explain something Peirce defined."

"Astute of you to pick up on that. You are probably right. However, Peirce's explanation of this region would require an extensive explanation of the interaction of continuity, fallibilism, and evolution. I use the word 'matrix' because I can relate it to something that people can remember without having to give a lengthy explanation. If anyone wants to become a Peirce scholar, we can just transfer this concept over into his language. The concept of matrix is important because it is the region where value and purpose reside. Since we usually use the matrix unconsciously, few people understand that value directs the formation of all of our purposes. And a great many people do not realize that the way they form purposes affects the outcomes that they produce. I use Dewey's term for this hypothetical region because my goal is teaching people how to use these concepts, not how to recite them."

"Then, I guess I will permit you to use the word 'matrix,'" he teased.

"Thank you. So, from the perspective of the matrix, you can re-think any matter in terms of value and purpose as well as content. From the matrix, you can construct a hypothesis and make adjustments to both the hypothesis and to the means for testing it, before you act. Using abduction in that way would be called retroducing."

"Would that be part of what Peirce says is ethical?"

"Which part?"

"The part that says you can get out of the system and see how things should or could be in some other way?"

"Good question! Yes. The element of deliberate choice sets Peirce apart from Hegel. Hegel argued for the *status quo*. His philosophy held that whatever is, is what is supposed to be at that time and within that system. That takes the responsibility for ethics, and all other consequences, out of the hands of choice. It relegates the norms for personal and social conduct to following whatever rules or norms already exist."

"Regardless of whether they are right or wrong?"

"If a norm is in place, then it is right, according to Hegel. If the norm is wrong, the system will take care of it through conflict."

"That does not leave much room for gradual improvements."

"Good point. Now, a word about the term 'absolute idealism.' Hegel thought that the absolute ideal reality was reached by this process of synthesizing the best from opposing thoughts."

"I thought that Peirce did not believe in absolutes."

"He did not believe that you could know for sure when you had the absolute ideal reality. That is not the same thing as believing that such an absolute does not exist."

"Then, in what way did he agree with Hegel's idealism?"

"Hegelian absolute idealism contends that absolute truth exists, and that this truth may be found by means a particular system, or method. For Hegel, this method involved synthesizing the best from each side of a conflict between contraries."

"What are contraries?"

"Contraries are near opposites, but not complete contradictions of one another. Complete contradictions leave nothing to synthesize. The *yin* and *yang* symbol is an example of contraries. The dark side of the symbol has a piece of lightness in it, and the light side has a piece of darkness. Because each side contains an element in common with the other, you have something from which to synthesize a new outcome. For Hegel, this synthesis comes from a clash between the thesis, say the *yin*, and the antithesis, say the *yang*."

"I see that. Things do appear to work the way Hegel said. At least they appear that way to me."

"Many things in the human social arena appear to work that way," I conceded, "and in nature too. Things swing too far in one direction, then too far in another. They usually land somewhere just left or right of center. That does not mean that everything is guided by this principle, however, nor that it should be. Nor does it mean that reaching synthesis through conflict is the best or most natural way to operate. Remember, we are talking about differing beliefs concerning what is ultimately true or not. Hegel proposed that something could be valid during one historical era and invalid during another because the historical context had changed. His was a logic of dynamics, determining truth by employing the oppositional nature of dark and light, right and wrong, too much and too little. He sought to demonstrate how this opposition between forces plays out within contexts."

"It still sounds a lot like the *yin* and *yang* symbol to me," Hal commented. "Surely Peirce would have agreed with the context part?"

"Yes, but Peirce would not have agreed that truth changes from one historical context to another. Remember Peirce believed that there is an ultimate ideal reality and that any truth we uncover needs to be considered as a provisional truth, not an absolute. The reason we cannot assume that we have the absolute truth about something is that we, as fallible human beings, cannot trust that we know anything absolutely. Peirce dealt in probabilities. Thus, a truth is more or less certain to be true, based in large part upon the method by which it was ascertained. Its effect upon human conduct ultimately determines the meaning of that truth. For Peirce, truth does not change. We change our understanding through self-correction and growth in the course of inquiry."

"That makes sense."

"Other pragmatists went even further in this truth and context matter. Peirce was upset with John Dewey over this issue. He even called Dewey a 'nominalist,' which is a dirty word in most philosophical circles. Dewey said that a conclusion is either warranted or not, depending upon how a proposition is formulated. A different conclusion could be reached by re-formulating the qualities of a particular proposition. For Dewey, the issue was not so much a matter of truth changing through self-correction. He said we should consider the usefulness of a particular concept or piece of knowledge within a particular context for a particular purpose. For Dewey, when the purpose changes, then what you are going to consider as true is going to change, too."

"Then, Peirce and Hegel were saying that we are headed more and more toward some ultimate truth, but Dewey said that what is true or not depends on the situation and the purpose?"

"Yes. Peirce and Hegel were both idealists who believed there was an absolute truth out there and Dewey was not."

"What was he then?"

"Dewey called himself an instrumentalist. He held that natural laws and propositions, as well as facts, sensations, and actual things, were the materials of knowledge. These were tools, or instruments, for inquiring into matters." Upon saying this, I then remembered a comment that had just surfaced on my email Dewey list that morning. "Listen to what Frank Ryan, who is a philosophy professor at Kent State University, wrote about this."

> Dewey rejected the suggestion that the dependence of reality upon mind led to a cosmological Absolute or world Soul. Dewey perceived the conditions of experience as methodological rather than as cosmological, as explanatory of what it means to be an object of experience, not an account of the contents of the natural universe. As this organic unity evolved into the movement of inquiry, Dewey's transition from idealism to instrumentalism was complete.[15]

"Does that mean then, for Dewey, you can aim for nothing, not even a greater good? Heading toward an ideal would keep you on your toes. It would keep you striving toward bettering yourself."

"Not necessarily. Ryan also mentioned that, although Dewey rejects the notion of an absolute ideal good, he believed that by using his method of inquiry, you can progressively accumulate ever greater goodnesses. These are not the idealist's unattainable *summum bonum*, or greatest goods. They are accessible, human goodnesses. Dewey even suggested that the progressive nature of his inquiry methods might eventually cause a future concept of greatest good to surpass previous concepts. Ryan pointed out that you can use Dewey's methods, regardless of what doctrine you believe in."

"Doctrine?"

"I mean idealism, spiritualism, realism, materialism. You can take your pick of 'isms.' Though Dewey was not aiming toward an absolute ideal, he was seeking to define the best methods for defining purposes, for selecting the means for achieving those purposes, and for evaluating results along the way. Listen to this." I found my copy of John Shook's book, *Dewey's Empirical Theory of Knowledge and Reality*, and read from it:

> Peirce held that in knowing the world, the knower does not alter the reality known. Dewey held the instrumentalist view that for humans to have knowledge, the known object had to be created by the knower's actions altering the environment. In other words, the known object could not possess existence prior to being known.[16]

"Dewey saw no point in warranting something as true from a strictly logical perspective. For Peirce, however, scientific hypotheses should only be entertained from the perspective of reason and logic, though they should be developed in an ethical way for an admirable purpose."

"What other way would there be for something to be true?" Hal argued. "Surely something has to be logical to be true?"

"I said Dewey saw no point from a 'strictly logical' perspective," I reminded him, then recalled a statement I had read in Howard Callaway's book *Context for Meaning and Analysis*. "Listen to this:"

> Dewey's theory of the valuable involves a generalization of scientific method...from the usual sphere in which this is applied to the social and moral sphere. This point is crucial to understanding Dewey's concept of inquiry. We cannot think of value claims merely posited and not subject to revision, no more than other claims. As experience expands, new information and new situations give us grounds for revision of our values and value claims.[17]

"But," Hal argued, "something still has to be logical to be true, otherwise it would just be nonsense."

"Something can be logical and not be true," I reminded him. "Just think of *Alice in Wonderland*."

"Oh, right. I keep forgetting about that."

"In Dewey's logic, the criteria for proof resides in the formulation of qualities and the methods for examining these qualities for a particular purpose. Every purpose has aesthetic as well as ethical and logical components. For Dewey, when the purpose changes, so does everything else, as well as the shape of whatever truth is warranted or not." I changed course at this point. "But, we should not be talking about Dewey here. I only brought up his perspective so that I could give you a contrast for absolute idealism. One of the reasons that Peirce wrote this essay was that he did not like Dewey's interpretations of pragmatism. First though, let me just give a brief summary of these different perspectives on truth."

"That is fine with me."

"For Hegel, history is the unfolding of reason. Reason gives us access to truth. For Hegel, reason, which also meant order in terms of form and relationships, was fixed. This meant that something could only be one way and no other. So, history unfolds according to a fixed plan, according to destiny. Any contradictions that might occur in the course of this unfolding are only appearances because reason is ordered, and it orders whatever is."

"Ah! That would be hardening of the categories."

"Yes it would," I agreed. "For Peirce, truth is an unchanging reality distinct from our experience. Truth is something that you approach by means of inquiry. Peirce, too, believed in an ultimate ideal reality. This is to say that Peirce believed that there is an absolute truth and that we are forever coming closer to it by means of inquiry. We cannot, however, ever be absolutely certain that we have reached the truth. For Peirce, like Hegel, reason brings us toward something that is really there and, by means of right reasoning, we are moving towards greater permanence and fixity. Unlike Hegel, though, Peirce believes that truth resides in the future, not in history."

"What about Dewey?"

"Dewey believed that the natural world is impermanent and made up of changing events. All we can have are guaranteed expectations, warranted truths, which have been established by means of a series of experiments. Dewey did not like to use the word 'true.' He called truths 'warranted assertions.' For Dewey, an assertion is either warranted or not depending upon whether it has satisfied the purpose for which it was designed. A warranted assertion is true because it permits the resolution of a problematic situation. Unlike Peirce, Dewey did not believe that reality was moving toward greater permanence and fixity."

"That is a lot to remember!"

"There is no need to remember it," I assured him. "You just need to have a general idea of the differences."

"I think I have that."

"Then, I am going to return to Peirce's statement."

The truth is that pragmaticism is closely allied to the Hegelian absolute idealism, from which, however, it is sundered by its [pragmaticism's] vigorous denial that the third category (which Hegel degrades to a mere stage of thinking) suffices to make the world, or is even so much as self-sufficient.

"By sundered, Peirce means that, although his pragmaticism is closely allied to Hegel's absolute idealism, he disagrees with Hegel on other issues. The main disagreement is with Hegel's contention that synthesis, the outcome of the conflict between thesis and antithesis, can stand on its own as reality. Peirce means that you would not have a synthesis without the action and reaction that create it. How such actions and reactions occur, or are made to occur, are vital to the eventual outcome."

"What does Peirce mean by Hegel's 'third category'?"

"The category of synthesis. That is the category that Peirce called thirdness. By 'thirdness,' Peirce meant ideas, representations, relationships, and results. He meant all of those things that most of us think of as being real."

"I remember thirdness, and secondness and firstness as well," he said, confidently. "Firstness is quality, or feeling, or energy, where everything just has the potential for being. Secondness is action without any connections. And thirdness is the pattern of relationships between things."

"Good!" I said, pleased again at his memory. "Peirce did not agree with Hegel's position that the third category of the triad, synthesis, is the most significant. This is what Peirce was referring to when he said that his pragmaticism is 'sundered' from Hegel's absolute idealism. Here is more of what Peirce says about this:"

Had Hegel, instead of regarding the first two stages with his smile of contempt, held on to them as independent or distinct elements of the tri-une Reality, pragmaticists might have looked up to him as the great vin-dicator of their truth. (Of course, the external trappings of his doctrine are only here and there of much significance.)

"Peirce is referring again here to Hegel's thesis and antithesis, since Hegel contended that truth resided in synthesis, which Peirce would have called thirdness."

"Thesis is the initial force, and antithesis is the anti-force. Right?"

"Right. Peirce's complaint against Hegel was that he dismissed the first two, thesis and antithesis, as irrelevant in terms of their contributions to real-ity," I explained. "Instead, Hegel settled on the outcome, the synthesis or what we might call the result of the conflict, as reality."

"That sounds like 'the meaning of something is in its consequences'."

"Contending that the meaning of a conflict is in the synthesis is not the same thing as contending that the rational meaning of a word or other expres-sion resides in its conceivable bearing upon the conduct of life."

"Because of the conduct issue?"

"Exactly! The activity of qualifying and relating among things based upon their qualitative similarities and differences are the parts that enable us to think matters out in advance of doing them. If only the category of thirdness, or representation, were real, then no way would exist for figuring out how to change your conduct in the future. That is one of the main problems with Hegel's theory. Also, meaning could only be one way and no other for Hegel, because he saw reason as a fixed order in terms of form and relationships."

"Then Hegel must have suffered from hardening of the categories," Hal playfully commented, then asked: "For Peirce, then, are the categories of firstness and secondness the parts that make reality?"

"No. Firstness and secondness are integral parts of reality. Quality, rela-tion, and representation are all indispensable aspects of reality. Peirce dis-dained Hegel for ignoring the place of the other two forces. Peirce's theory, remember, presumes the capability of conscious control. The faculty for that control resides in the ability of the mind to make relationships out of the inter-actions of firstness and secondness. Another way of saying this is that the in-teractions among feeling and action, which are brought into relationship as thought, habit, or representation, provides us with reality. Peirce called this relationship 'thirdness,' which corresponds to what Hegel called 'synthesis.' Once you have synthesized, that is, once you have established a habit or cre-ated a representation, your actions are no longer subject to self-control. Peirce's pragmaticism says you can only effectively control outcomes before you take action, and you cannot do this if you ignore the dynamic parts of the system that brings an outcome into being."

"That makes sense."

"We are almost finished. The ending is disappointing, by the way. This essay does not have an ending. It just stops. Here is the last sentence:"

For pragmaticism belongs essentially to the triadic class of philosophical doctrines, and is much more essentially so than Hegelianism is. (Indeed, in one passage, at least, Hegel alludes to the triadic form of his exposition as to a mere fashion of dress.)

"That is it. That is the end of the essay."

"You were right," he agreed. "It is disappointing. Peirce ended this essay so abruptly that I feel a little bit empty. It took so much effort to understand him, that I would at least have liked a more satisfying conclusion."

"Peirce was a thinker, not a writer," I commented, as if Hal needed reminding. "Besides, now you have a good grasp of Peirce's pragmaticism."

"I may have a good grasp, but I sure wish he had tied things together."

"Maybe we can do that for him. We could talk about how Engaged Intelligence training teaches people to become the sorts of pragmaticists that would make Peirce proud. Engaged Intelligence training is just an educational expression of Peirce's pragmaticism and Relational Thinking Styles."

"I would like that. As much as I know about Engaged Intelligence training, I am still missing the direct link between the exercises in that training program and Peirce's pragmaticism."

"Then that is what we will discuss tomorrow."

Eighteen
ENGAGED INTELLIGENCE

This would be our final day of discussing Peirce's essay. Since Hal appeared to have understood what Peirce had been trying to explain during our discussions, I felt sure he would have little trouble seeing how Peirce's pragmaticism connects to Engaged Intelligence training. I knew I would have to do some summarizing, though, before we could begin connecting the two.

"Today," Hal commented as we settled in that next morning, "you are going to lay the transatlantic cable."

"I am going to 'what'?"

"Lay the transatlantic cable. You said that you were going to connect Peirce's pragmaticism with Engaged Intelligence training. So far, I see an ocean of difference between them."

"I doubt you will think that by the time we are finished," I assured him.

"Fire away, then."

"Do you remember early in our discussion of the essay that Peirce said that his pragmaticism 'eliminated the phenomenal, or sense based, equivalents of words and ideas'? He said that his pragmaticism only dealt with finding the rational meaning of words and general ideas?"

"Sure I remember. You said that we parted company with Peirce there."

"Good memory! When I said that we parted company with him on that point, I was referring to Relational Thinking Styles. I meant Dottie's non-verbal model of *logica utens*. Peirce would have argued that these everyday reasoning habits cannot properly be called reasoning methods."

"Why not?"

"Because they are habits and they are instinctual. All reasoning, according to Peirce, is 'voluntary, critical, and controlled, all of which...can only be done if it is done consciously.' Listen to this." I read a statement by Peirce from K. T. Fann's book *Peirce's Theory of Abduction*:

> A mental operation which is similar to reasoning in every other respect except that it is performed unconsciously cannot be called 'reasoning'...because it is idle to criticize as good or bad that which cannot be controlled.... Since reasoning is a kind of voluntary and deliberate conduct, we are held responsible for its consequences. It is clear such conduct comes under the domain of ethics for ethics is the theory of self-controlled or deliberate conduct.[18]

"Peirce contended that we acquire the bulk of our knowledge by means of our *logica utens*. These reasoning instincts work well for us for most things. However, sometimes we come across things that instinct cannot handle. For these matters, we need to have access to trained reasoning methods, *logica do-*

cens. Peirce's pragmaticism is about *logica docens*. From what I have seen, he apparently did not address *logica utens* in any systematic way. In any case, a theory of *logica utens* was not his purpose. He was seeking to develop formal methods of reasoning. You and I know that different people have different habits of reasoning and that we cannot successfully teach people how to reason more effectively unless we know what these habits are. Relational Thinking Styles lays out the method for determining these habits by which people determine the rational meaning of the 'phenomenal equivalents' of words and ideas. We can demonstrate that all reasoning begins with, and is guided by, a non-verbal reasoning habit of one sort or another. These reasoning habits conform to Peirce's description of the processes of induction, deduction, and abduction. We cannot teach people what these are and how to use them more effectively unless we have a verbal system with which to discuss them. That verbal system comes to us through Peirce's *logica docens*. Engaged Intelligence training teaches people how to think rationally using Peirce's verbal method of *logica docens* so that they can become conscious of their mental habits. Once conscious, we can learn to deliberately adapt our mental habits, our *logica utens*, as a situation requires.

"Then is Engaged Intelligence training the same as *logica docens* and Relational Thinking Styles, *logica utens*?"

"Engaged Intelligence training is not exactly *logica docens*. It is a way of teaching people how to perform all of the mental activities needed to effectively perform each of the inference-making methods that comprise Peirce's *logica docens*."

"Oh."

"Relational Thinking Styles demonstrates that, in addition to verbal reasoning methods, parallel non-verbal reasoning methods exist. Although the verbal methods are necessary for communicating meaning, the non-verbal methods are primary to all reasoning. If someone does not also learn to reason well non-verbally, then the verbal training will be useless. Engaged Intelligence training helps people to develop greater skill with both."

"With both verbal and non-verbal reasoning?"

"Yes. The concept that reasoning is non-verbal tends to be obvious to people who are artists, dancers, and auto-mechanics. However, people like philosophers, who deal almost entirely with language, often have a difficult time recognizing the fundamental influence of non-verbal mental processes on all reasoning. From the non-verbal perspective, experience-based activities involve the same sorts of mental processes as verbal ones."

"And Peirce would not agree with that?"

"Peirce believed that, if we do not have conscious control of an activity, we are not reasoning, which does not automatically exclude non-verbal activities. However, most people do not have deliberate control of their non-verbal activities, especially their non-verbal reasoning processes. That is why Engaged Intelligence training is so valuable. This training helps people to gain a measure of control over their normally habitual processes."

"What about people who habitually use abductive reasoning?"

"As long as they use the abductive process habitually, Peirce would not view what they do as reasoning. Peirce was investigating formal logical processes, which he considered to be verbal and applicable primarily to mathematical and scientific issues. Although Peirce recognized that pragmatism had universal applications, he did not flesh out the broad-based applications of his theory as we have. It took him a whole lifetime just to lay out this system in the verbal and logical sense."

"Yet, the Engaged Intelligence exercises cover all sorts of matters."

"Good point. Peirce's concept of a deliberate, verbal method of reasoning and our concept of non-verbal reasoning habits both require the same underlying reasoning methods. Whether you do so deliberately or habitually, if you follow these methods, you will reason rightly, regardless of whether you are trying to prove a theorem or figure out how to build a patio in the back yard. If you do not follow the methods of right reasoning, you greatly lower your odds of getting good results, no matter how intelligent you are. The seventeenth-century philosopher, Francis Bacon, had a good metaphor for this. Bacon said that if a fast runner travels down the wrong path, he is not going end up where he needs to be, although he may get there quickly. However, a slow traveler, following the right path will eventually reach the correct end."

"That sounds like the old I.Q. problem," Hal commented, "certifiably smart people who make unbelievably bad decisions."

"That would be it. Engaged Intelligence training can help to make teachers and students aware of the different reasoning skills necessary for making different kinds of decisions. The exercises for this program show how Peirce's reasoning methods can be applied to all sorts of problems, including those about political, social, and environmental issues as well as body intelligence."

"What is body intelligence?"

"Body intelligence is reflected by the way we use our bodies in space. It comes out when we interact with physical tools and raw materials, including our bodies themselves, as in athletics and dance. Dancers and football players reason with their bodies, parallel to the ways that logicians reason with language. We need to use language to explain this non-verbal reasoning, however. Dottie's model does not include a rigorous treatment of language and meaning, like Peirce's theory does. We need the verbal aspect of Peirce's model of right reasoning to communicate the non-verbal aspects of Dottie's model. Since non-verbal reasoning underlies verbal reasoning, we need an effective way of identifying how non-verbal reasoning works in order to effectively improve both verbal and non-verbal reasoning."

"Ah," he said, seeing my point then, "the non-verbal problem. As Dottie says, 'How much is there to say about something you cannot talk about'?"

"Yes. Without a way to communicate distinctly and unambiguously about non-verbal meaning-making, there is no way to be sure we are understanding one another, and no basis for testing out whether our ideas are sound."

"Are you saying that people need to understand Peirce in order to understand Relational Thinking Styles?"

"No, I am saying that people need to understand Peirce's theory of verbal meaning in order to be able to talk about Dottie's non-verbal model."

"Does Engaged Intelligence training make it possible to do this?"

"Yes it does, because it provides a common language and a way to have a set of common experiences within the framework that both Peirce and Dottie use. This allows people to develop better reasoning skills in both the verbal and non-verbal realms."

"I see that now."

"Both verbal and non-verbal right reasoning matter for everything we think and do. As you know, my primary interest is education, especially improving teacher education. I want this information to be used for inspiring teachers to develop their own critical-thinking abilities. I want to wake up the will to learn in educators so that they can be better prepared to inspire and guide students through the learning process. I believe that Peirce has what is needed to construct the solutions to our educational problems."

"How would you apply Engaged Intelligence training to young children?"

"The same way we did for our own children, by taking the fundamental principles of Engaged Intelligence training and finding ways of developing appropriate expectations and learning situations."

"As we did with chores?"

"Exactly! We set up household chores as learning situations by applying our knowledge of *logica docens*, based on Engaged Intelligence training, to the particular *logica utens* of each child. We gave each child chores that provided opportunities to develop the particular reasoning skills that child needed. We knew what these needs were based on their non-verbal reasoning habits."

"But we did not put each of the children through Engaged Intelligence training," Hal argued. "I mean, Tonya still cannot read or do math."

"That is true, but she can reason intelligently in spite of her severe learning disabilities. She has made a fine life for herself and her family because she learned how to engage her intelligence for making good decisions in her day-to-day living. She learned to do this because we adapted materials, expectations, and skills for her needs."

"I guess I am confused. Just who is Engaged Intelligence training intended for, then? Is it just for people who can read?"

"The formal Engaged Intelligence training program is for people who can read, mostly for people who are college-educated or planning to go to college. This is a course for people who plan to teach, or to manage other people or projects. It is designed to help people learn how to figure out general principles and abstract concepts and then apply these effectively. However, we do not need this particular class to teach people how to engage their intelligences. We can help people learn these skills in many different ways. These skills are, after all, basic to everything we do."

"Then why not make a class for people like Tonya?"

"Once others know the principles of Engaged Intelligence and how to apply them, they can take these principles and develop all sorts of programs, including programs for those who are severely learning disabled, like Tonya. I emphasize the verbal training program because I want to help educators build 'a loosely compacted individual,' a community of learners as Peirce proposed, instead of a collection of individual teachers. We should all be exploring and developing ways to bring about the will to learn within everyone associated with an educational system. This includes administrators, coaches, secretaries, janitors, and cafeteria workers, as well as teachers, students, and parents. When everyone who is involved in education comes to understand the basic principles of Peirce's version of pragmatism and Dottie's non-verbal expression of it, they can begin to apply its principles to develop competencies in all sorts of areas. Once that process begins, teachers will discover their own ways of encouraging the intellectual, aesthetic, ethical, and social development of their students. Peirce's pragmaticism should be used to provide educational norms. Once established, these norms can go a long way in helping us to build the minds we need to formulate and implement good solutions. This world is in desperate need of good solutions that do not cause bigger problems down the road, the kinds of good solutions that right reasoning can produce."

He nodded thoughtfully at this.

"I think I mentioned yesterday," Hal said, "that as much as I know about Engaged Intelligence training, I still do not see the direct connection between Peirce's philosophy and those exercises in the training program."

"That may be because no obvious doctrine of educational philosophy exists within Peirce's writings. Peirce gave his opinions on education in a few letters and manuscript notes, but he did not formulate any specific doctrine concerning educational theory. We have to consider that his philosophy of education is embedded within the totality of his doctrine, instead of distinctly stated. We need to take his whole theory as a theory of learning."

"Why not? Everything else has been embedded, too."

"Do you remember what Peirce said about the formation of a belief?"

"I think so. He said something about beliefs being formed by repetition, like habits, until you think there is no other way to believe."

"Yes. The same process of repetition holds true for non-verbal reasoning habits. The longer you tend to think in a particular way, the more it appears to you that this is the only way in which to think. We become experts at getting along by means of our mental habits. Engaged Intelligence training helps people to disengage those habits by retraining their mental muscles. It works in much the same way that weight training retrains physical muscles."

"That is a strange way to think about Engaged Intelligence training, as building mental muscles."

"That is exactly what it does," I assured him, "and it takes as much effort and practice as weight training, especially when someone does not naturally think as an experimentalist."

"I guess it would."

"Here is how Engaged Intelligence training connects to Peirce's doctrine of pragmaticism," I began. "Peirce contended that all rational thought comes out of a particular interaction among his three categories. Those are the categories of firstness, secondness, and thirdness. In another essay, Peirce referred to these categories as 'The Three Universes of Experience' because these are the arenas in which we experience reality. The first universe, which corresponds to the category of firstness, which he also called by the terms 'quality,' 'value,' and 'purpose,' is the 'Universe of Ideas.' Peirce said that this universe is filled with the kind of 'airy nothings' that exist only in the mind. These would be the kinds of thoughts that a poet or a pure mathematician might think and even give a name."

"What about the second universe?"

"The second universe corresponds to Peirce's category of secondness or actuality, which he also called action. This is the 'Universe of the Brute Actuality' of things and facts. This is the universe of actual stuff and actual events that actually occur but have no connections among one another. This is the state in which everything is an unrelated individual."

"And the third universe?"

"The third universe of experience corresponds to Peirce's thirdness, or relationship. Peirce called this the 'Universe of the Power to establish connections among things and ideas.' This third universe is the one that allows us to make relationships between things and qualities within the same universe and among the other universes as well. I call this third Universe of Experience, the 'Universe of Inbetweeness.' In this third universe, we make and discover relationships, this is where things connect with one another. Peirce used the word 'mediation' for this connecting-up concept. His theory of knowledge resides in this ability of minds to form and understand inbetweenesses. These relationships, which can be either actual or possible, are the result of the interactions between objects and minds. Peirce believed that we could train our minds to discover these relations. Engaged Intelligence training teaches people how to understand these relationships, so that they can discover, and describe them. They learn how to create original relationships as well. The making of relationships produces inferences, which are the vehicles of meaning making."

"Do you mean that inference-making is the vehicle of all meaning making, or just of reasoning? You must be able to make meaning in other ways besides reasoning, like in art, for example."

"I sure do mean that inference-making is the vehicle of all meaning making. When we are making meaning, we are reasoning. Art requires reasoning as much as science does. We discussed inferences earlier when we talked about Peirce's theory of signs, remember?"

"I remember that discussion. But I am sure you did not say then that all meaning-making is done by means of inferences."

"Maybe I thought you might infer this from our discussions," I teased. "Inference-making is the vehicle for non-verbal meaning-making as well as for verbal understanding. We could just as easily have called Dottie's non-verbal reasoning habits 'non-verbal inference-making habits.' Engaged Intelligence training could just as easily have been called 'inference-making training.' Any application of Peirce's doctrine to educational theory must focus upon teaching those inference-making skills necessary for producing what he called rational thought."

"I think I am starting to see the connection."

"Good. Most people think of inferences differently than Peirce."

"How so?"

"As we discussed earlier, Peirce held that abduction is its own unique form of inference-making, just as induction and deduction are. He proposed that deduction should be subordinate to abduction and that induction should be subordinate to deduction. He called the proper use of these 'right reasoning'."

"So?"

"This is a difficult concept for most people to understand."

"How come?"

"Because you cannot teach people how to reason rightly until they have mastered the basic skills which underlie all three types of reasoning. In Dottie's model we use the word 'retroduction' to refer to this process of right reasoning. People who do not have an innate capability to reason abductively usually do not understand the process of abductive reasoning. The Davis Non-verbal Assessment makes the abductive inference-making process visible, which enables others to see what it is and how it works. You must be able to reason abductively, as well as deductively and inductively in order to have the capability for applying right reasoning to a situation."

"Does that mean, if someone does not know how to do all three kinds of reasoning, they cannot do right reasoning?"

"That is what it means. That is also why it is so important to be able to demonstrate abductive reasoning with the same clarity that deduction and induction can be demonstrated."

"That makes sense."

"Anytime you make any kind of an inference, you are traveling within Peirce's third universe of experience. Engaged Intelligence training helps people to develop the mental skills necessary for performing all three sorts of inferences. With these skills, people can engage this third universe of experience more effectively to produce right reasoning. Different levels of exercises build up your abilities for performing the skills needed for making good inferences."

"And these skills are?"

"Qualification, analysis, and interpretation."

"Those are the main sections of Engaged Intelligence training."

"Yes, they are. These three categories of skills correspond to Peirce's three categories of firstness, secondness, and thirdness. I should probably mention that, by the very fact that we are discussing these categories, we are operating in Peirce's category of thirdness, or representation. So, even as we teach people how to be more facile with the first two categories, we are really teaching them thirdness skills."

"Then is Engaged Intelligence training really thirdness training?"

"Just call it *logica docens* training and leave it at that. We will begin with the category of firstness, which as you know, Peirce also called 'being,' 'quality,' 'feeling,' and 'impulse.' By the way, as we go along, you may notice that the skills within each of the three sections of Engaged Intelligence training are, themselves, organized according to Peirce's three categories. Thus, the category of qualification is organized into the qualities of firstness, secondness, and thirdness. We call them qualities of feeling, sensing, and reason."

"Yes, I see that connection."

"Facility with this first category requires the ability to make distinctions among the qualities of things, so we teach the skills and the vocabulary of noticing. These qualification skills are essential for good reasoning because we can only reason about the similarities and differences among what we notice. Abductive reasoning, especially, requires the ability to notice subtle qualitative differences. Abduction also requires the ability to establish unique and unusual similarities among things, as you must do with metaphorical relationships."

"What about deduction?"

"Deductive reasoning relies upon a back-and-forth sorting of both similarities and differences. This back-and-forth sorting of deductive reasoning is done to develop categories and set up analyses. We use inductive reasoning for making generalizations and to sort things into pre-set categories."

"I see how Peirce connects with the qualification section and with similarities and differences. Now, what about the next part?"

"Analysis skills provide the tools of relating, which are the tools for engaging Peirce's category of secondness. Secondness, remember, is also called 'action' and 'relating.' Various forms of analysis provide tools for selecting and relating qualities among things as we form and examine values, purposes, goals, and other ideas. Thus, analysis is a relational tool for relating qualities, forming purposes, and making inferences. Analysis can help us to understand what something means and to figure out how to explain what we mean more effectively. That 'something' can itself be a purpose, or it can be a process for thinking out whatever has been, or is going to be, done for a purpose."

"That must mean you can use analysis while you construct a conditional purpose," he suggested, "and when you make plans to prove it, or achieve it."

"Wow! I am impressed!"

He shrugged diffidently, and I continued.

"We teach three forms of analysis in Engaged Intelligence training. They are classifications, basic structure analysis, and basic systems analysis."

"I know all of those," Hal interjected. "Let me see if I can define them. Classifications sort out kinds of things, structure analysis shows part-whole relationships, and systems analysis has to do with things that operate in time."

"Yes, analysis provides a set of tools for forming relationships."

"Surely there are other ways of forming relationships?"

"Sure there are. Painting is another way of forming relationships, as are dancing, cooking, constructing a sentence, and any other kind of activity. Whenever we make, say, or do something, we are forming relationships. The important thing to keep in mind about Peirce's category of secondness is that it stands for action and movement. Secondness is the category of action, including the action part of any activity of relating things and their qualities."

"Then, why analysis?"

"Because analysis allows us to carefully examine an idea in advance of doing something. It is a relational tool for organizing, comparing, and contrasting the qualities of things. With analysis we can figure out what was done in the past and to make changes before we act again in the future. We can also use analysis to discover and evaluate new possibilities. Just as for qualification, Peirce's three categories are contained within the analysis portion of Engaged Intelligence training. Analysis always begins with qualification for determining the purpose of, and categories for, the activity. Qualification is followed by the act of relating things and their qualities according to a particular form. The conclusion, or outcome, of an analysis corresponds to thirdness."

"What about the interpretation section?"

"The interpretation section of Engaged Intelligence training corresponds to Peirce's category of thirdness, which he also called 'representation,' 'thought,' 'mediation,' and 'relationship.' The interpretation section is designed to teach people how to comprehend and define the meaning of words and other signs. As you know, we have this section broken into two steps. Step one concerns learning how to identify Peirce's three main types of signs. Step two involves learning how to identify and apply the principles of context and matrix when interpreting the meaning of a sign. Context is what some people call the 'sign situation'."

"Does the matrix come in here too?"

"Yes. The matrix corresponds to Peirce's firstness, or state of potentials and possibilities. Matrix is where everything else in the universe resides."

"Everything else?"

"Everything except for the sign. The matrix contains a whole lot of possibilities. It is a hypothetical region from which we explore possibilities and form purposes. Interpretation is a process of building up a theory about the matrix and context surrounding whatever we want to figure out."

"What is the matrix good for?"

"Everything, but especially abduction. Abductive inferences are driven by acts of valuation. Learning to maneuver effectively within the matrix means learning the skills of valuation. The matrix is a category-less place. It provides no distinct markers or signposts to guide your thinking, as the context does."

"I remember all of that."

"The interpretation portion of Engaged Intelligence training is also organized according to Peirce's three categories. The matrix corresponds to firstness, the context to secondness, and the content, which is the sign, to thirdness. The thirdness category, filled as it is with conclusions, outcomes, and representations, always appears as the most real to us. Qualification and analysis, which we could call 'noticing' and 'doing,' are sometimes difficult to recognize as essential to the reasoning process. They are mostly invisible activities because we usually only see the results of what people notice and do, not how the noticing and doing is done. Dottie's non-verbal assessment identifies these invisible activities while they are being performed. As you know, we do not pay attention to 'what' people create during the assessment process, but rather to how they select and reject among options as they are doing it."

"Is that why you use Dottie's non-verbal assessment in the classes?"

"Yes. I find it useful to know which of the mental habits a person is using, especially when I am working with someone who is having difficulty mastering the reasoning skills. The non-verbal assessment is necessary whenever we are working with people who do not speak English well, or who are mentally retarded, learning disabled, or have other language-based problems. Since the assessment is a diagnostic tool, it helps me better understand what each participant needs. It helps participants understand themselves better, too."

"All of this is perfectly clear. I find it hard to believe that the connection of Engaged Intelligence training to Peirce is that simple. How did I miss the connection as we discussed this essay?"

"Probably because Engaged Intelligence training is skill-based. The exercises do not teach theoretical 'whys' and 'wherefores.' Once people know how to perform the skills we teach in this training, they can apply them to improve upon their reasoning habits and to develop their abilities for using the deliberate reasoning skills of Peirce's *logica docens*, as well."

We ended our discussions of the essay at this point. We had been doggedly discussing it for nearly six weeks. It was late fall by this time. Soon Halloween would be upon us and then, right around the corner, Thanksgiving and Christmas. I felt it would be a good thing to give Peirce's pragmaticism a chance to settle in for a while. We would let it hibernate during the long rainy winter that we are always sure to have here in the Pacific Northwest.

EPILOGUE

It is spring again. Our tulips and daffodils are in full bloom. The vegetable garden has been planted, but it is still too soon to fill the planter boxes in front of our house. Over the winter we had lots of time to think and read. Hal has discovered that he can better understand other essays by Peirce, now that we have completed our discussion of this one.

"I think I have become used to the language," he told me one day. "It must be a lot like Shakespeare."

Shakespeare had been our project the previous winter.

We began our long discussion of Peirce's essay because I had wanted to explain the connection between Peirce's concept of belief and doubt to the work that I do. I wanted to show Hal how the Relational Thinking Styles non-verbal reasoning model and the Engaged Intelligence training program were both firmly rooted in Peirce's work. We were weeding the tulip bed that afternoon when I brought this topic up again.

"Over the long run, explaining how people habitually reason is going to be as essential as identifying how they should reason."

"I think knowing how people habitually reason is more essential," Hal countered. "We mostly use our everyday reasoning habits."

"But, do people want to know this about themselves?"

"Do you mean do they want to know what mental habits they use?"

"Yes."

"Probably not," he conceded. "I think that what Peirce said is true. Most people think that they already reason well. They might like to have a way of showing other people how to reason better, but until this information about reasoning habits and about how to reason better becomes common knowledge, people just cannot know that others habitually reason differently than they do. If they do not know this, they cannot possibly know that each habit is good for solving some kinds of problems, but not others."

I sighed at this. He was right, and I knew it.

"Just look at how few people are able to perform abductive reasoning, compared to those who claim to know what it is," Hal continued. "We would never have known if not for Dottie's non-verbal assessment. Think of all the multi-relational children you have uncovered who were thought to be just slow learners or lazy underachievers."

"True."

"Think too of what we have been able to do with this knowledge about reasoning habits and the Engaged Intelligence system. Can you imagine what a dilemma we would have been in raising all of our children if we had not had this information? Tonya would surely be in a sheltered living situation for the mentally disabled, not happily married with a child. And Greg would never have managed to graduate from high school in the top ten percent of students in the state. He would not have been able to perform so well in college either."

"You are right. Our biggest challenge now is the 'light bulb problem'."

"What light bulb problem?"

"How many psychologists does it take to change a light bulb?"

"Only one, but it has to really want to change. Is that the one you mean?"

"That is the one. Since most people think they reason perfectly well, thank you, they are not going to see any point in honing their reasoning skills."

"Sure it will be difficult getting this information out," he agreed, "but at least we will have something keeping us busy well into old age. Just think of what we are able to do with this information right now. Think of how we have been able to help people find jobs that are right for them and help managers understand how to better manage personnel and resources."

"And think how valuable this information is for people who want to improve the educational system!" I was beginning to catch his spirited optimism. "That is what I most want to do. I love teaching Engaged Intelligence to adult learners. It is like squirting oil onto rusted brains. Teachers can work magic with this information, even special education teachers. Just think of what this information could do for people who are trying to deal with other children like Tonya, especially learning specialists, psychologists, social workers, vocational rehabilitation specialists, as well as parents and foster parents."

"Do you see what I mean?" Hal said with great fervor. "It makes no difference how long it takes us to get this information out. What matters most is that this information eventually becomes common knowledge and that it is used correctly. Engaged Intelligence training and all of the applications of Dottie's non-verbal theory can be used to help save us all from ourselves."

We had nearly finished weeding the tulip bed by then, and we both fell silent. Perhaps we were weary of yard work; perhaps, of preaching to the choir. In any case, Hal and I had discussed these concepts long enough, not only during our discussions on these pages, but also during our endless conversations about mental habits and right reasoning over the years. Now it is time to find people who can master and teach Engaged Intelligence skills, and then boldly carry the power of Peirce's pragmaticism into the world at large. It is time to begin the real thrust, to build a bigger choir made up of voices from many disciplines. Perhaps one of these voices will be yours.

NOTES

1. Umberto Eco, "Introduction" to *The Meaning of Meaning* by C. K. Ogden and I. A. Richards (Orlando, Florida: Harcourt Brace Jovanovich, 1989), pp. x-xi.

2. Martin Goldstein and Inge F. Goldstein, *How We Know: An Exploration of the Scientific Process* (New York: Plenum Press, 1978), pp. 206-207.

3. Charles S. Peirce, "The First Rule of Logic," *Reasoning and the Logic of Things*, ed. Kenneth Laine Ketner (Cambridge, Mass.: Harvard University Press, 1992), p. 178.

4. Charles S. Peirce, "How to Make Our Ideas Clear," *Charles S. Peirce: Selected Writings*, ed. Philip P. Weiner (New York: Dover Publications, 1958), pp. 188-119.

5. Paul Engelmann, *Letters from Ludwig Wittgenstein, With a Memoir*, ed. B. F. McGuinness, trans. by L. Furtmüller (Oxford: Basil Blackwell, 1967), p. 97.

6. Sandra Rosenthal, *Charles Peirce's Pragmatic Pluralism* (Albany, N. Y.: State University of New York Press,1994), pp. 5-6.

7. Erica Goode, "Among the Inept, Researchers Discover, Ignorance Is Bliss," *New York Times* (18 January 2000), section F, p. 1.

8. Charles S. Peirce, "The Fixation of Belief," *Philosophical Writings of Peirce*, ed. Justus Buchler (New York: Dover, 1955), p. 5.

9. Peirce, "The First Rule of Logic," p. 171.

10. Jaakko Hintikka, "What Is Abduction? The Fundamental Problem of Contemporary Epistemology," *Transactions of the Charles S. Peirce Society*, 36:3 (Summer 1998), p. 503.

11. Tomas Kapitan, "Peirce and the Structure of Abductive Inference," *Studies in the Logic of Charles Sanders Peirce*, eds. Nathan Houser, Don D. Roberts, and James Van Evra (Bloomington: Indiana University Press, 1997), pp. 447-448.

12. Charles S. Peirce, "The Logic of Continuity," *Reasoning and the Logic of Things*, ed. Ketner, p. 246.

13. Jayne Tristan, personal communication, 8 November 1998.

14. *Ibid.*

15. Frank Ryan, personal communication, 1 August 1999.

16. John Shook, *Dewey's Empirical Theory of Knowledge and Reality* (Nashville, Tenn.: Vanderbilt University Press, 2000), p. 214.

17. H. G. Callaway, *Context for Meaning and Analysis* (Amsterdam: Editions Rodopi, 1993), p. 153.

18. K. T. Fann, *Peirce's Theory of Abduction* (The Hague, Netherlands: Martinus Nijhoff, 1970), pp. 38-39.

BIBLIOGRAPHY

Anderson, Douglas R. *Strands of System: The Philosophy of Charles Peirce.* West Lafayette, Ind.: Purdue University Press, 1995.

Ayim, Maryann and Goldwin J. Emerson. "Dewey and Peirce on Curriculum and the Three R's." *Journal of Educational Thought,* 14:1 (April 1980), pp. 23-37.

Brent, Joseph. *C. S. Peirce: A Life.* Bloomington, Ind.: Indiana University Press, 1993.

Buchler, Justus. *The Concept of Method.* New York: Columbia University Press, 1961.

Buchler, Justus, ed. *Philosophical Writings of Peirce.* New York: Dover, 1955.

Black, Max. *Models and Metaphors: Studies in Language and Philosophy.* Ithaca, N.Y.: Cornell University Press, 1962.

Callaway, H. G. *Context for Meaning and Analysis.* Amsterdam: Editions Rodopi, 1993.

Chiasson, Phyllis, "Charles Sanders Peirce and Educational Theory," *Encyclopedia of Educational Philosophy,* eds. Paulo Ghiraldelli and Michael A. Peters. Online publication: www.educacao.pro.br, 1999.

_____. "Revisiting A Neglected Argument for the Reality of God," Online publication: www.door.net/arisbe, 1999.

_____, Ben Konsynski, and Jay Nunamaker. "Thinking Style Assessment in Computer Personnel Evaluation." *Proceedings of the Sixteenth Annual Hawaii International Conference on Systems Sciences* (IEEE Computer Society, Los Alamitos, Cal., 1983), pp. 665-676.

_____ and Dorothy Davis. *Relational Thinking Styles Model and Assessment Tool.* Port Townsend, Washington: Davis-Nelson, 1996.

Davis, Dorothy S. "Style: Viable Construct of Thought Patterning." Dissertation, University of Arizona, Tucson, 1972.

_____ and Phyllis Chiasson Schwimmer. "Style: A Manner of Thinking," *Educational Leadership,* 38:5 (February 1981), pp. 376-377.

_____ and Phyllis Chiasson Schwimmer. "Relational Thinking Styles: Learning to See the Forest and the Trees." *Journal of Learning Disabilities,* 14:8 (October 1981), pp. 449-450.

Dewey, John. *Art as Experience.* New York: G. P. Putnam's Sons, 1980.

_____. *Logic: The Theory of Inquiry.* New York: Holt, Reinhart, and Winston, 1938.

_____. "Theory of Valuation." *International Encyclopedia of Unified Science.* Chicago: University of Chicago Press, 1939.

Dossey, Larry. *Healing Words: The Power of Prayer and the Practice of Medicine.* New York: Harper Collins, 1993.

Engelmann, Paul. *Letters from Ludwig Wittgenstein, With a Memoir,* ed. B. F. McGuinness, trans. by L. Furtmüller. Oxford: Basil Blackwell, 1967.

Fann, K.T. *Peirce's Theory of Abduction.* The Hague, Netherlands: Martinus Nijhoff, 1970.

Fishman, Stephen M. and Lucille McCarthy. *John Dewey and the Challenge of Classroom Practice.* New York: Teacher's College Press, 1998.

Garrison, Jim. *Dewey and Eros: Wisdom and Desire in the Art of Teaching.* New York: Teacher's College Press, 1997.

Goldstein, Inge and Martin Goldstein. *How We Know: An Exploration of the Scientific Process.* New York: Plenum Press, 1978.

Goode, Erica. "Among the Inept, Researchers Discover, Ignorance Is Bliss." *New York Times* (18 January 2000), section F, p. 1.

Hickman, Larry. *Dewey's Pragmatic Technology.* Bloomington: Indiana University Press, 1992.

Hintikka, Jaakko. "What Is Abduction? The Fundamental Problem of Contemporary Epistemology." *Transactions of the Charles S. Peirce Society,* 34:3 (Summer 1998), pp. 503-553.

Hoffmeyer, Jesper. *Signs of Meaning in the Universe.* West Lafayette, Ind.: Indiana University Press, 1996.

Houser, Nathan and Christian Klosesel, eds. *The Essential Peirce.* West Layfayette, Ind.: Indiana University Press, 1992.

Janik, Allan and Stephen Toulmin. *Wittgenstein's Vienna.* New York: Simon and Schuster, 1973.

Johnson, Mark. *The Body in the Mind.* Chicago: University of Chicago Press, 1987.

Jung, Carl. *Essays on Contemporary Events.* London: Kegan Paul, 1947.

Kapitan, Tomas. "Peirce and the Structure of Abductive Inference." *Studies in the Logic of Charles Sanders Peirce.* eds. Nathan Houser, Don D. Roberts, and James Van Evra (Bloomington, Ind.: Indiana University Press, 1997), pp. 447-496.

Kaptchuk, Ted J. *The Web That Has No Weaver.* Chicago: Congdon and Weed, 1983.

Ketner, Kenneth Laine, ed. *Reasoning and the Logic of Things.* Cambridge, Mass.: Harvard University Press, 1992.

_____. *His Glassy Essence: An Autobiography of Charles Sanders Peirce.* Nashville, Tenn.: Vanderbilt University Press 1998.

Lakoff, George and Mark Johnson. *Metaphors We Live By.* Chicago: University of Chicago Press, 1980.

Nubiola, Jaime. "Scholarship on the Relations Between Ludwig Wittgenstein and Charles S. Peirce." *Studies on the History of Logic.* eds. Ignacio Angelelli and Maria Cerezo (Berlin: Walter de Gruyter, 1996), pp. 281-294.

Ogden, C. K. and I. A. Richards, *The Meaning of Meaning.* Reprint of 1923 edition. Orlando, Fla.: Harcourt, Brace, Jovanovich, 1989.

Parret, Herman, ed. *Peirce and Value Theory.* Philadelphia: John Benjamins Publishing Company, 1994.

Prawat, Richard S. "Dewey, Peirce, and the Learning Paradox." *American Educational Research Journal,* 36:1 (Spring 1999), pp. 47-76.

Rosenthal, Sandra B. *Charles Peirce's Pragmatic Pluralism.* Albany: State University of New York Press, 1994.

Samson, Richard and Albert Upton. *Creative Analysis.* New York: E. P. Dutton, 1963.

Shook, John. *Dewey's Empirical Theory of Knowledge and Reality.* Nashville, Tenn.: Vanderbilt University Press, 2000.

Thompson, Manley. *The Pragmatic Philosophy of C. S. Peirce.* Chicago: University of Chicago Press, 1953.

Tristan, Jayne. "Dewey's Theory of Inquiry and the Aesthetics of Inference." Dissertation, Southern Illinois University at Carbondale, 1996.

Upton, Albert. *Design for Thinking.* Palo Alto, Cal.: Pacific Books, 1960.

Upton, Anne. *Teacher Manual* for *Design for Thinking.* Palo Alto, Cal.: Pacific Books, 1961.

Weiner, Philip P., ed. *Charles S. Peirce Selected Writings: Values in a Universe of Chance.* New York: Dover, 1958.

APPENDIX

WHAT PRAGMATISM IS

by Charles Sanders Peirce

The Monist, 15:2 (April 1905), pp. 161-181.

[This is a reproduction of the original publication with a few silent punctuation changes. Line numbers have been introduced to assist cross-referencing to each chapter of the present book.]

1   The writer of this article has been led by much experience to believe
2   that every physicist, and every chemist, and, in short, every master in
3   any department of experimental science, has had his mind molded by
4   his life in the laboratory to a degree that is little suspected. The ex-
5   perimentalist himself can hardly be fully aware of it, for the reason
6   that the men whose intellects he really knows about are much like
7   himself in this respect. With intellects of widely different training
8   from his own, whose education has largely been a thing learned out of
9   books, he will never become inwardly intimate, be he on ever so fa-
10 miliar terms with them; for he and they are as oil and water, and
11 though they be shaken up together, it is remarkable how quickly they
12 will go their several mental ways, without having gained more than a
13 faint flavor from the association. Were those other men only to take
14 skillful soundings of the experimentalist's mind—which is just what
15 they are unqualified to do, for the most part—they would soon dis-
16 cover that, excepting perhaps upon topics where his mind is tram-
17 meled by personal feeling or by his bringing up, his disposition is to
18 think of everything just as everything is thought of in the laboratory,
19 that is, as a question of experimentation. Of course, no living man pos-
20 sesses in their fullness all the attributes characteristic of his type: it is
21 not the typical doctor whom you will see every day driven in buggy or
22 coupé, nor is it the typical pedagogue that will be met with in the first
23 school-room you enter. But when you have found, or ideally con-
24 structed upon a basis of observation, the typical experimentalist, you
25 will find that whatever assertion you may make to him, he will either
26 understand as meaning that if a given prescription for an experiment
27 ever can be and ever is carried out in act, an experience of a given de-
28 scription will result, or else he will see no sense at all in what you say.
29 If you talk to him as Mr. Balfour talked not long ago to the British As-
30 sociation saying that "the physicist seeks for something deeper than
31 the laws connecting plausible objects of experience," that "his object

32   is physical reality" unrevealed in experiments, and that the existence
33   of such non-experiential reality "is the unalterable faith of science," to
34   all such ontological meaning you will find the experimentalist mind to
35   be color-blind. What adds to that confidence in this which the writer
36   owes to his conversations with experimentalists is that he himself may
37   almost be said to have inhabited a laboratory from the age of six until
38   long past maturity; and having all his life associated mostly with ex-
39   perimentalists, it has always been with a confident sense of under-
40   standing them and of being understood by them.
41   That laboratory life did not prevent the writer (who here and in
42   what follows simply exemplifies the experimentalist type) from be-
43   coming interested in methods of thinking; and when he came to read
44   metaphysics, although much of it seemed to him loosely reasoned and
45   determined by accidental prepossessions, yet in the writings of some
46   philosophers, especially Kant, Berkeley, and Spinoza, he sometimes
47   came upon strains of thought that recalled the ways of thinking of the
48   laboratory, so that he felt he might trust to them; all of which has been
49   true of other laboratory-men.
50   Endeavoring, as a man of that type naturally would, to formulate
51   what he so approved, he framed the theory that a *conception*, that is,
52   the rational purport of a word or other expression, lies exclusively in
53   its conceivable bearing upon the conduct of life; so that, since obvi-
54   ously nothing that might not result from experiment can have any di-
55   rect bearing upon conduct, if one can define accurately all the con-
56   ceivable experimental phenomena which the affirmation or denial of a
57   concept could imply, one will have therein a complete definition of the
58   concept, and *there is absolutely nothing more in it*. For this doctrine he
59   invented the name *pragmatism*. Some of his friends wished him to call
60   it *practicism* or *practicalism* (perhaps on the ground that πρακτικός is
61   better Greek than πραγματικός). But for one who had learned philoso-
62   phy out of Kant, as the writer, along with nineteen out of every twenty
63   experimentalists who have turned to philosophy, had done, and who
64   still thought in Kantian terms most readily, *praktisch* and *pragmatisch*
65   were as far apart as the two poles, the former belonging in a region of
66   thought where no mind of the experimentalist type can ever make sure
67   of solid ground under his feet, the latter expressing relation to some
68   definite human purpose. Now quite the most striking feature of the
69   new theory was its recognition of an inseparable connection between
70   rational cognition and rational purpose; and that consideration it was
71   which determined the preference for the name *pragmatism*.
72   Concerning the matter of philosophical nomenclature, there are a
73   few plain considerations, which the writer has for many years longed
74   to submit to the deliberate judgment of those few fellow-students of
75   philosophy, who deplore the present state of that study, and who are

76 intent upon rescuing it therefrom and bringing it to a condition like
77 that of the natural sciences, where investigators, instead of condemn-
78 ing each the work of most of the others as misdirected from beginning
79 to end, co-operate, stand upon one another's shoulders, and multiply
80 incontestable results; where every observation is repeated, and isolated
81 observations go for little; where every hypothesis that merits attention
82 is subjected to severe but fair examination, and only after the predic-
83 tions to which it leads have been remarkably borne out by experience
84 is trusted at all, and even then only provisionally; where a radically
85 false step is rarely taken, even the most faulty of those theories which
86 gain wide credence being true in their main experiential predictions.
87 To those students, it is submitted that no study can become scientific
88 in the sense described, until it provides itself with a suitable technical
89 nomenclature, whose every term has a single definite meaning univer-
90 sally accepted among students of the subject, and whose vocables have
91 no such sweetness or charms as might tempt loose writers to abuse
92 them,—which is a virtue of scientific nomenclature too little appreci-
93 ated. It is submitted that the experience of those sciences which have
94 conquered the greatest difficulties of terminology, which are unques-
95 tionably the taxonomic sciences, chemistry, mineralogy, botany,
96 zoölogy, has conclusively shown that the one only way in which the
97 requisite unanimity and requisite ruptures with individual habits and
98 preferences can be brought about is so to shape the canons of termi-
99 nology that they shall gain the support of *moral principle* and of every
100 man's sense of decency; and that, in particular (under defined restric-
101 tions), the general feeling shall be that he who introduces a new con-
102 ception into philosophy is under an obligation to invent acceptable
103 terms to express it, and that when he has done so, the duty of his fel-
104 low-students is to accept those terms, and to resent any wresting of
105 them from their original meanings, as not only a gross discourtesy to
106 him to whom philosophy was indebted for each conception, but also as
107 an injury to philosophy itself; and furthermore, that once a conception
108 has been supplied with suitable and sufficient words for its expression,
109 no other *technical* terms denoting the same things, considered in the
110 same relations, should be countenanced. Should this suggestion find
111 favor, it might be deemed needful that the philosophians in congress
112 assembled should adopt, after due deliberation, convenient canons to
113 limit the application of the principle. Thus, just as is done in chemis-
114 try, it might be wise to assign fixed meanings to certain prefixes and
115 suffixes. For example, it might be agreed, perhaps, that the prefix
116 *prope-* should mark a broad and rather indefinite extension of the
117 meaning of the term to which it was prefixed; the name of a doctrine
118 would naturally end in *-ism*, while *-icism* might mark a more strictly
119 defined acception of that doctrine, etc. Then again, just as in biology
120 no account is taken of terms antedating Linnaeus, so in philosophy it

121   might be found best not to go back of the scholastic terminology. To
122   illustrate another sort of limitation, it has probably never happened
123   that any philosopher has attempted to give a general name to his own
124   doctrine without that name's soon acquiring in common philosophical
125   usage, a signification much broader than was originally intended.
126   Thus, special systems go by the names Kantianism, Benthamism,
127   Comteanism, Spencerianism, etc., while transcendentalism, utilitari-
128   anism, positivism, evolutionism, synthetic philosophy, etc. have ir-
129   revocably and very conveniently been elevated to broader govern-
130   ments.
131   After awaiting in vain, for a good many years, some particularly
132   opportune conjuncture of circumstances that might serve to recom-
133   mend his notions of the ethics of terminology, the writer has now, at
134   last, dragged them in over head and shoulders, on an occasion when he
135   has no specific proposal to offer nor any feeling but satisfaction at the
136   course usage has run without any canons or resolutions of a congress.
137   His word "pragmatism" has gained general recognition in a general-
138   ized sense that seems to argue power of growth and vitality. The
139   famed psychologist, James, first took it up, seeing that his "radical
140   empiricism" substantially answered to the writer's definition of prag-
141   matism, albeit with a certain difference in the point of view. Next, the
142   admirably clear and brilliant thinker, Mr. Ferdinand C. S. Schiller,
143   casting about for a more attractive name for the "anthropomorphism"
144   of his *Riddle of the Sphinx*, lit, in that most remarkable paper of his on
145   *Axioms as Postulates*, upon the same designation "pragmatism," which
146   in its original sense was in generic agreement with his own doctrine,
147   for which he has since found the more appropriate specification "hu-
148   manism," while he still retains "pragmatism" in a somewhat wider
149   sense. So far all went happily, But at present, the word begins to be
150   met with occasionally in the literary journals, where it gets abused in
151   the merciless way that words have to expect when they fall into liter-
152   ary clutches. Sometimes the manners of the British have effloresced in
153   scolding at the word as ill-chosen—ill-chosen, that is, to express some
154   meaning that it was rather designed to exclude. So then, the writer,
155   finding his bantling "pragmatism" so promoted, feels that it is time to
156   kiss his child good-by and relinquish it to its higher destiny; while to
157   serve the precise purpose of expressing the original definition, he begs
158   to announce the birth of the word "pragmaticism," which is ugly
159   enough to be safe from kidnappers.[1]
160   Much as the writer has gained from the perusal of what other
161   pragmatists have written, he still thinks there is a decisive advantage in
162   his original conception of the doctrine. From this original form every
163   truth that follows from any of the other forms can be deduced, while
164   some errors can be avoided into which other pragmatists have fallen.
165   The original view appears, too, to be a more compact and unitary con-

166 ception than the others. But its capital merit, in the writer's eyes, is
167 that it more readily connects itself with a critical proof of its truth.
168 Quite in accord with the logical order of investigation, it usually hap-
169 pens that one first forms an hypothesis that seems more and more rea-
170 sonable the further one examines into it, but that only a good deal later
171 gets crowned with an adequate proof. The present writer having had
172 the pragmatist theory under consideration for many years longer than
173 most of its adherents, would naturally have given more attention to the
174 proof of it. At any rate, in endeavoring to explain pragmatism, he may
175 be excused for confining himself to that form of it that he knows best.
176 In the present article there will be space only to explain just what this
177 doctrine, (which, in such hands as it has now fallen into, may probably
178 play a pretty prominent part in the philosophical discussions of the
179 next coming years), really consists in. Should the exposition be found
180 to interest readers of *The Monist*, they would certainly be much more
181 interested in a second article which would give some samples of the
182 manifold applications of pragmaticism (assuming it to be true) to the
183 solution of problems of different kinds. After that, readers might be
184 prepared to take an interest in a proof that the doctrine is true,—a
185 proof which seems to the writer to leave no reasonable doubt on the
186 subject, and to be the one contribution of value that he has to make to
187 philosophy. For it would essentially involve the establishment of the
188 truth of synechism.
189   The bare definition of pragmaticism could convey no satisfactory
190 comprehension of it to the most apprehensive of minds, but requires
191 the commentary to be given below. Moreover, this definition takes no
192 notice of one or two other doctrines without the previous acceptance
193 (or virtual acceptance) of which pragmaticism itself would be a nul-
194 lity. They are included as a part of the pragmatism of Schiller, but the
195 present writer prefers not to mingle different propositions. The pre-
196 liminary propositions had better be stated forthwith.
197   The difficulty in doing this is that no formal list of them has ever
198 been made. They might all be included under the vague maxim, "Dis-
199 miss make-believes." Philosophers of very diverse stripes propose that
200 philosophy shall take its start from one or another state of mind in
201 which no man, least of all a beginner in philosophy, actually is. One
202 proposes that you shall begin by doubting everything, and says that
203 there is only one thing that you cannot doubt, as if doubting were "as
204 easy as lying." Another proposes that we should begin by observing
205 "the first impressions of sense," forgetting that our very percepts are
206 the results of cognitive elaboration. But in truth, there is but one state
207 of mind from which you can "set out," namely, the very state of mind
208 in which you actually find yourself at the time you do "set out"—a
209 state in which you are laden with an immense mass of cognition al-
210 ready formed, of which you cannot divest yourself if you would; and

211   who knows whether, if you could, you would not have made all
212   knowledge impossible to yourself? Do you call it *doubting* to write
213   down on a piece of paper that you doubt? If so, doubt has nothing to
214   do with any serious business. But do not make believe; if pedantry has
215   not eaten all the reality out of you, recognize, as you must, that there is
216   much that you do not doubt, in the least. Now that which you do not at
217   all doubt, you must and do regard as infallible, absolute truth. Here
218   breaks in Mr. Make Believe: "What! Do you mean to say that one is to
219   believe what is not true, or that what a man does not doubt is *ipso*
220   *facto* true?" No, but unless he can make a thing white and black at
221   once, he has to regard what he does not doubt as absolutely true. Now
222   you, *per hypothesiu*, are that man, "But you tell me there are scores of
223   things I do not doubt. I really cannot persuade myself that there is not
224   some one of them about which I am mistaken." You are adducing one
225   of your make-believe facts, which, even if it were established, would
226   only go to show that doubt has a *limen*, that is, is only called into be-
227   ing by a certain finite stimulus. You only puzzle yourself by talking of
228   this metaphysical "truth" and metaphysical "falsity," that you know
229   nothing about. All you have any dealings with are your doubts and be-
230   liefs,[2] with the course of life that forces new beliefs upon you and
231   gives you power to doubt old beliefs. If your terms "truth" and "fal-
232   sity" are taken in such senses as to be definable in terms of doubt and
233   belief and the course of experience (as for example they would be, if
234   you were to define the "truth" as that to a belief in which belief would
235   tend if it were to tend indefinitely toward absolute fixity), well and
236   good: in that case, you are only talking about doubt and belief. But if
237   by truth and falsity you mean something not definable in terms of
238   doubt and belief in any way, then you are talking of entities of whose
239   existence you can know nothing, and which Ockham's razor would
240   clean shave off. Your problems would he greatly simplified, if, instead
241   of saying that you want to know the "Truth," you were simply to say
242   that you want to attain a state of belief unassailable by doubt.
243   Belief is not a momentary mode of consciousness; it is a habit of
244   mind essentially enduring for some time, and mostly (at least) uncon-
245   scious; and like other habits, it is, (until it meets with some surprise
246   that begins its dissolution), perfectly self-satisfied. Doubt is of an alto-
247   gether contrary genus. It is not a habit, but the privation of a habit.
248   Now a privation of a habit, in order to be anything at all, must be a
249   condition of erratic activity that in some way must get superseded by a
250   habit.
251   Among the things which the reader, as a rational person, does not
252   doubt, is that he not merely has habits, but also can exert a measure of
253   self-control over his future actions; which means, however, *not* that he
254   can impart to them any arbitrarily assignable character, but, on the
255   contrary, that a process of self-preparation will tend to impart to ac-

256 tion, (when the occasion for it shall arise), one fixed character, which
257 is indicated and perhaps roughly measured by the absence (or slight-
258 ness) of the feeling of self-reproach, which subsequent reflection will
259 induce. Now, this subsequent reflection is part of the self-preparation
260 for action on the next occasion. Consequently, there is a tendency, as
261 action is repeated again and again, for the action to approximate in-
262 definitely toward the perfection of that fixed character, which would
263 be marked by entire absence of self-reproach. The more closely this is
264 approached, the less room for self-control there will be; and where no
265 self-control is possible there will be no self-reproach.

266 These phenomena seem to be the fundamental characteristics
267 which distinguish a rational being. Blame, in every case, appears to be
268 a modification, often accomplished by a transference, or "projection,"
269 of the primary feeling of self-reproach. Accordingly, we never blame
270 anybody for what had been beyond his power of previous self-control.
271 Now, thinking is a species of conduct which is largely subject to self-
272 control. In all their features (which there is no room to describe here),
273 logical self-control is a perfect mirror of ethical self-control,—unless it
274 be rather a species under that genus. In accordance with this, what you
275 cannot in the least help believing is not, justly speaking, wrong belief.
276 In other words, for you it is the absolute truth. True, it is conceivable
277 that what you cannot help believing to-day, you might find you thor-
278 oughly disbelieve tomorrow. But then there is a certain distinction
279 between things you "cannot" do, merely in the sense that nothing
280 stimulates you to the great effort and endeavors that would be re-
281 quired, and things you cannot do because in their own nature they are
282 insusceptible of being put into practice. In every stage of your excogi-
283 tations, there is something of which you can only say, "I cannot think
284 otherwise," and your experientially based hypothesis is that the impos-
285 sibility is of the second kind.

286 There is no reason why "thought," in what has just been said,
287 should be taken in that narrow sense in which silence and darkness are
288 favorable to thought. It should rather be understood as covering all ra-
289 tional life, so that an experiment shall be an operation of thought. Of
290 course, that ultimate state of habit to which the action of self-control
291 ultimately tends, where no room is left for further self-control, is, in
292 the case of thought, the state of fixed belief, or perfect knowledge.

293 Two things here are all-important to assure oneself of and to re-
294 member. The first is that a person is not absolutely an individual. His
295 thoughts are what he is "saying to himself," that is, is saying to that
296 other self that is just coming into life in the flow of time. When one
297 reasons, it is that critical self that one is trying to persuade; and all
298 thought whatsoever is a sign, and is mostly of the nature of language.
299 The second thing to remember is that the man's circle of society,
300 (however widely or narrowly this phrase may be understood), is a sort

301   of loosely compacted person, in some respects of higher rank than the
302   person of an individual organism. It is these two things alone that ren-
303   der it possible for you—but only in the abstract, and in a Pickwickian-
304   sense,—to distinguish between absolute truth and what you do not
305   doubt.
306   Let us now hasten to the exposition of pragmaticism itself. Here
307   it will be convenient to imagine that somebody to whom the doctrine
308   is new, but of rather preternatural perspicacity, asks questions of a
309   pragmaticist. Everything that might give a dramatic illusion must be
310   stripped off, so that the result will be a sort of cross between a dia-
311   logue and a catechism, but a good deal more like the latter,—some-
312   thing rather painfully reminiscent of *Mangnall's Historical Questions.*
313   Questioner: I am astounded at your definition of your pragma-
314   tism, because only last year I was assured by a person above all suspi-
315   cion of warping the truth—himself a pragmatist—that your doctrine
316   precisely was "that a conception is to be tested by its practical effects."
317   You must surely, then, have entirely changed your definition very re-
318   cently.
319   Pragmatist: If you will turn to Vols. VI and VII of the *Revue*
320   *Philosophique*, or to the *Popular Science Monthly* for November 1877
321   and January 1878, you will be able to judge for yourself whether the
322   interpretation you mention was not then clearly excluded. The exact
323   wording of the English enunciation, (changing only the first person
324   into the second), was: "Consider what effects that might conceivably
325   have practical bearings you conceive the object of your conception to
326   have. Then your conception of those effects is the WHOLE of your
327   conception of the object."
328   Questioner: Well, what reason have you for asserting this is so?
329   Pragmatist: That is what I specially desire to tell you. But the
330   question had better be postponed until you clearly understand what
331   those reasons profess to prove.
332   Questioner: What, then, is the *raison d'être* of the doctrine?
333   What advantage is expected from it?
334   Pragmatist: It will serve to show that almost every proposition of
335   ontological metaphysics is either meaningless gibberish—one word
336   being defined by other words, and they by still others, without any real
337   conception ever being reached—or else is downright absurd; so that all
338   such rubbish being swept away, what will remain of philosophy will
339   be a series of problems capable of investigation by the observational
340   methods of the true sciences—the truth about which can be reached
341   without those interminable misunderstandings and disputes which
342   have made the highest of the positive sciences a mere amusement for
343   idle intellects, a sort of chess—idle pleasure its purpose, and reading
344   out of a book its method. In this regard, pragmaticism is a species of

345   prope-positivism. But what distinguishes it from other species is, first,
346   its retention of a purified philosophy; secondly, its full acceptance of
347   the main body of our instinctive beliefs; and thirdly, its strenuous in-
348   sistence upon the truth of scholastic realism, (or a close approximation
349   to that, well stated by the late Dr. Francis Ellingwood Abbot in the In-
350   troduction to his *Scientific Theism*). So, instead of merely jeering at
351   metaphysics, like other prope-positivists, whether by long-drawn-out
352   parodies or otherwise, the pragmaticist extracts from it a precious es-
353   sence, which will serve to give life and light to cosmology and phys-
354   ics. At the same time, the moral applications of the doctrine are posi-
355   tive and potent; and there are many other uses of it not easily classed.
356   On another occasion, instances may be given to show that it really has
357   these effects.
358   Questioner: I hardly need to be convinced that your doctrine
359   would wipe out metaphysics. Is it not as obvious that it must wipe out
360   every proposition of science and everything that bears on the conduct
361   of life? For you say that the only meaning that, for you, any assertion
362   bears is that a certain experiment has resulted in a certain way: Noth-
363   ing else but an experiment enters into the meaning. Tell me, then, how
364   can an experiment, in itself, reveal anything more than that something
365   once happened to an individual object and that subsequently some
366   other individual event occurred?
367   Pragmatist: That question is, indeed, to the purpose—the purpose
368   being to correct any misapprehensions of pragmaticism. You speak of
369   an experiment in itself, emphasizing "*in itself.*" You evidently think of
370   each experiment as isolated from every other. It has not, for example,
371   occurred to you, one might venture to surmise, that every connected
372   series of experiments constitutes a single collective experiment. What
373   are the essential ingredients of an experiment? First, of course, an ex-
374   perimenter of flesh and blood. Secondly, a verifiable hypothesis. This
375   is a proposition[3] relating to the universe environing the experimenter,
376   or to some well-known part of it and affirming or denying of this only
377   some experimental possibility or impossibility. The third indispensa-
378   ble ingredient is a sincere doubt in the experimenter's mind as to the
379   truth of that hypothesis. Passing over several ingredients on which we
380   need not dwell, the purpose, the plan, and the resolve, we come to the
381   act of choice by which the experimenter singles out certain identifiable
382   objects to be operated upon. The next is the external (or quasi-
383   external) ACT by which he modifies those objects. Next, comes the
384   subsequent *reaction* of the world upon the experimenter in a percep-
385   tion; and finally, his recognition of the teaching of the experiment.
386   While the two chief parts of the event itself are the action and the re-
387   action, yet the unity of essence of the experiment lies in its purpose
388   and plan, the ingredients passed over in the enumeration.
389   Another thing: in representing the pragmaticist as making ra-

390 tional meaning to consist in an experiment (which you speak of as an
391 event in the past) you strikingly fail to catch his attitude of mind. In-
392 deed, it is not in an experiment, but in *experimental phenomena*, that
393 rational meaning is said to consist. When an experimentalist speaks of
394 a *phenomenon*, such as "Hall's phenomenon," "Zeemaun's phenome-
395 non" and its modification, "Michelson's phenomenon," or "the chess-
396 board phenomenon," he does not mean any particular event that did
397 happen to somebody in the dead past, but what *surely will* happen to
398 everybody in the living future who shall fulfill certain conditions. The
399 phenomenon consists in the fact that when an experimentalist shall
400 come to *act* according to a certain scheme that he has in mind, then
401 will something else happen, and shatter the doubts of skeptics, like the
402 celestial fire upon the altar of Elijah.
403   And do not overlook the fact that the pragmaticist maxim says
404 nothing of single experiments or of single experimental phenomena,
405 (for what is conditionally true *in futuro* can hardly be singular), but
406 only speaks of *general kinds* of experimental phenomena. Its adherent
407 does not shrink from speaking of general objects as real, since what-
408 ever is true represents a real. Now the laws of nature are true.
409   The rational meaning of every proposition lies in the future. How
410 so? The meaning of a proposition is itself a proposition. Indeed, it is
411 no other than the very proposition of which it is the meaning: it is a
412 translation of it. But of the myriads of forms into which a proposition
413 may be translated, what is that one which is to be called its very
414 meaning? It is, according to the pragmaticist, that form in which the
415 proposition becomes applicable to human conduct, not in these or
416 those special circumstances, nor when one entertains this or that spe-
417 cial design, but that form which is most directly applicable to self-
418 control under every situation, and to every purpose. This is why he lo-
419 cates the meaning in future time; for future conduct is the only conduct
420 that is subject to self-control. But in order that that form of the propo-
421 sition which is to be taken as its meaning should be applicable to every
422 situation and to every purpose upon which the proposition has any
423 bearing, it must be simply the general description of all the experi-
424 mental phenomena which the assertion of the proposition virtually
425 predicts. For an experimental phenomenon is the fact asserted by the
426 proposition that action of a certain description will have a certain kind
427 of experimental result; and experimental results are the only results
428 that can affect human conduct. No doubt, some unchanging idea may
429 come to influence a man more than it had done; but only because some
430 experience equivalent to an experiment has brought its truth home to
431 him more intimately than before. Whenever a man acts purposively, he
432 acts under a belief in some experimental phenomenon. Consequently,
433 the sum of the experimental phenomena that a proposition implies
434 makes up its entire bearing upon human conduct. Your question, then,

435 of how a pragmaticist can attribute any meaning to any assertion other
436 than that of a single occurrence is substantially answered.
437   Questioner: I see that pragmaticism is a thorough-going phenom-
438 enalism. Only why should you limit yourself to the phenomena of ex-
439 perimental science rather than embrace all observational science? Ex-
440 periment, after all, is an uncommunicative informant. It never expi-
441 ates: it only answers "yes" or "no"; or rather it usually snaps out 'No!"
442 or, at best, only utters an inarticulate grunt for the negation of its "no."
443 The typical experimentalist is not much of an observer. It is the stu-
444 dent of natural history to whom nature opens the treasury of her confi-
445 dence, while she treats the cross-examining experimentalist with the
446 reserve he merits. Why should your phenomenalism sound the meagre
447 jews-harp of experiment rather than the glorious organ of observation?
448   Pragmaticist: Because pragmaticism is not definable as "thor-
449 ough-going phenomenalism," although the latter doctrine may be a
450 kind of pragmatism. The *richness* of phenomena lies in their sensuous
451 quality. Pragmaticism does not intend to define the phenomenal
452 equivalents of words and general ideas, but, on the contrary, elimi-
453 nates their sential element, and endeavors to define the rational pur-
454 port, and this it finds in the purposive bearing of the word or proposi-
455 tion in question.
456   Questioner: Well, if you choose so to make Doing the Be-all and
457 the End-all of human life, why do you not make meaning to consist
458 simply in doing? Doing has to be done at a certain time upon a certain
459 object. Individual objects and single events cover all reality, as every-
460 body knows, and as a practicalist ought to be the first to insist. Yet,
461 your meaning, as you have described it, is *general*. Thus, it is of the
462 nature of a mere word and not a reality. You say yourself that your
463 meaning of a proposition is only the same proposition in another dress.
464 But a practical man's meaning is the very thing he means. What do
465 you make to be the meaning of "George Washington"?
466   Pragmaticist: Forcibly put! A good half dozen of your points
467 must certainly be admitted. It must be admitted, in the first place, that
468 if pragmaticism really made Doing to be the Be-all and the End-all of
469 life, that would be its death, For to say that we live for the mere sake
470 of action, as action, regardless of the thought it carries out, would be to
471 say that there is no such thing as rational purport. Secondly, it must be
472 admitted that every proposition professes to be true of a certain real
473 individual object, often the environing universe. Thirdly, it must be
474 admitted that pragmaticism fails to furnish any translation or meaning
475 of a proper name, or other designation of an individual object.
476 Fourthly, the pragmaticistic meaning is undoubtedly general; and it is
477 equally indisputable that the general is of the nature of a word or sign.
478 Fifthly, it must be admitted that individuals alone exist; and sixthly, it

479 may be admitted that the very meaning of a word or significant object
480 ought to be the very essence of reality of what it signifies. But when,
481 those admissions have been unreservedly made, you find the prag-
482 maticist still constrained most earnestly to deny the force of your ob-
483 jection, you ought to infer that there is some consideration that has es-
484 caped you. Putting the admissions together, you will perceive that the
485 pragmaticist grants that a proper name, (although it is not customary to
486 say that it has a *meaning*), has a certain denotative function peculiar, in
487 each case, to that name and its equivalents; and that he grants that
488 every assertion contains such a denotative or pointing-out function. In
489 its peculiar individuality, the pragmaticist excludes this from the ra-
490 tional purport of the assertion, although *the like* of it, being common to
491 all assertions, and so, being general and not individual, may enter into
492 the pragmaticistic purport. Whatever exists, ex-sists, that is, really acts
493 upon other existents, so obtains a self-identity, and is definitely indi-
494 vidual. As to the general, it will be a help to thought to notice that
495 there are two ways of being general. A statue of a soldier on some
496 village monument, in his overcoat and with his musket, is for each of a
497 hundred families the image of its uncle, its sacrifice to the Union. That
498 statue, then, though it is itself single, represents any one man of whom
499 a certain predicate may be true. It is *objectively* general. The word
500 "soldier," whether spoken or written, is general in the same way; while
501 the name "George Washington" is not so. But each of these two terms
502 remains one and the same noun, whether it be spoken or written, and
503 whenever and wherever it be spoken or written. This noun is not an
504 existent thing: it is a *type*, or *form*, to which objects, both those that are
505 externally existent and those which are imagined, may *conform*, but
506 which none of them can exactly be. This is subjective generality. The
507 pragmaticistic purport is general in both ways.
508 As to reality, one finds it defined in various ways; but if that
509 principle of terminological ethics that was proposed be accepted, the
510 equivocal language will soon disappear. For *realis* and *realitas* are not
511 ancient words. They were invented to be terms of philosophy in the
512 thirteenth century, and the meaning they were intended to express is
513 perfectly clear. That is *real* which has such and such characters,
514 whether anybody thinks it to have those characters or not. At any rate,
515 that is the sense in which the pragmaticist uses the word. Now, just as
516 conduct controlled by ethical reason tends toward fixing certain habits
517 of conduct, the nature of which, (as to illustrate the meaning, peace-
518 able habits and not quarrelsome habits), does not depend upon any ac-
519 cidental circumstances, and *in that sense*, may be said to be *destined*;
520 so, thought, controlled by a rational experimental logic, tends to the
521 fixation of certain opinions, equally destined, the nature of which will
522 be the same in the end, however the perversity of thought of whole
523 generations may cause the postponement of the ultimate fixation. If

524   this be so, as every man of us virtually assumes that it is, in regard to
525   each matter the truth of which he seriously discusses, then, according
526   to the adopted definition of "real," the state of things which will be
527   believed in that ultimate opinion is real. But, for the most part, such
528   opinions will be general. Consequently, *some* general objects are real.
529   (Of course, nobody ever thought that all generals were real; but the
530   scholastics used to assume that generals were real when they had
531   hardly any, or quite no, experiential evidence to support their assump-
532   tion; and their fault lay just there, and not in holding that generals
533   could be real.) One is struck with the inexactitude of thought even of
534   analysts of power, when they touch upon modes of being. One will
535   meet, for example, the virtual assumption that what is relative to
536   thought cannot be real. But why not, exactly? *Red* is relative to sight,
537   but the fact that this or that is in that relation to vision that we call be-
538   ing red is not *itself* relative to sight; it is a real fact.
539   Not only may generals be real, but they may also be *physically*
540   *efficient*, not in every metaphysical sense, but in the common-sense
541   acception in which human purposes are physically efficient. Aside
542   from metaphysical nonsense, no sane man doubts that if I feel the air
543   in my study to be stuffy, that thought may cause the window to be
544   opened. My thought, be it granted, was an individual event. But what
545   determined it to take the particular determination it did, was in part the
546   general fact that stuffy air is unwholesome, and in part other *Forms*,
547   concerning which Dr. Carus has caused so many men to reflect to ad-
548   vantage—or rather, *by* which, and the general truth concerning which
549   Dr. Carus's mind was determined to the forcible enunciation of so
550   much truth. For truths, on the average, have a greater tendency to get
551   believed than falsities have. Were it otherwise, considering that there
552   are myriads of false hypotheses to account for any given phenomenon,
553   against one sole true one (or if you will have it so, against every true
554   one), the first step toward genuine knowledge must have been next
555   door to a miracle. So, then, when my window was opened, because of
556   the truth that stuffy air is malsain, a physical effort was brought into
557   existence by the efficiency of a general and non-existent truth. This
558   has a droll sound because it is unfamiliar; but exact analysis is with it
559   and not against it; and it has besides, the immense advantage of not
560   blinding us to great facts—such as that the ideas "justice" and "truth"
561   are, notwithstanding the iniquity of the world, the mightiest of the
562   forces that move it. Generality is, indeed, an indispensable ingredient
563   of reality; for mere individual existence or actuality without any regu-
564   larity whatever is a nullity. Chaos is pure nothing.
565   That which any true proposition asserts is *real*, in the sense of
566   being as it is regardless of what you or I may think about it. Let this
567   proposition be a general conditional proposition as to the future, and it
568   is a real general such as is calculated really to influence human con-

569   duct; and such the pragmaticist holds to be the rational purport of
570   every concept.
571   Accordingly, the pragmaticist does not make the *summum bonum*
572   to consist in action, but makes it to consist in that process of evolution
573   whereby the existent comes more and more to embody those generals
574   which were just now said to be *destined*, which is what we strive to
575   express in calling them *reasonable*. In its higher stages, evolution
576   takes place more and more largely through self-control, and this gives
577   the pragmaticist a sort of justification for making the rational purport
578   to be general.
579   There is much more in elucidation of pragmaticism that might be
580   said to advantage, were it not for the dread of fatiguing the reader. It
581   might, for example, have been well to show clearly that the pragmati-
582   cist does not attribute any different essential mode of being to an event
583   in the future from that which he would attribute to a similar event in
584   the past, but only that the practical attitude of the thinker toward the
585   two is different. It would also have been well to show that the prag-
586   maticist does not make Forms to be the only realities in the world, any
587   more than he makes the reasonable purport of a word to be the only
588   kind of meaning there is. These things are, however, implicitly in-
589   volved in what has been said. There is only one remark concerning the
590   pragmaticist's conception of the relation of his formula to the first
591   principles of logic which need detain the reader.
592   Aristotle's definition of universal predication, which is usually
593   designated, (like a papal bull or writ of court, from its opening words),
594   as the *Dictum de omni,* may be translated as follows: "We call a predi-
595   cation, (be it affirmative or negative), *universal*, when, and only when,
596   there is nothing among the existent individuals to which the subject af-
597   firmatively belongs, but to which the predicate will not likewise be re-
598   ferred (affirmatively or negatively, according as the universal predica-
599   tion is affirmative or negative)." The Greek is: λέγομεν τὸ κατὰ παντὸς
600   κατηγ ορεῖσθαι ὅταν μηδὲν ᾖ λαβεῖν τῶν τοῦ ὑποκειμένου καθ' οὗ θάτερον οὐ
601   λεχθήσεται· καὶ τὸ κατὰ μηδενὸς ὡσαύτως. The important words "existent
602   individuals" have been introduced into the translation (which English
603   idiom would not permit here to be literal): but it is plain that existent
604   individuals were what Aristotle meant. The other departures from lit-
605   eralness only serve to give modern English forms of expression. Now,
606   it is well known that propositions in formal logic go in pairs, the two
607   of one pair being convertible into another by the interchange of the
608   ideas of antecedent and consequent, subject and predicate, etc. The
609   parallelism extends so far that it is often assumed to be perfect; but it
610   is not quite so. The proper mate of this sort to the *Dictum de omni* is
611   the following definition of affirmative predication: We call a predica-
612   tion *affirmative*, (be it universal or particular), when, and only when,
613   there is nothing among the sensation affects that belong universally to

614   the predicate which will not be, (universally or particularly, according
615   as the affirmative predicate is universal or particular), said to belong to
616   the subject. Now, this is substantially the essential proposition of
617   pragmaticism. Of course, its parallelism to the *dictum de omni* will
618   only be admitted by a person who admit the truth of pragmaticism.
619   Suffer me to add one word more on this point—for, if one cares
620   at all to know what the pragmaticist theory consists in, one must un-
621   derstand that there is no other part of it to which the pragmaticist at-
622   taches quite as much importance as he does to the recognition in his
623   doctrine of the utter inadequacy of action or volition or even of resolve
624   or actual purpose, as materials out of which to construct a conditional
625   purpose or the concept of conditional purpose. Had a purposed article
626   concerning the principle of continuity and synthesizing the ideas of the
627   other articles of a series in the early volumes of *The Monist* ever been
628   written, it would have appeared how, with thorough consistency, that
629   theory involved the recognition that continuity is an indispensable
630   element of reality, and that continuity is simply what generality be-
631   comes in the logic of relatives, and thus, like generality, and more than
632   generality, is an affair of thought, and is the essence of thought. Yet
633   even in its truncated condition, an extra-intelligent reader might dis-
634   cern that the theory of those cosmological articles made reality to con-
635   sist in something more than feeling and action could supply, inasmuch
636   as the primeval chaos, where those two elements were present, was
637   explicitly shown to be pure nothing. Now, the motive for alluding to
638   that theory just here is, that in this way one can put in a strong light a
639   position which the pragmaticist holds and must hold, whether that
640   cosmological theory be ultimately sustained or exploded, namely, that
641   the third category—the category of thought, representation, triadic re-
642   lation, mediation, genuine thirdness, thirdness as such—is an essential
643   ingredient of reality, yet does not by itself constitute reality, since this
644   category, (which in that cosmology appears as the element of habit),
645   can have no concrete being without action, as a separate object on
646   which to work its government, just as action cannot exist without the
647   immediate being of feeling on which to act. The truth is that pragmati-
648   cism is closely allied to the Hegelian absolute idealism, from which,
649   however, it is sundered by its vigorous denial that the third category,
650   (which Hegel degrades to a mere stage of thinking), suffices to make
651   the world, or is even so much as self-sufficient. Had Hegel, instead of
652   regarding the first two stages with his smile of contempt, held on to
653   them as independent or distinct elements of the triune Reality, prag-
654   maticists might have looked up to him as the great vindicator of their
655   truth. (Of course, the external trappings of his doctrine are only here
656   and there of much significance.) For pragmaticism belongs essentially
657   to the triadic class of philosophical doctrines, and is much more es-
658   sentially so than Hegelianism is. (Indeed, in one passage, at least,

659 Hegel alludes to the triadic form of his exposition as to a mere fashion
660 of dress.)

661   NOTES

662   1. To show how recent the general use of the word "pragmatism"
663 is, the writer may mention that, to the best of his belief, he never used
664 it in copy for the press before today, except by particular request, in
665 *Baldwin's Dictionary*. Toward the end of 1890, when this part of the
666 *Century Dictionary* appeared, he did not deem that the word had suffi-
667 cient status to appear in that work. But he has used it continually in
668 philosophical conversation since, perhaps, the mid-seventies.

669   2. It is necessary to say that "belief" is throughout used merely as
670 the name of the contrary to doubt, without regard to grades of certainty
671 nor to the nature of the proposition held for true, i. e., "believed."

672   3. The writer, like most English logicians, invariably uses the
673 word *proposition*, not as the Germans define their equivalent, *Satz*, as
674 the language-expression of a judgment (*Urtheil*), but as that which is
675 related to any assertion, whether mental and self-addressed or out-
676 wardly expressed, just as any possibility is related to its actualization.
677 The difficulty of the, at best, difficult problem of the essential nature
678 of a Proposition has been increased, for the Germans, by their *Urtheil*,
679 confounding, under one designation, the mental *assertion* with the *as-*
680 *sertible*.

681   C. S. Peirce.

682   MILFORD, Pa., September, 1904.

683   POSTSCRIPT. During the last five months, I have met with ref-
684 erences to several objections to the above opinions, but not having
685 been able to obtain the text of these objections, I do not think I ought
686 to attempt to answer them. If gentlemen who attack either pragmatism
687 in general or the variety of it which I entertain would only send me
688 copies of what they write, more important readers they could easily
689 find, but they could find none who would examine their arguments
690 with a more grateful avidity for truth not yet apprehended, nor any
691 who would be more sensible of their courtesy.
692   C. S. P.
693   Feb. 9, 1905.

ABOUT THE AUTHOR

Phyllis Chiasson completed her bachelor's degree in speech and theater education, and her master's degree in secondary education, at the University of Arizona. She taught speech, directed plays, and coached the forensics team at Salpointe High School in Tucson before joining the Tucson Unified School District in 1970. There, Chiasson taught speech and English classes, first at Pueblo High School and then at Palo Verde High School, until 1980.

In January of 1980 she became co-director of Educational Consultations, also in Tucson. While with this agency she assisted parents, teachers, foster parents, social workers, and counselors in helping students improve their reasoning capabilities. She also provided workshops and wrote for professional journals.

In the fall of 1983, Chiasson relocated to the Seattle area where, after a brief stint as a corporate writer, she co-founded the Davis-Nelson consulting group. This agency addresses learning and performance issues within the business community.

Chiasson and her husband, Hal Leskinen, raised a blended family of five unique children: natural, adopted, step, gifted, average, learning-disabled, and biracial. They applied the Engaged Intelligence methods and the non-verbal model referenced in this book while raising their children. Most significant was the usefulness of this information for determining how to parent two of their adopted children. These two were drug and alcohol-exposed *in utero*, causing behavioral and learning problems due to fetal alcohol syndrome and cocaine effects, as well as early abuse prior to adoption. In May 1997, due in great part to the successful raising of these children, Chiasson was featured as one of four "Moms of a Lifetime" in a nationally televised program.

In addition to her work with the Relational Thinking Styles (RTS) model, the Davis Non-verbal Assessment, and Engaged Intelligence training, Chiasson is author of the Chiasson Temperament Indicator (CTI), a computerized temperament test based upon Carl G. Jung's typology.

In 1996, she and her husband moved to Port Townsend, Washington, where Chiasson is affiliated with Peninsula College. Her first contact with other pragmatism scholars came in the spring of 1998 when she joined the Peirce and Dewey discussion groups on the Internet. Although she occasionally teaches for Peninsula College and provides workshops for interested groups, her primary efforts continue to be focused upon the explication and application of the Relational Thinking Styles model of non-verbal reasoning habits and its accompanying non-verbal assessment tool.

INDEX

VIBS

The **Value Inquiry Book Series** is co-sponsored by:

1. Noel Balzer, *The Human Being as a Logical Thinker.*

2. Archie J. Bahm, *Axiology: The Science of Values.*

3. H. P. P. (Hennie) Lötter, *Justice for an Unjust Society.*

4. H. G. Callaway, *Context for Meaning and Analysis: A Critical Study in the Philosophy of Language.*

5. Benjamin S. Llamzon, *A Humane Case for Moral Intuition.*

6. James R. Watson, *Between Auschwitz and Tradition: Postmodern Reflections on the Task of Thinking.* A volume in **Holocaust and Genocide Studies.**

7. Robert S. Hartman, *Freedom to Live: The Robert Hartman Story,* edited by Arthur R. Ellis. A volume in **Hartman Institute Axiology Studies.**

8. Archie J. Bahm, *Ethics: The Science of Oughtness.*

9. George David Miller, *An Idiosyncratic Ethics; Or, the Lauramachean Ethics.*

10. Joseph P. DeMarco, *A Coherence Theory in Ethics.*

11. Frank G. Forrest, *Valuemetrics^N: The Science of Personal and Professional Ethics.* A volume in **Hartman Institute Axiology Studies.**

12. William Gerber, *The Meaning of Life: Insights of the World's Great Thinkers.*

13. Richard T. Hull, Editor, *A Quarter Century of Value Inquiry: Presidential Addresses of the American Society for Value Inquiry.* A volume in **Histories and Addresses of Philosophical Societies.**

14. William Gerber, *Nuggets of Wisdom from Great Jewish Thinkers: From Biblical Times to the Present.*

15. Sidney Axinn, *The Logic of Hope: Extensions of Kant's View of Religion.*

16. Messay Kebede, *Meaning and Development.*

17. Amihud Gilead, *The Platonic Odyssey: A Philosophical-Literary Inquiry into the* Phaedo.

18. Necip Fikri Alican, *Mill's Principle of Utility: A Defense of John Stuart Mill's Notorious Proof.* A volume in **Universal Justice.**

19. Michael H. Mitias, Editor, *Philosophy and Architecture.*

20. Roger T. Simonds, *Rational Individualism: The Perennial Philosophy of Legal Interpretation.* A volume in **Natural Law Studies.**

21. William Pencak, *The Conflict of Law and Justice in the Icelandic Sagas.*

22. Samuel M. Natale and Brian M. Rothschild, Editors, *Values, Work, Education: The Meanings of Work.*

23. N. Georgopoulos and Michael Heim, Editors, *Being Human in the Ultimate: Studies in the Thought of John M. Anderson.*

24. Robert Wesson and Patricia A. Williams, Editors, *Evolution and Human Values.*

25. Wim J. van der Steen, *Facts, Values, and Methodology: A New Approach to Ethics.*

26. Avi Sagi and Daniel Statman, *Religion and Morality.*

27. Albert William Levi, *The High Road of Humanity: The Seven Ethical Ages of Western Man,* edited by Donald Phillip Verene and Molly Black Verene.

28. Samuel M. Natale and Brian M. Rothschild, Editors, *Work Values: Education, Organization, and Religious Concerns.*

29. Laurence F. Bove and Laura Duhan Kaplan, Editors, *From the Eye of the Storm: Regional Conflicts and the Philosophy of Peace.* A volume in **Philosophy of Peace.**

30. Robin Attfield, *Value, Obligation, and Meta-Ethics.*

31. William Gerber, *The Deepest Questions You Can Ask About God: As Answered by the World's Great Thinkers.*

32. Daniel Statman, *Moral Dilemmas.*

33. Rem B. Edwards, Editor, *Formal Axiology and Its Critics.* A volume in **Hartman Institute Axiology Studies.**

34. George David Miller and Conrad P. Pritscher, *On Education and Values: In Praise of Pariahs and Nomads.* A volume in **Philosophy of Education.**

35. Paul S. Penner, *Altruistic Behavior: An Inquiry into Motivation.*

36. Corbin Fowler, *Morality for Moderns.*

37. Giambattista Vico, *The Art of Rhetoric* (*Institutiones Oratoriae,* 1711-1741), from the definitive Latin text and notes, Italian commentary and introduction by Giuliano Crifò, translated and edited by Giorgio A. Pinton and Arthur W. Shippee. A volume in **Values in Italian Philosophy.**

38. W. H. Werkmeister, *Martin Heidegger on the Way,* edited by Richard T. Hull. A volume in **Werkmeister Studies.**

39. Phillip Stambovsky, *Myth and the Limits of Reason.*

40. Samantha Brennan, Tracy Isaacs, and Michael Milde, Editors, *A Question of Values: New Canadian Perspectives in Ethics and Political Philosophy.*

41. Peter A. Redpath, *Cartesian Nightmare: An Introduction to Transcendental Sophistry.* A volume in **Studies in the History of Western Philosophy.**

42. Clark Butler, *History as the Story of Freedom: Philosophy in Intercultural Context,* with Responses by sixteen scholars.

43. Dennis Rohatyn, *Philosophy History Sophistry.*

44. Leon Shaskolsky Sheleff, *Social Cohesion and Legal Coercion: A Critique of Weber, Durkheim, and Marx.* Afterword by Virginia Black.

45. Alan Soble, Editor, *Sex, Love, and Friendship: Studies of the Society for the Philosophy of Sex and Love, 1977-1992.* A volume in **Histories and Addresses of Philosophical Societies.**

46. Peter A. Redpath, *Wisdom's Odyssey: From Philosophy to Transcendental Sophistry.* A volume in **Studies in the History of Western Philosophy.**

47. Albert A. Anderson, *Universal Justice: A Dialectical Approach.* A volume in **Universal Justice.**

48. Pio Colonnello, *The Philosophy of José Gaos.* Translated from Italian by Peter Cocozzella. Edited by Myra Moss. Introduction by Giovanni Gullace. A volume in **Values in Italian Philosophy.**

49. Laura Duhan Kaplan and Laurence F. Bove, Editors, *Philosophical Perspectives on Power and Domination: Theories and Practices.* A volume in **Philosophy of Peace.**

50. Gregory F. Mellema, *Collective Responsibility.*

51. Josef Seifert, *What Is Life? The Originality, Irreducibility, and Value of Life.* A volume in **Central-European Value Studies.**

52. William Gerber, *Anatomy of What We Value Most.*

53. Armando Molina, *Our Ways: Values and Character,* edited by Rem B. Edwards. A volume in **Hartman Institute Axiology Studies.**

54. Kathleen J. Wininger, *Nietzsche's Reclamation of Philosophy.* A volume in **Central-European Value Studies.**

55. Thomas Magnell, Editor, *Explorations of Value.*

56. HPP (Hennie) Lötter, *Injustice, Violence, and Peace: The Case of South Africa.* A volume in **Philosophy of Peace.**

57. Lennart Nordenfelt, *Talking About Health: A Philosophical Dialogue.* A volume in **Nordic Value Studies.**

58. Jon Mills and Janusz A. Polanowski, *The Ontology of Prejudice.* A volume in **Philosophy and Psychology.**

59. Leena Vilkka, *The Intrinsic Value of Nature.*

60. Palmer Talbutt, Jr., *Rough Dialectics: Sorokin's Philosophy of Value,* with Contributions by Lawrence T. Nichols and Pitirim A. Sorokin.

61. C. L. Sheng, *A Utilitarian General Theory of Value.*

62. George David Miller, *Negotiating Toward Truth: The Extinction of Teachers and Students.* Epilogue by Mark Roelof Eleveld. A volume in **Philosophy of Education.**

63. William Gerber, *Love, Poetry, and Immortality: Luminous Insights of the World's Great Thinkers.*

64. Dane R. Gordon, Editor, *Philosophy in Post-Communist Europe.* A volume in **Post-Communist European Thought.**

65. Dane R. Gordon and Józef Niznik, Editors, *Criticism and Defense of Rationality in Contemporary Philosophy.* A volume in **Post-Communist European Thought.**

66. John R. Shook, *Pragmatism: An Annotated Bibliography, 1898-1940.* With Contributions by E. Paul Colella, Lesley Friedman, Frank X. Ryan, and Ignas K. Skrupskelis.

67. Lansana Keita, *The Human Project and the Temptations of Science.*

68. Michael M. Kazanjian, *Phenomenology and Education: Cosmology, Co-Being, and Core Curriculum.* A volume in **Philosophy of Education.**

69. James W. Vice, *The Reopening of the American Mind: On Skepticism and Constitutionalism.*

70. Sarah Bishop Merrill, *Defining Personhood: Toward the Ethics of Quality in Clinical Care.*

71. Dane R. Gordon, *Philosophy and Vision.*

72. Alan Milchman and Alan Rosenberg, Editors, *Postmodernism and the Holocaust.* A volume in **Holocaust and Genocide Studies.**

73. Peter A. Redpath, *Masquerade of the Dream Walkers: Prophetic Theology from the Cartesians to Hegel.* A volume in **Studies in the History of Western Philosophy.**

74. Malcolm D. Evans, *Whitehead and Philosophy of Education: The Seamless Coat of Learning.* A volume in **Philosophy of Education.**

75. Warren E. Steinkraus, *Taking Religious Claims Seriously: A Philosophy of Religion,* edited by Michael H. Mitias. A volume in **Universal Justice.**

76. Thomas Magnell, Editor, *Values and Education.*

77. Kenneth A. Bryson, *Persons and Immortality.* A volume in **Natural Law Studies.**

78. Steven V. Hicks, *International Law and the Possibility of a Just World Order: An Essay on Hegel's Universalism.* A volume in **Universal Justice.**

79. E. F. Kaelin, *Texts on Texts and Textuality: A Phenomenology of Literary Art,* edited by Ellen J. Burns.

80. Amihud Gilead, *Saving Possibilities: A Study in Philosophical Psychology.* A volume in **Philosophy and Psychology.**

81. André Mineau, *The Making of the Holocaust: Ideology and Ethics in the Systems Perspective.* A volume in **Holocaust and Genocide Studies.**

82. Howard P. Kainz, *Politically Incorrect Dialogues: Topics Not Discussed in Polite Circles.*

83. Veikko Launis, Juhani Pietarinen, and Juha Räikkä, Editors, *Genes and Morality: New Essays.* A volume in **Nordic Value Studies.**

84. Steven Schroeder, *The Metaphysics of Cooperation: The Case of F. D. Maurice.*

85. Caroline Joan ("Kay") S. Picart, *Thomas Mann and Friedrich Nietzsche: Eroticism, Death, Music, and Laughter.* A volume in **Central-European Value Studies.**

86. G. John M. Abbarno, Editor, *The Ethics of Homelessness: Philosophical Perspectives.*

102. Bennie R. Crockett, Jr., Editor, *Addresses of the Mississippi Philosophical Association.* A volume in **Histories and Addresses of Philosophical Societies.**

103. Paul van Dijk, *Anthropology in the Age of Technology: The Philosophical Contribution of Günther Anders.*

104. Giambattista Vico, *Universal Right.* Translated from Latin and edited by Giorgio Pinton and Margaret Diehl. A volume in **Values in Italian Philosophy.**

105. Judith Presler and Sally J. Scholz, Editors, *Peacemaking: Lessons from the Past, Visions for the Future.* A volume in **Philosophy of Peace.**

106. Dennis Bonnette, *Origin of the Human Species.* A volume in **Studies in the History of Western Philosophy.**

107. Phyllis Chiasson, *Peirce's Pragmatism: The Design for Thinking.* A volume in **Studies in Pragmatism and Values.**